MARIA SANCTISSIMA:

OUR LIFE, OUR SWEETNESS, OUR HOPE;

OR,

A RECORD OF

150 𝔖𝔭𝔦𝔯𝔦𝔱𝔲𝔞𝔩 𝔞𝔫𝔡 𝔗𝔢𝔪𝔭𝔬𝔯𝔞𝔩 𝔉𝔞𝔳𝔬𝔲𝔯𝔰

GRANTED BY

OUR BLESSED LADY.

𝔖𝔢𝔩𝔢𝔠𝔱𝔢𝔡 𝔞𝔫𝔡 𝔞𝔡𝔞𝔭𝔱𝔢𝔡 𝔣𝔯𝔬𝔪 𝔱𝔥𝔢 𝔊𝔢𝔯𝔪𝔞𝔫

OF

THE VERY REV. J. A. KELLER, D. D.

BY O.S.B.,

TRANSLATOR OF 'THE SACRED HEART,' 'ANGELI DEI,'
'CHRISTMAS LEGENDS,' AND 'ST. JOSEPH'S HELP.'

𝕹𝖎𝖍𝖎𝖑 𝖔𝖇𝖘𝖙𝖆𝖙.
GULIELMUS L. GILDEA, S.T.D.,
CENSOR DEPUTATUS.

𝕴𝖒𝖕𝖗𝖎𝖒𝖆𝖙𝖚𝖗.
HERBERTUS CARDINALIS VAUGHAN,
ARCHIEPISCOPUS WESTMONAST.

Die I, *Martii*, 1899

Originally printed by R. & T. Washbourne, LTD.
Republished December 2015 © AMDG
ISBN 978-1519589477

Printed in the United States of America

PREFACE.

THIS record of spiritual and temporal favours, granted by the gracious Queen of Heaven, will, we feel confident, be welcomed by Mary's clients as a witness to the power and compassion of one who is dearer to them than all other creatures; while every incident which manifests the boundless love of their Mother, cannot fail to interest and stir the hearts of those, whose greatest pride lies in the fact that they are, in very deed—her children.

This little work has not, however, been undertaken only for them, but rather in the hope of re-enkindling in cold and dormant souls, a real and filial devotion to the blessed Mother of God. It is surely the ambition of every English Catholic, worthy of the name, to see this, our land, not Ruler of the world, or Arbiter of the nations, but worthy to possess once more the glorious title which she alone was privileged to bear in the age of Faith—the title of "Mary's Dowry."

It has often been said, and with truth, that an Englishman is not a man of many words, but eminently one of deeds, and that one solid example appeals to him more than an impassioned flow of rhetoric; it may be, then, that this collection of plain facts, told in simple words, without any pretension, beyond their authenticity, will strike a chord in some souls which more effective writers have failed to touch, and so do its own work in promoting a cause we all have so much at heart.

This book is a translation from Father Keller's "Maria Geschicten." His works have attained great popularity in Germany and America; three of them, on St. Joseph, the Angels and the Sacred Heart, have already been given to English readers by the translator, and in all three cases a second edition

i

has been called for.

Nineteen centuries ago, it was St. Joseph and the Angels who prepared the poor stable at Bethlehem for the Virgin Mother, and may we not believe that, in our own day also, they have been softening, by their gentle influence, the rough hearts of sinners, and preparing them to open their doors and receive once again into their midst—the Mother and Child.

May our dear Lady bless this labour of love—and may it help to prove how, even in this incredulous age, her arm is not shortened, nor the power of her intercession with her Divine Son diminished.

CONTENTS.

I.

QUEEN OF THE HOLY ROSARY.

II.

MARY'S HABIT—THE HOLY SCAPULAR.

iii

III.
OUR LADY'S MEDALS.

IV.
SALUS INFIRMORUM.

V.
REFUGIUM PECCATORUM.

VI.
CONSOLATRIX AFFLICTORUM.

vi

VIII.

MARY, THE COUNSELLOR OF HEARTS.

IX.

MARY, THE MERCIFUL MOTHER OF THE DYING.

X.

PRIVILEGED PLACES AND THEIR MIRACLES.

XI.

LOURDES.

XII.

RETRIBUTIVE JUSTICE.

MARIA SANCTISSIMA.

I.

QUEEN OF THE HOLY ROSARY.

1. *The Power of the United Recital of the Rosary.*

HOW often has not the destruction of the Church and Papacy been prophesied, and even their dirge been sung? But, vain delusion! the Papacy is not dead yet. From the rocky slopes of the Apennines to the rough mountain ridges of the Himalayas; from the charming towns of Liguria to the Empire of Brazil; from Catholic Belgium, and the most lonely castle on the hills of Switzerland, to the poorest little huts in Ireland and Scotland; from Rome to Manila; from Lima to Berlin, a mighty song of praise resounds, a reverberating melody is taken up by two hundred and sixty million voices, forming one sweet unison, one harmony, in one and the same language. It is the praise of the Queen of the Universe in the Angelical Salutation, which, throughout the month of October, re-echoes on the lips of millions of children of the Catholic church. It is the tender love-song to the "Blessed among women," the Mother of Sinners, the Virgin Mother of God. The Rosary of Mary witnesses to a heavenly, not an earthly, science, it rejoices heaven, and fills the pilgrims of earth with hope.

But who is he, I ask, who possesses the power and skill to command the wills and voices of such a multitude of God's creatures? An old man, who has now seen nearly ninety summers—weak in body, and robbed of his earthly dominions—an old man who, though a prisoner in the Vatican, and awaiting with sighs and tears, the mercy of God, has raised his paternal voice; a voice which draws a super-human power from the Wounds of Christ, whose Vicar he is—it is he who has compelled the admiration and respect of friends and enemies alike, who has silenced the adherents of Luther, Voltaire, and Rousseau, and obliged them to own that the Papacy is not a thing of the past, and that the Catholic church—far from being annihilated by their efforts—exists, ever living and vigorous.

True, urged on by an evil spirit, men are always to be found ready to carp at, or ridicule, the power of the Rosary, one of the strongest and most valued spiritual weapons of the Holy Father, Pope Leo XIII., and of all his predecessors, but we, who have read in history of two mighty princes, the proud Count Raymund, of Toulouse, and King James, of Arragon, who raised a similar laugh of contempt and scorn against the meek and peace-loving Pope, Innocent III., and his Crusade, when, at the head of a hundred thousand furious and sacrilegious Albigenses, they besieged the last bulwark of the Crusaders, namely, the stronghold of Müret, on the Garonne, in which they were immured. But in the Cistercian Church, at Müret, there happened to be, at that time, the great Apostle, and the first preacher of the Rosary, the servant of God, Dominic Guzman. On that memorable day, the 12th of September, 1213, Saint Dominic was saying the Rosary, together with the old men, women, and children, and all know the result. How he obtained for the bravest Crusader, and most valiant knight of his time, the noble Count Simon de Montfort, that renowned triumph, which he gained with only a thousand Catholic Knights over a hundred thousand heretics. On one and the same day, the head of the Albigensian serpent was cut off, and the princedom taken from the excommunicated Raymund, whilst the stiff-necked and obdurate king met with a shameful death. From that time the Albigenses were silenced, and scoffed no longer at the Pope and the Rosary.

The savage and cruel Selim also derided, with cynical sarcasm, the Pope, and the Rosary crusade, when, at the head of a formidable Turkish army, made insolent by a recent victory, he prepared to invade Europe, and to overrun it from end to end, in order to subject it to the shameful Mahometan rule. But the reigning Pope, Saint Pius V., a worthy son of Saint Dominic, took up the invisible arms of the holy Rosary, repeating it with all the fervour of his heart, as only a saint can pray, and ordered it to be recited by all the Confraternities in Rome, and other Christian cities. By its power, the memorable victory of Lepanto was gained on the first Sunday of October, 1571, a victory which saved the Faith of Europe, and the whole of Christian civilization, from the barbarous yoke of the Crescent.

Again, the Grand Vizier, Kara Mustapha, satanically scoffed at the Pope and the Rosary, when, at the head of three hundred thousand Turks, with a destructive artillery, he laid low all the towns which resisted his march. With the intention of marching into Rome, and converting St. Peter's into a Mosque, he besieged and stormed Vienna, the bulwark of Christendom. But the Pope at that time was the great and magnanimous Innocent XI., who had preached the Crusade of the Rosary of the Blessed Virgin Mary. And to these Rosaries we may attribute the glorious triumph of King John Sobieski, of Poland, over the Turks, on the 12th of September, 1683, the remembrance of which the entire Catholic world celebrated, by Thanksgivings to God, the Giver of all good gifts. Ever since that day the enemies of the Christian name have no longer ridiculed the Pope and the Rosary. For those who to-day scoff at the Pope and the Rosary are not Turks and Albigenses but, alas! some who still call themselves Christians, the degenerate children of the Church of Christ. They oppose us everywhere with their modern idols and heroes, but we know well how to value them since they are heroes without God, without Faith, and too often are only led by personal interests, and the low aims of selfish ambition.

The Rosary is not merely a weapon for the uneducated and for peasants—no, it forms the essential prayer of the whole Church; it is the shield of Christian souls, who are fighting in the army of this mortal life, and it is a sign of faith in Christ and His Virgin Mother. The Rosary is a prayer for all who reverently kneel to honour with a hymn of praise, their Saviour, and the Co-Redemptress of the human race, as the holy Fathers rightly call the Virgin Mary. In other kinds of prayer, man is called upon to meditate on his own misery as a finite being, before the Infinite, he acknowledges his own nothingness, and represents his necessities to God, with the confidence of a child who has recourse to the best of Fathers. But in the Rosary, multitudes of people, diversified by

4

language, descent, colour, manners and customs, have recourse to the "Blessed among women," the Mother of sinners, in one and the same sentiment of love, in one harmonious song of many voices. The Rosary is the song of Virginity, the hymn of praise, the greeting of an Archangel, and is now repeated by at least two hundred and sixty million voices.

This stamp of universality which the Rosary possesses, a mark peculiar to it (which we might almost call cosmopolitan, as being the common prayer of the world) unfolded itself with new beauty and splendour before the eyes of those who, in a certain October, came to visit the still unfinished sanctuary of the Rosary in the valley of Pompeii. In the hearts and on the lips of all, only two ideas dominated, only two sentiments dwelt, and only two expressions were heard—namely, those of honour paid to Leo XIII., the new standard bearer of the holy Rosary, and praise and glory to the Queen of Victory. Let us, also, form part of this two-fold element in the Catholic Church—love and veneration for the Pope, love and veneration towards the Blessed Virgin Mary. Where these two supports are wanting, there can be no longer a question of Catholicism, nor a true Christianity.

2. A Mother's Prayer.

Alfred V— — was an officer in the army, and as he was rich and unmarried, he gave himself up to every enjoyment which a refined and worldly life can afford; but his heart was not entirely dead to religion. His mother, with whom he lived, was a good pious widow; she wept in silence and prayed very earnestly for her son, especially by saying the Rosary for him, in order to obtain the intercession of Mary, Queen of the holy

Rosary.

"Mother," said Alfred one day, "why do you pray for my conversion? I am an honest man, I have no debts, I perform my duties regularly, and I never come home intoxicated. Why then do you say the Rosary, which only befits ignorant people?"

"Why do I pray for you, my son?" answered his mother, sorrowfully. "Because you have time for many other things, but none for God and your poor soul. Why do I say the Rosary? In this prayer lies a hidden power. Through its means many a sick person is cured, and many a sinner brought to repentance; the devout recital of the Rosary has saved many dying persons from dangers of soul and body."

"Really!" said Alfred, mockingly, "if the Rosary ever saves me from any danger, I will say it daily, and become altogether a new man."

Some weeks later, a striking change began to show itself in our hero; he became daily more serious and reserved, and one eventful morning he retired from his room, put his papers in order, and wrote several letters. In the afternoon he sought out his mother, whom he found in her room on her knees saying the Rosary.

"Mother," said Alfred, deeply moved, "why are you praying?"

"A strange presentiment is tormenting me," answered his mother, "a dreadful misfortune seems to be hanging over you. I have long lost your confidence, my son, but I pray God to deliver you, and bring me consolation."

"Calm yourself, mother," replied her son, "all is well," but the tone of his voice belied his words. Some hours had passed, when Alfred burst again into his mother's room, holding a letter in his hand. Very weary, the old lady was sitting in an arm-chair still saying the Rosary.

"Mother," cried Alfred, excitedly, "read this letter, or rather let me tell you its contents. My passionate character had involved me in an affair of honour, which would have ended to-morrow at day-break in a duel. My opponent, Captain F——, is a first-rate shot, and has killed a man in a duel before this. Being the offended party, he would have had the first shot, and his ball would most infallibly have killed me. Now he has voluntarily withdrawn his challenge, not from cowardice, as he writes, but because his conscience pursued him with the bitterest reproaches for his past misdeeds. He is now going to do penance in a monastery for the rest of his life. Dear mother! I am indebted to your earnest recital of the Rosary for my deliverance from this danger. I solemnly promise you, before God and Mary, the Queen of the Rosary, to become a better Christian."

Mother and son then knelt down, and said the Rosary with burning tears of gratitude. Some weeks later, Alfred took his departure, and likewise effected the salvation of his soul in the cloister.

3. *An Edifying Story of the Rosary.*

A priest was called to a sick person, who lived at number twenty-eight in X—— street, but by mistake he went to number eighteen. He only found closed doors on the first story, so he mounted to the second, where a child showed him a room in which lay a sick person. There he found a poor woman, by whose bed a man of perhaps some fifty years of age was sitting. The priest kindly asked him how his wife was.

"That does not concern you," he answered gruffly. "What are you doing here, and who sent for you?"

"Someone called me to a sick person, but perhaps I have made a mistake in the number of the house. In any case, I believe I can be of use here also, for it is undoubtedly God's will that I should come to your wife."

"Yes, indeed," whispered the woman in a dying voice, "Almighty God has led you here, and I will willingly make my confession."

"That you shall not!" called out her husband. "For ten years no priest has put his foot in the house, so leave us in peace, reverend sir, and do not trouble yourself about our affairs."

"My friend," answered the priest, "your wife's soul does not belong to you. So I will hear her confession and do my duty; please leave us alone for a time."

The man continued to grumble, but at length he went out. Then the woman showed the priest a Rosary, hanging near her, and said:—

"Look, Father, this Rosary must have saved me. For ten years I have turned my back on God and religion, for fear of my husband, but every day I have faithfully said a decade of the Rosary." Thereupon the dying woman prepared herself by a contrite confession, for her departure out of this world, and died soon after.

4. A Rosary in a Military School.

Some years ago, a pupil of a French military school found a Rosary on the floor of a class room.

"Look here! A Rosary in a military school!" he cried out. "What a marvelous occurrence!"

This was on the eve of an examination at which an old French Marshal was going to preside. Amongst all the pupils who were examined, one youth especially signalized himself, as much by his modest demeanour as by his knowledge and steady behaviour. After the examination, the Marshal walked past the students who were arranged in order of rank. As soon as this was over, they were allowed to leave their places, and the one who had found the Rosary, pushing forward, exclaimed mockingly, "Now, who has lost this Rosary? Who can be so stupid as to use such a thing?"

Then the pupil, who had answered the best at the examination, stepped forward and said: "The Rosary is mine, so give it back to me at once; it was a gift of my mother's, and I promised her to keep it carefully, and to say it every day of my life." The Marshal, to whom this occurrence was related, approached the youth and said to him: "My friend, I wish you joy that you have shown as much courage and noble determination in regard to your Rosary, as you gave proofs of talent and industry at the examination. Be ever as courageous in the fulfillment of your duties, and you will gain the esteem of all around you."

5. Say the Rosary.

Not very long ago, a gentleman who was very much esteemed in the eyes of the world, but unfortunately quite alienated from the practice of Religion, was in the company of several ecclesiastics on the occasion of a grand festival.

In the course of conversation he let slip this avowal: "I would willingly believe in the true Faith, but it is quite impossible for me to attain to it." One of the priests present, who was sitting near, whispered in his ear: "You have no faith? Then say the Rosary!" The conversation continued without any further mention of this subject.

Three years afterwards, this same priest received a letter, which ran as follows: "You will perhaps still remember that about three years ago, I was in a company with some priests, of whom you were amongst the number. I then expressed my regret that I could not *believe*, whereupon you advised me to say the Rosary. Those words which seemed so strange at first, remained in my memory, always ringing in my ear, with a singular fascination. By degrees they touched my heart, and at length they became sweet and lovable to me. I began to say the Rosary, and to-day I *believe*. I am now happy, and joyfully fulfill my religious duties."

Such was the result of only a few words dropped, as it were, casually, into the ears of a stranger, and points to the efficacy of persevering prayer above arguments or exhortations. Say one prayer, however small; *keep up* one practice, however little, in honour of Mary, and whatever your want may be, it will surely be fulfilled.

6. *The Musician Gluck and the Rosary.*

The music-master of the unfortunate Marie Antoinette of France, was as distinguished a Christian as he was a brilliant musician. Like most great composers, Gluck began to learn music under the mystical dome of a Cathedral. One day, when he was leaving the choir, where he had sung the praises of God in a marvelous manner, he was met by a poor religious, who, full of emotion, embraced him, congratulating him on his splendid talent.

"Truly, I have nothing to give you as a proof of my appreciation, my friend," said the priest, "nothing but this Rosary, keep it in remembrance of Brother Anselm, and promise me to say it daily in honour of the beloved Mother of God. This practice will bring you happiness, my young friend, and if you are faithful to it, I have a sure presentiment that heaven will bless your endeavours, that you will become great before men, and one day worthy to join in the heavenly songs of Paradise." Moved by these words, the young choir-boy took the Rosary, promising to say it as long as he lived.

Entering on man's estate, Gluck had already given such splendid proofs of his intellect, that his parents made up their minds to send him to Rome, there to continue his musical studies. But how could anyone without means accomplish the journey from the Imperial City on the Danube, to the Metropolis of the Christian world? Gluck did not, however, lose courage, but humbly and full of confidence he told his beads. His prayer was heard, and some days later, he and a companion, started for their wished-for goal.

He remained twenty years in Italy, and faithfully kept his promise to Brother Anselm. In after years, during his frequent stays at the Courts of Vienna and Versailles, he often had the courage to tear himself away from the delights of a brilliant entertainment, or an attractive conversation, in order to say his Rosary in a recess of the royal salôn. Thus Gluck sanctified his life, and on the day that the renowned musician gave up his soul to God, his hand still clasped the Rosary of Brother Anselm.

7. *The Discovered Rosary.*

Two students were once walking briskly along the high road, which led through a forest; the conversation had been at a standstill for some time, when one of them saw something lying on the ground. He picked it up, and then said contemptuously, "A Rosary! and one apparently worn out and of little worth." With these words, he was about to throw it down again, when his companion snatched it from him and put it in his pocket. "Eugène," he said in a reproachful tone, "I will not suffer religious objects to be handled in that contemptuous way; I will restore the Rosary to its owner."

"So, Charles, you appear to know very decidedly to whom it belongs, but of course your sound sense must tell you that not even uneducated men, and certainly not enlightened University Students, like us, except, perhaps, with a few exceptions, attach their hearts to such things. But how will you find the owner? Do you intend to have the bell rung by the parish clerk, announcing that you have found a Rosary, in every village which we pass through on our holidays?"

"Every Rosary," replied Charles, earnestly, "is consecrated to the great Queen of Heaven; therefore, I will place this one before the picture of the Immaculate Virgin in the next chapel which I find open."

A little later, the travellers came to a roadside chapel. Charles went in, but Eugène preferred to wait outside. After some time, however, as Charles did not reappear, Eugène went to look after him, and there he saw him kneeling before the picture of the Mother of God, his hands clasped in devout prayer. Eugène reminded him that it was time to come out. He at once arose, and both went again into the open air. After a long silence, Charles began: "I did not leave the Rosary before our Lady's picture after all, but I intend to keep it myself, as a remembrance of one of the most important hours of my life. Until now, I have hesitated in the choice of a state of life, but whilst kneeling before the picture of the Mother of God, it was made clear to me that I am called to the Priesthood."

Charles carried out this resolution, and after he had finished his studies, and had been ordained, full of zeal for the honour of God, he laboured in various parishes, first as assistant priest; then, later on, he was given a mission to work by himself. The spiritual care of a hospital was also entrusted to him, and here he felt in his element. With each consoling visit he raised up many an oppressed spirit; by persuasions and exhortations he brought many sick people, hardened in sin, to the last Sacraments, thus preparing them for their passage to eternity.

In this hospital there was a man dangerously ill, who was fully aware of his hopeless condition, yet, nevertheless, would not hear of receiving Holy Viaticum. Charles had gained nothing by persuasions or exhortations, but, in spite of this, the good priest prayed very earnestly, and invoked the intercession of the blessed Mother of God, for the grace of conversion for this poor hardened sinner. Strengthened by fervent prayer, and as if enlightened by Divine inspiration, he one day asked him: "Did not your mother teach you to say the Rosary when you were little?"

"Do not remind me of the Rosary!" cried the sick man, despairingly. "I owe to a Rosary all the unhappiness which has pursued me for so many years."

"A Rosary!" repeated the priest. "Unhappy man, you are deceiving yourself."

"No, no!" replied the sick man, passionately. "I used to say

13

the Rosary every evening with my pious parents, when I was a good and obedient son. But my father died early; bad company and bad books ruined my morals, and I became deaf to the warnings of my dear mother. Before setting out on my travels, my mother gave me her blessing and a Rosary. She admonished me to return to my religion and to virtue, and she begged and implored of me to say the Rosary daily, or at least one decade. To pacify her, I promised to do so, but scarcely had I made an hour's journey from my home, than I threw away the Rosary, and stamped on it with my feet. Since that day, peace of soul and all earthly happiness left me. Never shall I forget that day. It was—"

"It must have been the 23rd of June, 18—," interrupted Father Charles, "for that day also is indelibly impressed on my heart. I was the happy finder of the Rosary."

Hereupon, the priest accurately described the place, and then continued eagerly. "I hastened to the nearest chapel, with this Rosary, and then, in fervent prayer, it became clear to me that Almighty God called me to the Priesthood, and now, with the same Rosary which brought me peace and happiness, I shall seek to win the soul of a brother for heaven. Oh, my dear friend, take back your long-lost Rosary, which I always carry about with me, and know that by this same Rosary, you have challenged the Justice of God, and have experienced His Mercy in your own regard."

Sobbing, and with trembling hands, the sick man grasped the Rosary presented to him, and covered it with kisses. Full of glowing devotion and heartfelt repentance and contrition, he received the Last Sacraments, and shortly afterwards breathed forth his soul into the hands of his Maker.

8. *The Rosary on the Scaffold.*

Some years ago, in a town of Alsace, a young criminal, barely twenty-two years of age, was condemned to death. A large crowd stood around the place of execution, while an intense silence reigned. Before his death, the criminal besought the priest who accompanied him, to be pleased to fulfill a request for him. The unfortunate youth then drew a Rosary from his pocket, saying in a low voice to the priest: "My mother gave me this on the day of my First Communion as a little souvenir. In my boyhood, she said it with me daily, implanting a thousand good lessons in my heart. Later, I had to leave her, and went into a world full of dangers and temptations. I gave myself up to every kind of evil, and at last committed the dreadful crime for which I am condemned to death. For a long time I remained in prison, resolving never to be converted, until one day, I came across this Rosary, at the sight of which, all my dear mother's teaching recurred to my memory. For many, many years I had not said the Rosary, but I began it then, and scarcely had I done so, when tears came to my eyes at the thought of all the grief and sorrow I had caused my good mother by my wicked life. Take it to her, Father, and tell her of my repentance and tears, and also tell her I was brought back to God before my death."

9. *B. Clement Maria Hofbauer, Redemptorist.*

This pious priest was the first German Member of the Redemptorist Order founded by Saint Alphonsus Liguori, and he, it was, who first brought this Order into his native land. Like his master, he always said the Rosary to himself, when he was in the streets; he called it his "library," finding it the most powerful means for the conversion of sinners, especially for the dying. He used to say, "If I am called to a sick person, whom I know beforehand is not prepared to go to Confession, or will not hear of making his peace with God, then I say the Rosary on the way, and all is sure to go well as soon as I arrive. Believe me, the holy Mother of God assists all, and no one is forsaken, who truly confides in her intercession."

Once he returned home quite tired from a suburb of Vienna, and related that he had been with a sick person, who had not been to Confession for seventeen years, but who had nevertheless died repentant. "Yes," he said, "all goes well if the person lives in the suburbs, for then I have time to say the Rosary on the way, and I do not remember any sinner dying without Confession, if I have had time to say my beads beforehand."

10. *An Old Woman's Constancy.*

In the year 1863, Bishop Pichon, Vicar-Apostolic of Southern Tschuen, addressed a letter to the Director of the Guild of the Holy Childhood, in which he tells the following story:—

"Revolutionists, or I might rather call them wild beasts, are ravaging the whole country. In their frenzy, they have already seized upon, and slaughtered over three hundred converts. Yet God has been very merciful to us, and we have much to thank Him for. I will give as an example, a remarkable circumstance, which astonished even the heathens.

The rebels had taken possession of a town almost entirely Christian, numbering some ten thousand inhabitants. Fortunately, with one exception, all had contrived to leave the city before the arrival of the insurgents, and had saved themselves by flight. Only one solitary old woman remained, she was lame and infirm, and it had been quite impossible to get her away, so she stayed behind, and fell into the hands of the barbarians. For two long months, they continued sole masters of the town, and employed themselves in devastating and ravaging everything they could lay hands on, till the whole place was one great wreck. Meantime, the poor old woman never lost her confidence in God and in our Lady, though she felt that every day must be her last; she recited the Rosary unceasingly, and, strange to say, the rebels, ruffians as they were, not only left her unmolested, but even provided her with food, clothing, and other necessities.

At length the district was freed from the invaders, and the inhabitants came flocking back again. Among them was the grandson of the steadfast old woman, who, on his return, hastened to her former dwelling, though without the slightest hope of finding her alive. His surprise was unbounded, when he perceived that her house was uninjured, and, on entering, he could scarcely believe his eyes when he saw his grandmother standing before him. Her relatives, supposing her dead, had already had a Requiem Mass said for her, and now, in their delight at having her once more in their midst, they could not do enough for her. But she had only one desire, one aim, and that, to see a priest and approach once again to the Holy Sacraments before rendering her soul into the hands of her Creator. In order to accomplish this desire, she asked to start on a journey to the nearest resident priest. He lived eighteen miles away, and a dangerous river had to be crossed. Although the frightful circumstances of the last long weeks, and the joy of the unexpected meeting had told much on the declining powers of the old matron, yet she courageously resolved to undergo all these difficulties in order to satisfy the longings of her soul, as she felt her last hour fast approaching. Whilst her relations were preparing to fulfill her holy wish, a priest opportunely arrived, sent thither, we doubt not, by the compassionate intervention of Mary. His first steps were directed to the house of the sick person, so wonderfully saved, to whom he administered the consolations of Holy Church, just in time to strengthen her for the last journey she would ever have to take. R.I.P."

11. *Always carry your Rosary with you.*

In the year 1808, on the 2nd of May, a dreadful rebellion broke out in Spain, against the French, who had conquered that country, and in consequence the French were massacred relentlessly, especially in Madrid. Among them at that time was a doctor named de Klanby, who was a zealous servant of Mary, and who had on the above-mentioned day received Holy Communion in honour of the most holy Virgin, in a chapel consecrated to her, before betaking himself to his duties. On the way back he was suddenly seized by a clamorous multitude, who recognized him as a French officer. They were already drawing their swords to strike him down, when, seeing himself in this extreme danger, he invoked the protection of Jesus and Mary. Remembering how the French were stigmatized as unbelievers and defamers of God—as, indeed, at that time many among them were—a thought suddenly struck him—"No," he cried to the infuriated people, "I am no infidel, and here is a proof!" With these words he drew from his pocket his Rosary, which he always carried with him, and on which hung a silver medal blessed by Pope Pius VII.

Hardly had the Spaniards caught sight of the Rosary than they lowered their swords. Nevertheless, some were not yet appeased—but at that moment a man rushed into their midst, whom God had sent to save the client of Mary. It was the sacristan of the chapel, in which the doctor had performed his morning devotions. "Do that man no harm, my friends," he said, "for I myself have seen how he received Holy Communion to-day, in honour of the Mother of God." Scarcely had the sacristan spoken than the Spaniards, shortly before so incensed, overwhelmed the doctor with civilities, then, taking the Rosary, they kissed it respectfully, and presented it also to the doctor to kiss; he pressed it to his lips with most fervent love and gratitude for the speedy assistance he had just received from our Blessed Lady. They then conducted him to a place of safety, where he was secure from all other dangers.

When Dr. de Klanby returned to France, he related everywhere the wonderful benefit which the Queen of the holy Rosary had conferred upon him, and he assisted with most heartfelt gratitude at a Novena in honour of the most Holy Virgin, which was made solemnly in one of the Churches of Versailles, in thanksgiving for his wonderful deliverance.

12. Two Christian Brothers Rescued from Death.

A brother of the Congregation of the Christian Schools relates his experiences during the terrible Revolution which took place in Paris, in 1870, in the following account:—

"I was seized one day by the Communists, together with another brother, and shut up for a fortnight in the prison of Mazas; we were then released and allowed to return to the

House of our Congregation. However, shortly after, when Paris was attacked by the government troops, we were again forced, contrary to our principles, to work at the barricades, and to carry arms against the government. Thus armed, and apparently in the service of the Commune, we were taken prisoners by the victorious troops of Versailles, and marched off to the prison of la Roquette. It was a weary march, we were thoroughly tired out by the hard work which we had been compelled to do, and faint from want of food, added to which we were now overwhelmed with threats and insults. My feet were so swollen that I could scarcely drag myself along, but in that hour of humiliation and pain, I gathered comfort from the remembrance of my Saviour, and thought of His love and patience as He trod the infinitely more humiliating Way of the Cross.

"At length we reached an old building, which looked like a medieval castle—it was La Roquette. I glanced up as we entered the gate, and saw the inscription, 'Prison for the Condemned.' This, then, was to be the end of my earthly pilgrimage, to die for siding with the revolutionists whom we held in execration, to be murdered by men whose cause we had made our own.

"The heavy iron door closed behind us, and we were led into a dark cell, there to await our doom, together with many other poor wretches. At intervals during the day, a jailor entered the cell and summoned the prisoners, five by five, to receive their sentence. We were not long left in ignorance as to their fate, for presently our prison walls resounded with the shots which sent them—many, alas! so little prepared—into eternity. At length our turn came—the jailor led my companion and myself into a room where we were to undergo a short examination. On being questioned as to our names and profession, we replied that we were Brothers of the Christian Schools. At this our judges smiled incredulously, and well they might, for our clothes were torn and dirty, our faces disfigured and covered with mud, and our whole appearance betokened anything rather than Religious men. Then the hopelessness of our situation came home to us, the courage I had hitherto shown utterly failed me, and I broke down. Some member of the court martial, compassionating my evident despair, asked if I could not prove my assertion by producing my certificates. 'Alas!' I answered, 'all my papers were seized by the Communists when they locked us up in the Mazas Prison.' . . . . A hasty consultation followed, then the judges gave a sign to the soldiers, which could not be mistaken—the trial was over—our doom was sealed—we were to be led out and shot. Oh! the agony of that moment, I shall never forget. Suddenly an inspiration flashed across my mind—'Stay,' I exclaimed, 'I have proof of the truth of my statement,' so saying, I snatched the Scapular from my neck, and the Rosary from my pocket, and holding them up, 'there,' I continued, 'are my witnesses.' My companion followed my example, for the jailor at Mazas had not thought it worth while to take these from us. The expression of our judges instantly changed. 'Wait,' they said, 'we will enquire further into this matter.'

"Thereupon, we were taken into an adjoining room and examined by a private commission. There we explained how we had come to be among the rioters—how we had been taken prisoners in the first instance by the Communists, and subsequently compelled by them to bear arms and fight in an unjust cause. Having heard our story, the commission declared itself satisfied, and our former judges immediately acquitted us. We were saved! we were free! Words cannot describe the sensation of relief we experienced after that terrible suspense, and our joy and gratitude were unbounded at the thought that our Blessed Lady had delivered us by means of her Rosary.

"Leaving the prison, our first act was to seek out a church, where, with overflowing hearts, we solemnly promised that the remainder of our lives, which we owed to our Lady, should be wholly consecrated to her service, and that of her Divine Son."

13. *The Soldiers' Favourite Prayer Book.*

In the autumn of 1871, the year of the Franco-Prussian war, an alarming mortality spread among the German soldiers then in France. In consequence of unceasing rain and damp, in spite of which they had to live continually out of doors, added to the great fatigues they were then enduring, dysentery and typhoid, together with other infectious diseases, became prevalent, and wrought greater havoc among the troops than all the powder and shot of the enemy.

The most robust and healthy fell victims to the epidemic, death ensuing in most cases after one or two days' illness. The greater part of the Hesse division were at this time quartered at Gorze, a little town near Metz, and all the principal buildings had been turned into temporary hospitals, and were filled with sick and dying soldiers. All that human skill could devise was done to check the mortality, but comparatively few lives were saved. Day by day the death roll increased; even in that one small place, there were as many as twenty or thirty victims each day. The corpses had to be buried outside the town, in great, huge pits, which held from four to five hundred.

It was a sad, weary time, and the thought of death weighed on everyone's mind, while a look of apprehension appeared on every face. Never shall I forget how, morning after morning, two large wagons went through the streets, bent on their ghastly errand of collecting the lifeless bodies of those who had succumbed during the night. They stopped at each plague-stricken dwelling, and the dead were carried out and placed in the cart, without coffin or shroud, and thus buried in the pit. No mourners stood around the last resting place of those whom they had loved, only one self-sacrificing priest ventured near that awful grave, and daily read the burial service.

Yet, though the misery was so great, and the nature of the disease so dreadful, there were many consolations. The patience and piety of many of the poor suffering soldiers edified all those who had to do with them, especially the chaplains, while the immediate presence of death made everyone think of his own end, realizing that any moment he too might be struck down. Often in the course of a few days a whole ward had died off, and the beds refilled with fresh cases.

Under such circumstances, no one had much time for preparation, but the greater number ended their lives more piously than if they had been attended with every care at their own homes, their fervour making up for the shortness of time. And as the fewness of the chaplains made it impossible for them to give much attention to each patient, the sufferers contented themselves with a prayer book, which seemed to supply all their wants. This was the Rosary. Night and day they held it tightly clasped in their emaciated hands, now and again pressing it lovingly to their lips; it was their one consolation in their hour of need, and the devotion with which they repeated over and over again the Hail Mary, drew tears from the hardest heart. Even in death they still clung to this, their only treasure, and we may surely believe that when their souls appeared before the judgment seat of our Divine Lord, His Blessed Mother claimed them as her own.

14. *Eliodatus.*

During a war between the Spaniards and the Saracens, in the kingdom of Granada, Eliodatus, the son of a Turkish captain, was taken prisoner, and sold at Compostella. He had scarcely reached his twentieth year, when this disaster befell him, making him repine under his misfortunes all the more grievously, as from being the son of a nobleman, he had become the poorest of slaves. His prospects, which seemed to open so gloriously, were now all blighted, and, to crown his other miseries, the wounds which he had received whilst fighting, emitted such noxious odours, that no one would remain near him. Satan took advantage of his unfortunate state, and tormented him with visions of hell open to receive him; the unhappy youth, knowing no one to succour him, called upon the Prince of Darkness to come to his aid, and, his condition becoming more and more miserable, he sought means to take away his life, but, fortunately for his salvation, his weakness prevented him from carrying out his design. St. Dominic heard of his sad state, and, moved with his burning zeal for souls, set out on a journey to Compostella. Here he found the sick man, and after lovingly saluting him and winning his confidence, he said: "Do you wish to be well again? If so, be baptized, and become a Christian." "By no means," answered the distressed youth. "Never will I be unfaithful to the principles and doctrines of my parents." After this decided refusal, the Saint continued: "Well, if you will not be a Christian, nevertheless, if you desire to be soon restored to health, I will, out of compassion, teach you two consoling little songs, which possess a wonderful power, provided you repeat them a hundred and fifty times daily." "I will willingly do that," said Eliodatus, "if there is nothing contained in them against my religion." "These little songs," said St. Dominic, "are in no wise contrary to the law of God. They cannot possibly harm you." "If there is nothing about the Christian's God, i.e., of Jesus Christ and His Mother Mary, then I pray you teach me them." "The Mussulman believes," replied the Saint, "that Christ was at least a great Prophet, and His Mother a very holy woman; you also certainly hold that both have much power with God, and, I am sure you will agree, that my little songs possess, even for heathens and Jews, a very wonderful and health-giving unction."

Being won by the sweetness and tender manner of the Saint, the poor prisoner put aside his prejudices, and allowed himself to be taught the "Our Father" and the "Hail Mary." He did his best to repeat them and to commit them to memory, but he was so weak that he seemed quite unable to retain anything. At last, tired out by his endeavours, he fell asleep. Meanwhile the Saint besought God to give grace and strength to this poor soul, who needed it so much, and as he prayed, Eliodatus awoke, and to his joy and astonishment, repeated the Pater and Ave, without any hesitation. St. Dominic then gave him a few more instructions as to the manner of saying them, and left him.

The prisoner at once began to say his first Rosary, and his heart was thereby filled with such consolation, that he imagined he must already be tasting the joys of paradise. The next day he sang his little songs with greater confidence, and was rewarded by a wonderful increase of bodily strength. Continuing thus to pray daily, he at length resolved to ask for baptism. On the sixth day, when he had finished saying his Rosary, he beheld a marvelous vision; he saw the Divine Judge seated upon His throne, and heard Him pronounce the sentence of damnation against himself; suddenly, however, a lady of surpassing beauty threw herself at our Lord's feet, imploring mercy for him. And, being questioned as to what good he had ever done, his loving pleader answered: "During the last week he has daily said my Rosary with great devotion." Upon this the sentence was immediately revoked. Overjoyed, the youth returned to himself, and found that he was completely cured.

His one wish now was to receive holy Baptism, and, in consideration of the supernatural favour bestowed upon him by Mary, it was not long deferred. Shortly after becoming a Christian his liberty was restored to him, and he dedicated the remainder of his life to the service of his Benefactress, and to the promotion of her Rosary. When, in course of time, he came into possession of his vast estate, he disposed of its revenues, under the direction of St. Dominic, in founding Hospitals, Alms-Houses, and other similar works of charity, and after a most edifying life, he died the "death of the Saints," towards the middle of the XIII. century.

15. *The Rosary Wins the Day.*

The pious author of the book entitled "The Secret of obtaining Graces," relates how on one occasion, St. Vincent Ferrer went to visit a dying man, for whose salvation he much feared, and the following conversation took place: "Why," said the Saint, "do you insist on plunging yourself for ever into hell, when Jesus Christ your Redeemer longs to save you?" "I shall be damned in spite of Jesus Christ," exclaimed the unhappy man. "Say rather," replied the Saint, "that you will be saved in spite of yourself." Then St. Vincent invited the by-standers to join with him in saying the Rosary, and no sooner was it finished, than the poor sinner begged to make his peace with God, and, having confessed his sins, with many tears, died in the best dispositions.

16. Werner the Merchant.

All Catholics know, or ought to know, by experience, that the recitation of the Rosary is both useful and beneficial, hence it is that all Mary's clients make use of it in every necessity, and never fail to draw from it help and consolation. It is most advisable that parents should accustom their children from their tenderest years to have recourse to Mary, by daily reciting a portion of the Rosary. People are apt to consider this practice useless, alleging that children cannot understand it, and that a prayer like the Rosary is altogether above their capacity. Yet, after all, it is of small consequence whether they perfectly grasp the meaning of their prayer, provided they realize that they are pleasing our Blessed Lady, in which case the practice cannot fail to foster in their baby hearts a tender love, and unbounded confidence in their heavenly Mother. It is indeed a touching sight to see little children reciting their beads, and invoking our Lady in their small needs, with that perfect trust which is so peculiar to the innocent. Such prayers are especially pleasing to the Queen of Heaven, as we see in the following example:

27

In a town situated on the Rhine, there lived a merchant named Werner, a man respected by all who knew him. He had but one child, his joy and his pride; she was a beautiful little girl, with a most lovable nature, and her parents endeavoured to bring her up in the practice of every virtue. The pious mother delighted to teach her about our Lord and our Blessed Lady, and no sooner had her baby lips learnt the Pater and the Ave, than she might have been heard lisping her Rosary at her mother's knee.

When little Mary was barely seven years of age she lost her good mother, and her father now transferred all the love of his heart to his one remaining treasure. Two years passed uneventfully for the father and daughter, when it happened that in some unaccountable way the merchant mislaid, as he thought, some most important documents. Knowing that their loss would cost him the greater part of his property, he went about sad and pre-occupied. Little Mary noticed that her father looked anxious, and asked him what was the matter. At first he put her off with an attempt at a smile, but she coaxed and pleaded till at length he told her the cause of his grief. The child was silent for a while, and seemed as though she were seeking for some way out of the difficulty—suddenly a bright thought struck her, and she exclaimed, "don't worry about it any more—I will say my Rosary for you three days running, and after that, our Lady will most certainly find the papers for you." The good father was much touched by his little daughter's simple faith, and kissing her tenderly, he said, "Yes, do so, my child, and all will be well."

The pious child was not disappointed in her trust, for on the evening of the third day, Werner received a pocket book containing the missing documents, together with a letter

28

informing him that a former servant of his had stolen them, out of revenge, but that his conscience had so tormented him for three days, that he felt compelled to return them to their rightful owner. The joy and relief experienced by the merchant can scarcely be described, and it is hardly necessary to add that both father and daughter offered most fervent prayers in thanksgiving for the favour they had received, and continued ever after most faithful to the daily recital of the Rosary.

17. *Do not be Ashamed of your Rosary.*

A very anti-christian spirit has developed in the higher schools of France during this last century; a spirit which, even in our own day, does not seem to be on the wane. When Louis Philippe occupied the throne, an edifying incident took place at the Paris "Polytechnique."

One day a student rushed into the recreation room, and jumping on to a desk, demanded silence, with an air of importance, his eyes the while twinkling with merriment. The scholars eager to hear what he had to say, gathered excitedly round him and listened with breathless attention. "Gentlemen," he began, satirically, "I have discovered a most valuable and rare article; so rare and so unexpected is my discovery that I challenge any of you to guess what it is, unless, perhaps, its owner is among us. But I would be rather inclined to think that the article belongs to an inhabitant of the moon, and not to a rational student of the Polytechnique. Now I call upon you to guess what I found in the passage of this very house." Then followed a string of impossible suggestions, one more ludicrous than the other, while peals of laughter rang through the hall.

29

At last the speaker again demanded silence, and continued: "I see, gentlemen, that you are fast losing patience, allow me, then, to satisfy your curiosity, without further delay, by producing the object." With these words, he pulled a Rosary from his pocket, and held it high in the air. It was greeted with shouts and riotous mirth. "What!" they cried, "who on earth has brought such a thing as that here. The washerwoman must have dropped it." "Well," said the former speaker, "at any rate, it is a splendid joke, and if the owner does not come at once to claim it, I will set the rare and precious article up for auction. So, for the first and last time, does anyone desire it back as his property?" At these words, a scholar, who was sitting before a table covered with books and drawings, looked up, he was surveying the unusual scene with a quiet composure, and a grave, sweet smile. His figure was noble, his forehead high, and a refined spirit shone through his intrepid and bright countenance. He was respected and beloved among his comrades. This youth now arose, forced his way to the place of the speaker, stretched out his hand, and with an unmoved countenance and firm tone, said: "The Rosary is mine, please give it back to me."

Immense astonishment ensued. "Do you not see," cried one, "that he is but keeping up the fun, he is jesting like the rest." "I am not jesting," answered the youth, "least of all, do I joke about such holy things. Yes, gentlemen, the Rosary belongs to me, and I ask for it back, it was given to me by my mother when dying, and I promised her to keep it always, and to be faithful to the practice of saying it. I have just now heard the holiest things spoken of here with a levity which is alone to be explained by the only too common ignorance which exists about our objects of devotion . . . .

"Yes, I am religious, after the example of Vauban, our celebrated master, after the example of Turenne, Condé and Villars, men of whom every Frenchman is justly proud. I glory to be in such company, and I have no reason whatever to blush on account of my religious opinions." This courageous answer made a great impression on the listeners. Some wavered, uncertain whether to continue their ridicule or to apologise for their rudeness, and a few turned on their heel and left the room. But the majority admired the manly courage and candour of the undaunted champion of his Faith, and began to cheer loudly. The former speaker, who had found the Rosary, was the first to come forward, and shaking him warmly by the hand, said: "I beg your pardon, Henry, I hope you are not angry with me." "Oh, not in the least," replied the boy, good-naturedly, "only, I must say, I think you are rather. . ." "Speak out," he cried, "I know I have behaved disgracefully, and I quite acknowledge myself in the wrong. Your words have made me realize that I have been talking absolute nonsense, and only made a fool of myself." Thus Henry gained the day, and his pluck was a lesson to many of the students, who though good at heart, had not possessed sufficient strength of mind to acknowledge their real sentiments in the face of ridicule.

Henry was a true child of the Rosary, and his obedience to the last wishes of his pious mother, in always carrying it with him and saying it, had not merely preserved him from temptation in the unchristian atmosphere of a French military school, but had also given him the courage to make an avowal of his Faith, and brought many of his comrades to a better way of living.

Christian parents! Do you desire your children to reap the

31

fruits of a good Catholic education? Do you wish them to withstand the temptations of human respect and worldliness? Then inspire them with a true love of the holy Rosary; teach them to say it well, and with loving hearts, and never to be ashamed of letting others know that they make use of it.

18. A Mother's Gift.

A renowned preacher of the last century was one night summoned to attend a nobleman who had been struck down by apoplexy. He hastened in great fear lest he should be too late, and, indeed, when he arrived the sufferer was unconscious.

Next day, Father D— — offered a Votive Mass of the Blessed Virgin for him, and, when he went into the sacristy, he was informed that the invalid had sent for him, and was waiting to make his confession. Full of delight, Father D— — was soon at his side, and found him penetrated with the deepest contrition, and fully resigned to leave his worldly possessions, and the so-called joys of this life, for the true and everlasting joys of heaven.

The priest, marveling at the great grace bestowed on the sick man, begged him to say how he had merited this favour. In a voice choked with sobs, he said: "Ah, Reverend Father, I can only ascribe this grace to the mercy of God, through the intercession of our Lady, for without doubt, she has deigned to hear your and my mother's prayers; when she was dying she confided to me the grief she felt at the thought of the many dangers I should encounter in the world, and her last words I have never forgotten, 'I leave you,' she said, 'under the protection of the holy Virgin, promise me only one thing, to prove your love for me, and that is, to say your Rosary every day.' I promised, and for ten years it has been the only religious act I have persevered in."

In a few days he died; having been faithful to Mary, she was faithful to him; for the dying are ever the dearest objects of her tender charity, and having gained for him the consolations of religion, she presented his soul to her merciful Son.

II.

19. A Healing Scapular.

VERONICA N— —, a woman living in Vienna, had suffered, for more than six years, from an extremely obstinate and painful disease. Treated in different ways, by the various doctors who had been consulted, Doctor Stork, physician of the public hospital, at length declared her malady to be "paralysis of the vocal chord," and she remained for two years under his direction and supervision, making use of every remedy which science could suggest.

Every new experiment was, however, equally fruitless, nor did a month's stay in the country do her any good. Weary of these complete failures on the part of physicians, she resolved to abandon further remedies. None had afforded her the slightest relief, and her deplorable condition was daily becoming more aggravated, her constitution was quite destroyed, her digestion so weakened that she could hardly eat anything, and it was a subject of astonishment how her life could be prolonged by taking only such a small quantity of liquid nourishment. Violent sickness, with convulsive symptoms, came on, and a cough was added to her other trials, which troubled her for many hours at a time, hardly leaving her a moment's peace, and causing her throat to swell, so that she could scarcely swallow a drop of water; sometimes even death by suffocation seemed so imminent that it was thought necessary to have the Last Sacraments administered without delay.

Those who saw her in this state, said that they had never come across such suffering. It was not, therefore, to be wondered at, that weary of life, she fell into the deepest melancholy, and became a burden to herself and an object of sorrow and compassion to those around her.

Still, where the need is greatest, God's help is sure to come most quickly and most effectually. It happened that for two consecutive nights her deceased grandfather appeared to her in a dream, and directed her to prepare for death. After this warning she found no longer any rest in bed, and one morning left her room quite early. Then her Guardian Angel led her into the Church, and she entered a confessional, where the priest sought to console and strengthen her in her sufferings. He advised her to be enrolled in the holy Scapular, and to seek for protection under the mantle of Mary. She could not follow this well-meant advice for eight days, as increased weakness made it impossible for her again to leave her room. At last, on the 13th of January, 1871, she dragged herself, with great fatigue, to the Carmelite Church at Vienna, in order to receive the holy Scapular. Scarcely had the ceremony been accomplished, and the priest concluded the prayers, when the illness, with all its symptoms, suddenly left her, and with a new feeling of life, such as she never before experienced, she hastened home, sound in body and light at heart. With tears of gratitude in her eyes, she ran to her mother and cried out, "I am perfectly well, the holy Mother of God has cured me in a wonderful way," and, returning thanks in our Blessed Lady's own words (who had, by means of her Scapular, thrown her protecting mantle over her), she exclaimed, "The Lord hath done great things for me, and holy be His Name."

Six months have passed since that memorable day, and not a

35

single attack of this painful illness has recurred. Veronica is changed in body and soul, her weakness and delicacy have given place to perfect health, and, no longer weary of life, her heart overflows with joy and gratitude.

Would that every sufferer might be encouraged, by this fresh manifestation of Mary's power, to have recourse to her with fullest confidence, and to invoke her in every necessity as the "Auxilium Christianorum." "Help of Christians, pray for us."

20. *At the Point of Death.*

An American newspaper relates the following interesting event:—

"On Good Friday, a Mr. MacGill, being 240 miles from Gainesville, where he believed there was a Catholic church, determined to go there and remain over Easter. Arriving at this place he found there was neither church nor a priest, and that the nearest town where he could receive the Sacraments was Pilatea-Putnamby. This was too far for him to go, so he engaged rooms at a hotel, where he stayed several days.

"On the morning after his arrival, he noticed that many persons went in and out of a certain room. He asked the landlord's daughter whether anyone was sick, and received the answer, that a young man from Massachusetts lay there, dying of consumption. Mr. MacGill asked to be taken to see him, and as his business was not urgent, and his visits appeared to be pleasing to the sick man, he often sat for hours by his bedside, rendering him all kinds of little services, by arranging his pillows and giving him water or medicine, etc. He spoke to him about anything he thought might interest him, but avoided the topic of religion, for he supposed the young man to be a Protestant.

"On the evening before his departure, Mr. MacGill visited the sick man once more, and just before leaving him, raised him in bed, in order to arrange the pillows and bed covering. He then caught sight of a Scapular, which, to his astonishment, the sufferer was wearing round his neck. Seeing, however, that he was exhausted and sleepy, he could not say anything more to him that night, but going to him early the next morning, he told the patient that he had noticed the Scapular, and asked if he were a Catholic. 'I am not one,' was the answer; 'my mother was, but she died when I was quite a child. Before her death, I attended the Church and Sunday-school, but afterwards, I gave no thought to religion. My father kept a boarding-house for sailors, in Boston, so you can imagine the kind of companions that surrounded my youth. I was nursed at the beginning of this illness by a Sister of Mercy, in a hospital, and before coming here she gave me the Scapular, recommending me to wear it, as it might perhaps be of use to me. I have worn it ever since, just to please her, because she was so kind to me, and I shall continue to do so, even if I return home.' On being asked whether he would like to see a priest, he said he would, but added he had nearly forgotten all he had ever known of the Catholic religion, but that, if he ever practiced any form of worship, he would prefer the religion of his mother to any other. His friend saw there was no time to lose, for the youth was in the last stage of consumption, so he hastened to the telegraph office, and sent a dispatch to Father Kenny, at Pilatea. The priest took the next train, and arrived in the morning at Gainsville; he went to the sick room, instructed the young man, heard his Confession, gave him Holy Communion, and administered Extreme Unction. The very day after, the poor sufferer died."

Is not this, again, a proof how the Holy Mother of God takes care of all who are in any way her servants? If this youth had not worn the Scapular, he would, most probably, have died without the opportunity of making his peace with God.

21. *A Story of the Picture of Besançon, and of the Marvellous Preservation of Roveredo, by means of the Scapular.*

In the monastery of St. Mary Magdalen, at Besançon, there is an old and venerable picture of the Holy Virgin, commonly called "Our Lady of Compassion." The devotion which was long borne towards it, was increased by its wonderful deliverance from fire. When the monastery was burnt down in 1624, the picture was afterwards found among the ruins, without any trace of damage; not even the veil, with which it was covered, had been touched by the flames, although the niche in which it was placed was burned.

During a long continuance of rainy weather, in the year 1647, the little river Lenno, on which the town of Roveredo is situated, became so swollen that it overflowed its banks, submerging fields, devastating vineyards, drowning the cattle, and, in several sad cases, even lives were lost. The broad lowlands around, resembled an immense lake, so that the inhabitants of the surrounding districts only thought of saving themselves and their property, leaving the unfortunate population of Roveredo quite deserted. Within the town, the danger increased hourly from the continual rising of the water, while the misery and distress caused by scarcity of food was very great.

Public processions and devotions were ordered, in order to appease the anger of God; yet, still the water continued to rise higher and higher. At last, Jerome de Dominis, Prior of the Carmelite Convent, deeply moved by the misery of the people, and, inspired by God, took a blessed Scapular, and exhorting all to confidence in the power and goodness of God, and the intercession of Mary, went to pray by the water. His brethren, and many of the laity, accompanied him, and they besought Almighty God and the Blessed Virgin to show themselves merciful in this dire misfortune. Then the Prior, in the sight of all, threw the holy Scapular—"The sign of salvation and safeguard in danger"—into the swollen waves, with great confidence. Immediately, the power of Mary's Badge and of the Prayer of Faith was manifested, for, at once, the flood decreased considerably, and from that time it diminished by degrees until it completely subsided, leaving the surrounding lands more fertile than they were before, and the buildings almost uninjured.

22. *The Great Fire at Donanstamf.*

We have a little incident given to us from the most reliable source, which happened during the great fire at Donanstamf, concerning a young girl who, like so many others, attempted to save her few belongings by carrying them to the cellar. Amongst other things which she tried to rescue from the flames, were her greatest treasures: a porcelain statue of the Mother of God, two lamps, together with a few clothes, and in the pocket of her Sunday dress, she put a new pair of Scapulars; these were all deposited carefully out of danger, before she, herself, left the burning house.

When the fire was extinguished, and the poor girl returned to see how much damage had been done, she found everything destroyed, and in a charred state. Sorrowfully she looked for the place where she had put her statue, when, to her surprise and delight, there it stood white and uninjured on the very spot where she had placed it, although the two lamps, standing near, had melted away.

Still greater was her joyful astonishment, when she perceived the pocket of her now shapeless dress on the ground, and lifting it up she found the Scapulars still unhurt, though the edge of the pocket was black as far as the Scapulars. The writer of this has convinced herself of the truth of the story with her own eyes, and asks all pious clients of the Mother of God to consider if such indications of Mary's help appear in a thing of such little worth, what marvels of grace and protection may we not expect, if we wear Mary's livery with a pure and penitent heart.

23. *Always Wear your Scapular.*

One evening as P. Leblane, a Jesuit Father, was making his rounds through the dormitory of a college, he found a boy kneeling by his bedside, who, on being asked why he was not in bed, replied: "I have given my Scapular to the porter to mend, and he has not yet returned it; I dare not go to bed for fear of dying without it."

"Never mind, my little man," said the Father, "you will get it to-morrow, so go to bed now, and sleep peacefully."

"O, I could not go to sleep, Father, for fear I might die to-night," and saying this, the poor child burst into tears. The good Father, moved by his distress and earnestness, went to the porter, and brought the little fellow his Scapular; whereupon he became cheerful and pacified, and having kissed it fervently, went to sleep.

The following morning, the Father noticed that this boy did not come down with the rest, and, filled with an indescribable dread, he went to call him, but got no answer. He took him by the hand—it was cold and stiff. The good little child had died in the night. He had fallen asleep kissing his Scapular, and was still holding it, pressed to his smiling lips, when the Father found him.

Let us also adopt this pious custom of kissing our holy Scapular before going to sleep, and ask Mary for the grace to wear it till death. Let us never put it aside under any pretext, for an infinite benefit is bound up with it, and through it, as servants of Mary, we have a special claim to her assistance.

24. On the Heights of Düppel.

The morning of the 18th of April, 1864, can never be erased from my memory. We were marching to attack an almost impregnable fortress on the heights of Düppel; the firing had already begun, the great cannons were playing on the bulwarks with most vociferous energy, and the din and roar of battle was like a fierce storm, making the very earth tremble beneath our feet.

The preceding evening, one of my comrades had asked me "Why I wore a little piece of cloth over my shoulders?" I confided to him that it was the coat of mail of the Queen of Victories, and that I placed more trust in it than even in my battalion. I fully relied on my Scapular to save me from all danger the next day. Nor was I disappointed, for as I stood in

41

the midst of a shower of bullets, with my comrades falling on either side of me in quick succession, I constantly invoked the Blessed Virgin with Saint Bernard's beautiful words: "Remember, O most holy Virgin Mary," etc., and when more than a third part of our company lay dead or wounded, I remained uninjured, which I owe to no other cause than the protection of our Lady.

25. Mary's Scapular, our Armour.

As I was reading the article on the Scapular in the July number of the *Blüten,* an interesting occurrence of the great fire at Paderborn, in 1875, occurred to my mind, when over one hundred houses were burnt down, and I will briefly relate what I saw and heard:

"When I came to the neighbourhood of Paderborn last autumn, some weeks after the fire, they showed me a house which had been preserved during the great conflagration, and which was commonly believed to have been saved through the agency of the holy Scapular. Naturally, I was much interested, and examined all the surroundings carefully; even at first sight, the house exhibited much that was curious, and led me to suppose that, humanly speaking, it would have been as quickly consumed as the neighbouring buildings, which were now only desolate heaps of ruins. As I stood there, picturing the scene to myself, a woman came out of the very house I was looking at, and I asked her for an explanation of what was reported to be the miraculous preservation of the building. She willingly acceded to my request, and made the following statement: 'On the right hand a large pile of logs, belonging to a baker, stood in dangerous proximity; this wood had been burning for three whole days, and you can imagine the danger which threatened our house, when I tell that it is covered with straw thatching. Just on the side where the pile of wood was burning, you can still see a part of the straw roof projecting, quite untouched by the flames.

" 'The danger was not less on the left side, for there grew a young plum tree, the branches of which hung close over the roof; the flames had scorched its leaves and roasted its fruit, but the roof remained untouched; yet we had still great cause to fear, from the knowledge that the garret was partly filled with hay and straw. Added to this, a window remained wide open during the fire, but not a single spark entered. We might certainly have expected that, with the intense heat, the window panes would at least have been cracked, or the paint on the doors and windows would have suffered, but no trace of any injury could be discovered.' "

"My astonishment was very great on hearing all this, so I then asked the woman what, in her opinion, was the cause of this miraculous preservation. She told me that for twenty-four years she had been in the Confraternity of the Scapular, and still had the very Scapular which she received on the day of enrolment (the strings, she was careful to tell me, had been renewed from time to time). On the morning of the eventful day, she had laid her Scapular aside when changing her clothes, and, from forgetfulness, had left it hanging at the window. It was only at mid-day, when everyone was astonished to find her house uninjured, that she suddenly thought of her Scapular at the open window. Then she realized what had happened, and gratefully promised a Mass in thanksgiving."

I was deeply moved by this woman's simple story, and I

exhorted her to be ever grateful to the Divine Mother; I left her with the firm resolution, not only to remain an ardent lover myself of the Queen of Heaven, but also to contribute to the increase of Her honour to the best of my abilities.

26. Escape from Death.

On the 8th of May, 1842, a fearful accident happened at the gates of Paris; a train, which was starting for Versailles, caught fire, and in remembrance of this event, the Chapel of "Notre Dame des Flammes," at Bellevue, was built. More than a hundred persons were burnt, and many suffered from very severe wounds caused by the flames. Three days after this awful catastrophe, we read in the *Union*, that a young student accompanied one of his wounded friends, named Necker, to the hospital. On reaching the room where his friend was to be laid, the student said to one of the Sisters of Mercy, "Oh, Sister, my Scapular has saved me! I owe my life to the Blessed Virgin Mary, for I am the only person who escaped death out of all who were in the same carriage with me. I have not a single scar, and I have every reason to thank God for saving my life."

27. Conversion through the Scapular.

The circumstances under which a renowned American General and his wife were converted to Catholicism, during the war between the North and South American States, are so noteworthy, and show so clearly that they owed this inestimable grace to the Mother of God, that it will be for the greater honour of our Lord, and the Blessed Virgin Mary, to make them known to all who have not yet heard or read about them.

Whilst the cannons roared, and the cries of the wounded and dying were heard on every side, a soldier who had been struck by a ball was led to the General. The latter found that though the ball had struck the man over his heart, yet he was not even wounded, and it was most evident that his Scapular, worn on the very spot where the ball had pierced, had been the means of saving his life. The General could account for the wonderful occurrence in no other way, and when the grateful soldier had unfolded to him more in detail the efficacy of wearing our Lady's livery under his uniform, the Mother of God vouchsafed to enlighten the understanding of the brave officer, who had so promptly acknowledged Her power, winning for him the grace of conversion, and, from being a zealous Protestant, he became a fervent Catholic.

His wife knew nothing of this change, for, as she was a bigoted Protestant, he concealed the fact from her; but he prayed very earnestly, and especially invoked our Lady on her behalf. Nevertheless, when he returned home after the war, he was not without anxiety, lest the peace of the house should be disturbed by his change of religion, so he resolved, at least at first, to keep it a secret.

On the first Sunday after his return, when the bells were calling the faithful to Mass, the General left the house unperceived, and went to the Catholic church. Here he knelt down in the bench assigned to him, and was soon absorbed in devout prayer. A little later a lady entered the same bench without the General perceiving anything, or taking notice of his companion. Mass being ended, he rose to leave the church, and saw, with joyful surprise, that his wife had been next to him, and had signed her forehead, mouth, and heart with the

45

cross.

Unknown to each other, they had embraced the Catholic religion, the wife naturally attributing the grace she had received to the prayers of her husband. Who can describe the happiness and joy of these two new converts, when side by side, they left the church! The love which bound them together as husband and wife, was now augmented by their union in the One True Fold.

Thus, did that faithful practice of wearing the Scapular, bear fruit a hundredfold.

* * * * *

The same General relates another interesting fact concerning a trumpeter, who was struck down near him. He declared that the ball had wounded him in the breast, but when the Captain examined him, he found that the ball had fastened itself to our Lady's Scapular, which the man wore, and had not penetrated into the flesh. The Captain held up the ball, and showed it to all who were standing near.

28. *An Adventure with a Bull.*

A workman sends the following communication of an adventure which happened to himself: —

"One beautiful Sunday in summer, about twenty-one years ago, I went to R— —, in order to visit my aged parents. The high road led me past a wood, where my father, an old man of eighty-two, tended the cattle belonging to Count O— —. Among the herd, was a furious bull, which had already attacked several people, and which my father, much against his will, was compelled to take along with the rest, although the police had forbidden it. When I came near the place where my father was taking his mid-day meal, under the shade of a tree, the bull saw me, and foaming furiously at the mouth, and pawing the ground with its feet, suddenly made a rush for me. I took my stick and tried to drive it away, but almost before I knew where I was, it had tossed me in the air, some six feet from the ground, and as I fell at some distance, it again came bounding towards me. My father seeing the danger, sprang from his seat, and ran to my assistance, while I, lying on the ground, saw with terror, the ferocious beast coming nearer and nearer, its head bent, its neck outstretched. At this supreme moment, my father gave a tremendous shout, which made the beast turn round; then to my surprise and relief, it quietly went off in an opposite direction. In spite of my fear, I had thought with confidence of the Scapular round my neck, and I firmly believe that, in that hour of danger, Mary proved my protectress and deliverer.

"When my father joined me, he said he had never witnessed such a narrow escape from imminent peril, and ascribed the sudden quieting of the bull, entirely to the intervention of our Heavenly Mother."

29. "He is not Dead, but Sleepeth."

In one of the most sanguinary battles of the Franco-Prussian war, during which so many died of their wounds that they were obliged to bury all the dead in a common grave, we have an instance of how wonderfully God watches over the faithful clients of His Blessed Mother. Among those who were lying on the field of battle, was a young officer, apparently dead, who was really only in a swoon, consequent on the sufferings produced by his wounds. The Colonel, seeing him in this condition, had hastened to find someone to assist in carrying him to a place of safety; but on his return, he found, to his distress, that the young man had already been borne away to be buried with numbers of his comrades. Greatly afflicted, he hurried to the place where the corpses were piled together, awaiting burial; but, alas! under such circumstances, it was almost impossible to distinguish the features of his friend, in spite of close examination, so disfigured were the bodies which lay before them. At last a sudden idea came into the Colonel's mind, and he called out: "Examine the clothes, for my friend wore a Scapular, and a medal of the Immaculate Conception." They did what he desired, and our Blessed Lady, guiding their search, they almost immediately found the young officer. He was then placed on a stretcher, and taken to the hospital, where he received proper attention, and completely recovered his health.

It is needless to say that, as soon as he was able, he gave due thanks to our Immaculate Queen, who had stayed the awful fate which seemed in store for him.

III.

30. "In the Day of Battle, we beseech Thee to hear us."

FATHER Maesty, a military Chaplain, relates the following incident, which happened in the year 1872:

"One winter evening, in the course of my customary rounds in the military hospital, I stopped at the bedside of a brave soldier, who had taken part in twelve battles during the Franco-Prussian war, and having pulled through a violent typhoid fever in France, he was at length brought as a convalescent to this Bavarian hospital. There were but few patients in the ward, but, close by the spot where I was standing, six invalids had clustered round the stove, and were playing cards with as much earnestness and excitement as if the fate of the whole nation was at stake. I seated myself by the bedside, and, seeing we should be neither overheard nor disturbed, I was soon engaged in conversation with the convalescent soldier. We talked of old times, of home and country, of peace and war, of the friends of our youth — and thus we soon became the best of friends. Before leaving, I presented my new friend with a medal; but he, drawing his purse from under his pillow, produced another, saying, 'I have one already, my dear mother gave it to me before I started for the French campaign.' 'Why not wear it round your neck?' I asked. 'It might possibly get lost,' was the reply, 'and I value it more than a gold sovereign, I shall always treasure it as a precious keepsake.'

" 'Will you tell me the reason?' I asked.

49

"With some hesitation, and seeming reluctance, the sick man said, 'I want to tell you about it, and also what I have on my conscience, but somehow, I cannot do so to-day; be so kind as to return to-morrow, and then I will tell you all—be sure and come.'

"The next day I returned to the hospital at the same time; I found the same group of card-players busily engaged in their game, round a bright fire. The keeper of the ward seeing I was willing to stay, left me in charge of the sick soldier, who was not yet able to leave his bed, and meantime went out to breathe the fresh air, which his duty in the ward seldom allowed him to enjoy.

" 'Now then,' I said to my friend, 'we shall be quite undisturbed, so let us have a quiet chat. Tell me first of all why you are so attached to your medal, perhaps you think that so long as it is in your purse it keeps the money from falling out. Have I guessed rightly?' 'Not so,' he replied, 'that would only be foolish superstition.' The soldier then raised himself, and taking the medal in his hand, began his story with visible signs of emotion. 'As I told you before, my dear mother, on the day of my departure, hung this medal round my neck without saying a word, for she was weeping too much to speak. When we parted, her last words to me were these—My son, I have often begged of you to mend your ways, but in vain; now, at last, I entrust you to the Blessed Mother of God. If you should forget me, at least never forget Her. I brushed away a tear, for these words went to my heart, and I can assure you that I have never forgotten either my earthly or my Heavenly Mother. I set out for the war without even going to Confession, for I was too reckless to think of any religious duty; there was no good about me but our Lady's medal. Yet, I have always, in my heart, venerated the Immaculate Virgin, and in spite of all my extravagance, the very thought of her would make me serious; in trouble it was my best comfort, and in anger it had power to soften me, and thus it was that I always wore her medal most faithfully.

" 'The first engagement, which was the memorable battle of Wörth, was a fierce one. We fought desperately, and in the bloody fight I was wounded, a bullet striking me on the chest; the shock dazed me, and I fell to the ground unconscious, while my comrades pushed forward. When I came to myself, I did not experience the slightest pain, and so I began to feel for the wound. My coat, vest, and shirt were pierced through, but I saw nothing, save a blue mark on my chest, and at once searching for the medal, I found it in my trouser pocket, with the string broken off. Then, in my boot, I found the bullet, as flat as a penny, on one side being engraved the image of our Lady, quite plainly, with the motto, 'Maria sine labe concepta, intercede pro nobis,' only that the letters were reversed. Look here! compare the bullet with the medal, and you will see that the stamp perfectly corresponds. This medal had undoubtedly saved my life, and now you understand why I could not possibly forget the Blessed Mother of God, or my own dear mother, who gave me Mary as a shield to protect me.'

"The recollection of this wonderful incident, had deeply moved the brave soldier, who became now more communicative, and he added that there was something else he wished to confide to me; he said I had won his confidence, and he desired to make a good Confession. At Easter he had been refused Absolution, and he then made up his mind never to approach the Sacraments again. But the Holy Mother of God had not forsaken him, and now he felt urged to enter into himself, and make a good Confession, so that when he went home to his old mother, she would find he was really a changed man.

"A few days later, having made a worthy and humble Confession, he wrote a long letter to his good mother, who was overjoyed, and poured out her heart, brimful of gratitude, before the altar of our Lady of Sorrows, who had restored to her her son."

31. A Miraculous Escape.

The following narrative is related by a French emigrant of noble extraction. During the "Reign of Terror" he, more fortunate than most of his countrymen, was able to rescue a great part of his vast possessions from the greedy grasp of the bloody tyrants then in power—Robespierre, Danton, and Marat, whose names will ever be held in execration by posterity:—

"For some time," he says, "I had been confined in a prison at Paris, and, together with many fellow prisoners, I was daily expecting the execution of the death warrant passed against me. One morning the gaoler entered the prison and read aloud the list of those who were to be led to the guillotine. I counted about fifty names, and mine was amongst the number. Then followed a scene of indescribable confusion; some of the prisoners wept, some howled, some cursed the tyrants, whilst others exulted and sang hymns of praise to God, thanking Him that the hour of their deliverance had come at last.

"All had already left the prison to meet their doom. I alone lingered behind, and calling to the gaoler, I said imploringly, 'Have patience with me, I lost my medal last night, and I cannot go without it.' 'Medal!' cried the man indignantly, 'what medal?' '*My* medal,' I answered, at the same time turning over the straw of my couch, and searching with desperate eagerness. 'Forward!' cried the gaoler, imperiously, 'you shall not have a moment's respite.' 'Oh, I beseech you, have pity, grant me one moment more!' I entreated, falling on my knees, 'I have worn that medal all my life on my breast, and now at my last hour—;' and grief choked my voice, the loss of my treasure was breaking my heart. I expected an outburst of angry threats from the gaoler, and that he would call in the guards to drag me out by force, when, lo! to my astonishment, he stood still, and smiling good naturedly said, 'Well, then, stay for to-day, but to-morrow, be ready to ascend the guillotine with your medal!' With these words he left the prison, and turned the key in the lock. At that very moment I found the medal, and, springing to my feet, I rushed to the door, and called after the gaoler, but he was already out of sight, and did not hear me. Then I pressed the medal to my lips and kissed it with a devotion such as I had never before experienced.

"The next morning, the prison door was again opened, but by a strange gaoler, whom I had not seen before. He walked in and read the list of victims to be executed that day. I was not named! Why I was spared has always been a mystery to me; perhaps I was supposed to have already suffered execution, or perhaps I was reckoned among the fugitives.

"One evening, about a week later, there suddenly arose, in the court adjoining the prison, the cry of 'Fire!' At the same moment the prison door was thrown open, and a powerful voice, which I recognized as that of the first gaoler, shouted, 'Save yourselves if you can!'

"Apparently the breaking out of the fire was no mere chance, it was intended to afford the prisoners a means of escape. We readily understood its meaning, and each one hastened to avail himself of so favourable an opportunity. I was one of the first to escape. But only very few succeeded in their flight, for the guards, soon recovering from the first alarm, at once secured all the outlets of the prison. Meanwhile, I hurried on, unmolested, through the streets of the town, being protected by the darkness of the night. A few days later, I crossed the frontier, and proceeded towards the Rhine.

"An old acquaintance whom I met in Strasburg, procured me the necessary means of subsistence, and now my one desire was to be re-united to my wife and two children. At the time of my arrest and condemnation, they had left the country, and taken up their abode in some part of Germany, choosing one of the Catholic provinces near the Rhine. I knew nothing more of their plans, and undoubtedly they had long given me up as having fallen a victim to the Revolutionary party.

"My search was untiring. I wandered up and down the Rhine, visiting every village and hamlet on my way, for life could afford me no happiness without my beloved ones. Two whole years had already elapsed, my wanderings had proved absolutely fruitless, and the hope of a re-union was gradually beginning to die away, when at last, one day, I entered a church in the small town of X— —, in order to hear Mass, as was my daily custom. The service being ended, the devout worshippers began to disperse, but a few still lingered in the holy place.

"On visiting the church for the first time, it was my habit to gratify my taste for art by walking all round, to discover if there were any paintings or remarkable objects deserving closer inspection. This time, animated by the same motive, and led also by my good Angel, I directed my steps to a side chapel, where a lady, clad in deep mourning, and accompanied by two little girls, attracted my attention by the fervour with which they were praying before a picture of our Blessed Lady. It was evident they were mother and daughters. As I was standing a little distance behind them, I could not see their faces; but the thought that they were perhaps my dear wife and children, took such a strong hold of me, that I began to tremble all over, and could scarcely contain myself. I quietly left the spot, and betook myself to a corner in the nave, where I could watch, unperceived, all who went out of the chapel.

"My emotion was indescribable, for in a few minutes my presentiment would either be changed to happy certainty or most bitter disappointment. A quarter of an hour passed, which seemed to me an eternity, and at last the group rose to leave the chapel. How can I describe my feelings, as I recognized the features of my beloved wife and darling children! My heart beat so fast, that I could hardly breathe; I leaned against a pillar for support, but there was no time to lose. Rousing myself, I followed the little party out of church, keeping some distance behind, until they disappeared into a secluded but comfortable-looking house. I lost no time in obtaining information from the owner of the house, who told me that these 'good people,' as he styled them, had been living there as lodgers for about a year.

"I refrained from following the impulse of my heart, which was to fold my dear ones in my arms immediately; the sudden shock, and joy at meeting, might have proved fatal. So hurrying back to my lodgings, I wrote the following letter to my wife:—'An old friend of your husband begs to communicate to you tidings, as important as they are joyful. Your husband happily escaped from prison in Paris, and has for two years been seeking you in the neighbourhood of the Rhine. It is most likely that in a short time you will have the happiness to welcome him in your midst.' This was followed by another note, which ran as follows:—'Your husband has just learned the place of your residence, and all being well, he will shortly be with you.' Both letters were written in a disguised handwriting, and signed by different names.

"And thus, at last, we were once more united, with a joy and happiness which no pen can describe. We poured out our hearts in gratitude to the kind Providence of God, and to our Blessed Lady, who had so directed every circumstance of our separation, that our reunion might be the happier.

"In conclusion, let me add that the blessed Medal, to which I owe my life, is still my daily companion, as it was in the prison, for neither death nor the grave shall ever separate it from me."

32. *A Wonderful Conversion.*

At Freiburg, in Breisgau, A. M—, the daughter of a well-to-do tradesman, was engaged to a man who professed no religion whatever. He made it his first care to extinguish every spark of faith from the heart of his affianced bride, and by giving her all kinds of irreligious books, he succeeded but too well, for she first became a very indifferent Catholic, and later lapsed into being a free-thinker. She was, some time after, seized with a very serious illness, which brought her to death's door, and finding herself on the brink of Eternity, her views changed, and in that awful hour, she earnestly begged for the Last Sacraments. That blessed moment was, at the same time, the turning point of her spiritual life, and of her illness, from which she recovered, becoming a fervent Catholic. Her future husband, however, remained unchanged in his infidelity; yet notwithstanding the wide difference in their views, they engaged in the bond of Matrimony. From that time the young woman made it her one aim to win the soul of her husband to God. For six years she prayed most assiduously, and every Easter she begged him, with tears and supplications, to fulfil his Paschal duties, but all in vain. Then she had an inspiration to commend the matter to the Blessed Mother of God, and with great trust and confidence, she confided the conversion of her husband to her special care. At Eastertide, she did not breathe a word to him about approaching the Sacraments, but she secretly fastened inside his coat a medal of the Immaculate Conception, and then redoubled her prayers. After a few days, she noticed that he was more than usually thoughtful, and seemed as if something was weighing on his mind. The good wife observed a change in his whole manner, and her hopes began to revive. But who can describe the joy, the intense gratitude she felt towards the Blessed Virgin, when one day her two little boys, returning home from school, eagerly ran to meet her with the joyful tidings: "Mother, we have just met Papa; he sends his love, and told us to let you know that he is on his way to Confession!"

And so it was, for in a few days the Immaculate Virgin had softened the heart of that hardened sinner. The conversion was entire, and, thanks to the Mother of God, remained a lasting one.

33. Mary, the Refuge of Sinners.

In the year 1839, an old man of seventy was lying at death's door, in the hospital of Dijon, in France. In spite of every kind of exhortation, he would not hear of going to Confession. The good Sister of Charity, who was nursing him, was very much grieved at his obstinacy, and as all her own efforts failed, she at last had recourse to a pious stratagem. Taking a small medal of the Immaculate Conception, she hid it under the sick man's pillow; but he discovering it, took it and flung it on the ground, with the most awful imprecations. Sister Gabriel was now quite discouraged, and she could not refrain from weeping at the sight of this poor sinner, who was about to enter Eternity in such a miserable state. She rose to leave the room, and as she did so, she said to her patient: "I will go, but the Mother of God will stay with you!" (meaning the medal).

These words entered like lightning into the soul of the dying man. "The Mother of God will stay with you" he kept repeating over and over again, until at last he fell into a deep slumber. After some hours, he awoke, and calling to Sister Gabriel, he asked for a priest, explaining the cause of this sudden change: "The Blessed Mother of God appeared to me in my sleep; she stood there close by the bed, and wept. When I asked her why she wept, she answered sorrowfully, 'For thy sake!', and I then also wept, and the scales fell from my eyes, for at that very moment, I saw my wretched state, I recognized the depth of my guilt. Therefore, I beseech you, my dear Sister, get me a priest, that I may make my Confession before it is too late."

With sincere and heartfelt contrition, the poor sinner made his Confession, and having received the Last Sacraments, died soon after, peacefully, and happily reconciled to his God.

How compassionate must be the heart of our Immaculate Queen, to weep at the deathbed of a sinner, who was thus going headlong to perdition! How powerful is she, also, to obtain the conversion of so obstinate and hardened a soul! The title "Queen conceived without original sin," is most fittingly placed at the end of the Litany, and it is perhaps the one which is dearest and most pleasing to our Blessed Lady, and one which is never uttered in vain.

34. Our Lady's Protegée.

An accident, which might have terminated fatally, happened in a vineyard near Freiburg, in Switzerland, at the time of the vintage. It was evening, and the labourers were in high spirits, as the loads of grapes were being carried through the flower garden, which re-echoed with the merry chorus of voices. The proprietor's little daughter, aged ten years, in order to amuse herself, attempted to climb a ladder which was resting against a sort of bower formed of vines, trained over a trellis, but which had no proper support. As soon as the child got up, the ladder began to slip backwards before anyone could come to the rescue, and the little one's cry of terror was heard above all the singing and laughing. Just under the ladder grew a rosebush, supported by a pointed stake; the point of the stake had already penetrated the child's throat, when the ladder caught in the bush, and was thus abruptly brought to a standstill; but the child had a heavy fall, being thrown off the ladder on to the flower bed below. She was picked up unconscious, the blood streaming from a ghastly wound in her throat. A physician was hastily summoned, and while he was examining her, the poor parents stood by, awaiting his opinion with dreadful anxiety. In a few minutes he turned round, and said to them cheerfully: "Never, in my long practice, have I come across a more wonderful escape! On one side of the wound, the nerve is quite unharmed, and on the other, the windpipe is likewise uninjured. Tell me, little one, under whose happy protection you were, when you fell?" The weeping mother, who was a Protestant, then showed him a medal of our Lady, still stained with blood, which she had taken from the child's neck. The good doctor Schwörer, who was a Catholic, said, with tears in his eyes, "Indeed, no harm could come with such a protectress, for where the Mother of God is, there are also the holy Angels, ever ready to assist! Listen, my child, a scar will always remain, but let it ever remind you to whom you owe your life."

IV.

35. *Saved by our Lady of the Sacred Heart.*

THE Reverend B. Meucci, having been appointed to the Priory of Saint Blaise, in Arezzo, had hardly taken possession of the parish, and solemnly consecrated it to our Lady of the Sacred Heart, when he was, one evening, seized with a stroke of apoplexy in the street. The people rushed to his assistance from all parts of the village, but, alas! little hope of his recovery could be entertained. However, some fervent souls organized a public triduum in honour of our Lady of the Sacred Heart, for, knowing that such a seizure is nearly always fatal, they felt all the more urged to commit their anxiety to the Advocate of desperate cases. Their confidence was soon rewarded, for, on the third day of the triduum, the young priest had so far recovered, as to be able to resume his parochial duties, and, by degrees, his health improved so much, that no trace was left of his alarming seizure.

About this time, another wonderful event happened in the same parish. Two little children, whilst playing in a garden, came across some fruit, which had been poisoned for the rats. With a greediness, natural to their age, they at once began to eat it, and before long, vomiting and other symptoms of poisoning appeared. The distracted mothers felt that all medical aid was useless, and in their extremity, knew not to whom to turn. Suddenly, their hope revived at the thought of our Lady of the Sacred Heart; they knew she was the patroness of their parish, and the Advocate of hopeless cases, and they invoked her as their only refuge in this dire necessity, placing, at the same time, two medals round the necks of their children, who, for some hours, lay unconscious, apparently at the point of death—a time which seemed an eternity to the anxious watchers round their beds. But our Lady's hour was at hand, and she was about to manifest to the sorrowing mothers and sympathizing neighbours, the power of her intercession, for, at length, the two children opened their eyes, as though awaking from a peaceful slumber, and raising their heads, looked round in amazement at the scene of desolation which met their gaze. All symptoms of poisoning had entirely disappeared, and the little ones joyfully threw themselves into their mothers' arms. "May our Lady of the Sacred Heart be praised a thousand times!" was the grateful cry of all present, especially of those two happy mothers.

36. *Frustrated through Prayer.*

From Spain we have the following testimony of our Lady's wonderful protection; it is given by the superior of the Brothers of Charity in that country:—

"For some time, I have felt in duty bound, to publish in the 'Annals of our Lady of the Sacred Heart,' the wonderful help I have experienced in critical circumstances, through invoking her under that beautiful title. At the end of the year 1867, I undertook the reform of our Institute, and founded a house in Barcelona. I gratefully acknowledge that I owe the completion and success of that work to the power and loving kindness of our Lady of the Sacred Heart, although the undertaking entailed very severe trials and difficulties. Oh, how well protected are they who are sheltered under the mantle of the

Queen of Heaven!

"My vocation as a priest and Brother of Charity, has brought me in contact with numberless cases of misery and misfortune, especially during the last Revolution and Civil War in Spain. In such distressing times, it behoves the Brother of Charity to be more than ever the comfort and support of the unfortunate victims of such public calamities. On three separate occasions I found myself surrounded by a number of blood-thirsty men, whose intentions toward me were manifestly of the worst kind. In the hour of danger, I never failed to call upon Mary, the dispenser of the inexhaustible treasures of the Sacred Heart, and I have ever been protected in the most marvelous manner.

"Once I was actually seized by several armed ruffians, who were determined to take my life. In this extremity, I felt urged to call on our Lady for help, and to promise that if I escaped from this danger, I would do all in my power to make her name known and honoured under the beautiful title of our Lady of the Sacred Heart. Hardly had I made this promise interiorly, when the ruffians, who surrounded me, most unexpectedly set me free. This happened in the very place where I had made that foundation, which cost me so much trouble and anxiety, and it seems to me all the more a striking and visible proof that our Lady accepted my promise, for not only did she then grant me my life and freedom, but, by a mysterious dispensation of Providence, this house eventually became the home of the Missionaries of the Sacred Heart, and the head-quarters of the Archconfraternity of our Lady of the Sacred Heart, in Spain."

37. *Cure of Anna Krebs.*

Anna Krebs was the daughter of an honest weaver, and from her infancy she had been a delicate and sickly child, suffering especially from scrofula, which was the cause of a constant soreness of the eyes. She was incapable even of the slightest labour, and only dragged herself occasionally to school; but, in spite of her thirst for knowledge, she was obliged at last to give this up as well. Finally, she became completely bedridden, for, besides scrofula, she was afflicted with most painful cramps and constant headaches, her entire body being swollen to an extraordinary size. Her eyes were so sore, that she could not endure the least glimmer of light, and her room had to be kept in total darkness. At length she became quite blind. The illness was daily growing more serious, and the child's voice had become so weak, that it was with the greatest difficulty anyone could understand her almost inaudible whispers; this state lasted for nine weeks. Two doctors had been in constant attendance, and they at length declared that there was no hope, as the child was in a decline. After this decision, the poor sufferer was prepared for the Last Sacraments, and, having been anointed, she longed to be released from her sufferings. A few days later, the illness took such an alarming turn, that the sorrowing parents were daily expecting the loss of their child, and had given up even the slightest hope of her recovery. At this juncture, a friend brought a medal of our Lady of the Sacred Heart, and bade the mother to hang it round the child's neck, as a last endeavour to save her life. This was about two o'clock in the afternoon, and before three, the dying girl raised herself, and called out in a perfectly distinct voice: "Mother, I am better, for our Blessed

Lady has helped me!" At the same moment she was able to distinguish the objects around her, and did not feel the slightest pain anywhere; in fact she was quite transformed. The swelling had already decreased, although none could take this as a certain sign of recovery. Unhappily, this sudden improvement was not a complete cure. The poor invalid was, indeed, able to sit up and do a little work, but her feet had lost all power, so that she could neither walk nor stand, and had to be carried from one place to another. A week later, she was taken to the shrine of our Lady of Philippsdorf, a pilgrimage which she most especially loved, in order to obtain from our Blessed Lady a complete cure. Another week passed, and still they persevered in their prayers; the poor mother was longing for her child's recovery, and in her impatience, she kept urging her to try and make some little effort, and endeavour to stand or walk, or at least to stretch out her foot. But Anna felt how utterly useless every attempt of this kind was, and so refused to comply with her mother's request. The latter having left the room for a short time, the child felt she had done wrong not to obey, and so made an attempt to stand up. She bade her brother give her a stick, and leaning upon it she raised herself; at the same moment the weakness in her legs disappeared, and she was able to walk.

It was no freak of imagination that had caused this helpless state, for all who knew the child's character and disposition were convinced that she was incapable of being deluded, either by fancy or nervous apprehension. The miracle was thus all the more evident, and within a few weeks her appearance was quite changed, and she became the very picture of health.

May all praise and thanks be given to the Blessed Mother of God, to whom alone Anna Krebs ascribes her miraculous cure, as she did the very first moment of her improvement in health, when she cried out, "the Blessed Virgin has helped me!"

38. Mary Immaculate, the Health of the Sick.

Father X— —, of the Society of Jesus, laboured for several years in Quito, as professor of chemistry. Whilst making an experiment, he had the misfortune to injure his face in such a dreadful manner, that his eyes projected from their sockets, and could only be set in again by means of a skilful operation. After undergoing this, it was found that one of the eyes remained completely sightless, whilst the other was so extremely weak that, according to the doctor's statement, the sight of this one would also be lost before long, unless the blind eye were taken out in time. But Father X— — would not hear of this, and hoping to obtain better advice from European oculists, he started for Paris. No fewer than eighteen medical men and specialists were consulted in France, and they all agreed that the taking out of the blind eye was unavoidable. But the Jesuit Father would not give in, so he begged some of the members of the Society to unite with him in making a Novena before the Feast of the Immaculate Conception, saying that Mary was the best doctor after all, and that with her there is still hope, even when all physicians have failed. He would make one last attempt by consulting the famous Doctor Mooren, and for this purpose, he journeyed to Düsseldorf, where that renowned specialist then resided. Doctor Mooren, after making a careful examination of Father X— —'s eyes, declared that, in his opinion, the taking out of the blind eye was not absolutely necessary to secure the preservation of the other, which was so much injured by the accident. The Father then remained for some time under his treatment, residing in the hospital of the Sisters of the Cross. On the eighth of December he said Mass in their chapel, and as he came to the solemn moment of the Consecration, the few persons who were present, saw that he was experiencing some violent emotion, and the Sisters, becoming alarmed, thought of calling another priest to his assistance. What had really happened? Whilst the Father was pronouncing the words of Consecration, he felt a strange sensation in his eyes, and presently it seemed to him as if scales had fallen from them, at the same moment, he could read plainly and distinctly, with both eyes, the words on the Altar card. At the end of the Novena, on the Feast of the Immaculate Conception, he was perfectly cured!

It can easily be imagined, the sensation created by this miraculous event. May it strengthen our own confidence in our Heavenly Advocate, and may she obtain for us, the cure of spiritual blindness, to which we are all more or less subject, and which is a greater misfortune by far than the one we have just related.

39. A Cure through our Lady of Lourdes in Manchooria.

The Reverend F. B——, an Apostolic Missioner, relates the following details of the miraculous cure of a heathen woman in Manchooria. His Lordship, Bishop Dubail, Vicar Apostolic of the Province, testifies to the truth of this account, which is dated April, 1880:

"In the year 1879, as I was making a visitation through my district, on the Monday after Christmas Day, I was informed that a marvelous favour had been granted by our Lady to a heathen woman. I thought it necessary to investigate the matter very closely, and with this intention, I sought every kind of information, from Christians as well as from heathens, with the following result: —

"The heathen family, known by the name of Leon, consisting of father, mother, daughter and three married sons, was visited in the course of last year with a strange malady, that had every appearance of leprosy. The mother was the worst victim to the disease, and towards the end of November, an abscess formed on her upper lip, which soon became so serious, that the inflammation spread all over the mouth, the tongue being so swollen, that the poor sufferer could neither take any nourishment, nor speak a single word. The doctor was sent for, and in order to relieve the inflammation, he pierced the tongue through with a needle more than fifty times, but without any success. At last he declared his inability to help the sick woman, and a second doctor was called in, but with no more favourable result. The young girl then said to her mother: 'I have seen the child of a Christian named Loung cured, when in a dying state, as soon as she had drunk of a certain water; I know not what kind of water it was, but will you not, at least, try to swallow some of it?' The woman made a sign in the affirmative, and, having obtained the father's consent, Agnes Loung was immediately sent for, and asked to bring some of the water to the sick woman. She, with great faith, admonished the heathen to put her trust in the Blessed Virgin, and gave her two small spoonfuls of Lourdes water. No sooner had the poor sufferer swallowed it, than she fell into a deep slumber, although for many days previously she had taken no rest. Shortly after midnight, her relations who were in attendance, wishing to hasten her recovery, urged the doctor to give her some remedies, but, to their dismay, the medicine only made her worse, and her condition again became so alarming, that she seemed to be in her agony. The Christian girl was once more hastily sent for; she again exhorted the poor heathen to have confidence in the Blessed Virgin, and to promise, there and then, she would become a Christian if her life was spared. She then drank a glass of Lourdes water, which effected a sudden and complete cure; the invalid, and her husband, loudly proclaimed their gratitude to the ever-blessed Virgin for this second favour.

"The whole family was soon numbered among the catechumens, and the news of this wonderful event spread throughout the entire district, causing great excitement. Heathens, as well as Christians, were forced to acknowledge the interposition of a Supreme Power, and all gave glory to God."

40. Miraculous Recovery in Florence.

In the account of the wonderful cure and events related here, we wish it to be well understood that, in accordance with the decree of Pope Urban VIII., we merely intend to state the facts, without in any way anticipating the decision of the Church, regarding their supernatural importance. The following favour we relate in the words of the person who was cured, for it illustrates once more the power of our Lady of the Sacred Heart: —

"In the year 1874, on the twenty-second of November, I was attacked with a serious disease of the lungs, accompanied by violent hemorrhage. The doctor, who visited me daily, ordered various remedies, but all in vain, for the illness grew worse and worse. On the Feast of the Epiphany, my condition was so precarious, that it was thought necessary to strengthen me with the Last Sacraments, and the grief and distress of my afflicted family cannot be expressed. A few days later, however, a marked change for the better came over me, and as the improvement continued, by the end of March I had so far rallied as to be able to sit up for a little time every day. Yet, for all that, I felt that the cure was not a permanent one, and, indeed, I was threatened with a dangerous relapse of the same malady. Soon I found myself again bedridden, and in a far worse state than before; the frequent spitting of blood, which no remedy could check, brought me to such an extreme state of exhaustion, that all hope of recovery was given up, and the end daily expected. My hands, feet, and in fact my whole body began to swell enormously, and my stomach could not retain the least nourishment. I was again anointed, but the constant sickness prevented me from receiving Holy Viaticum. I lay in this miserable condition, more dead than alive, until the twenty-fourth of May, when the doctor again declared there was no more hope, and that the end was nigh.

"All human aid having thus proved fruitless, I was hourly expecting death as a release from my pitiful condition, so, turning my last thoughts once more to our Blessed Lady, I begged one of my relations to have a candle lighted for me, before the Altar of our Lady of the Sacred Heart, and when my mother brought me a picture of Mary, I raised my feeble eyes to it with a feeling of intense love and deepest confidence. Nor was it long before the Blessed Virgin let me experience her maternal protection. I fell into a swoon, and it seemed to me as if, at the foot of my bed, I beheld our Lady of the Sacred Heart, clothed in a bright mantle, and holding the Infant-God in her arms. The Child's face bore a striking resemblance to His beautiful Mother; she was young and fair, shining like the sun, and with a look of indescribable sweetness and majesty, and both Mary and the Divine Child held lamps in their hands. Our Lady approached me and said: 'See if the picture you are holding is like me.' Then she showed me her lamp, and I noticed that it was on the point of going out, for there was hardly any oil in it. 'See!' said our Lady, 'This lamp is like your life. It is on the point of going out; but I do not wish your life to be extinguished.' She then gave me the Child's lamp, which burnt brightly, after which I said to myself: 'Surely, I am dreaming!' 'No,' said our Lady, 'you are not dreaming,' and passing her hand over my hands, feet, and body, the swelling immediately disappeared. 'Stand up!' she then said, 'for you are now perfectly cured; make good use of the time that is granted you, and retire from the world for a while.' After these words, the vision disappeared. My mother, who had heard me talking, thought I was delirious. I came to myself about four o'clock, when I asked for a drink of water, which I was able to take then, as well as some solid food. All my pains were gone; at six o'clock, I got up, and at eleven, I was on my way to the Church of our Lady, for I desired to give thanks, without delay, to my Heavenly Mother for my miraculous cure. The astonishment of all my friends may be imagined at seeing me well and strong, when a few hours before, they had left me apparently dying. I am not so much overjoyed at my bodily cure, as for the wonderful favour and privilege bestowed on my unworthy self by the merciful and gracious Queen of Heaven. I have written and signed this with my own hand.

"Elvira Nelli,

"E. de M— —."

71

41. *The Portrait of Pope Pius IX.*

A worthy and venerable priest writes from Bologna to the *Osservatore Cattolico* of Milan, the following:—

"Carolina Orsi, of Bologna, aged thirty years, while living in the Convent of Saint Joseph, was taken ill in January, 1878. She was stricken with a violent fever, and was troubled with such an incessant cough, that no doctor could relieve it. Within a few weeks, the symptoms of the disease became alarming, and the doctor declared that, even if her life were spared, the convalescence would last a very long time, and that she would always be in a precarious state of health. About this time, one of the sick person's friends, gave her a portrait of the late venerable Pontiff, Pope Pius IX, and related to her some of the marvelous cures obtained through his intercession. These accounts made a strong impression on Carolina, and having asked her Confessor if it were allowable to pray to the deceased Pontiff, he answered in the affirmative. Thereupon, she took the picture, and placing it on her chest, she said with great feeling, and a lively faith: 'O Lord, if it be for the good of my soul, heal me through the merits of the holy Pope, Pius IX!' After a short time, she felt herself much better, she breathed more freely, and by degrees, the anguish and pressure on the heart, which hitherto had been a torture to her, completely disappeared. She then took courage, and began to pray with greater earnestness and confidence. Lest she might be deceived by her imagination, she told no one of her improvement in health, after her first prayer. During the following night, she continued with ever-increasing faith, to invoke the intercession of the glorious Pontiff, firmly trusting that she would be heard, and in fact, she felt her chest so relieved, that she would have been quite well, but for the extreme exhaustion and weakness, caused by her long confinement to her bed. Towards noon the next day, she fell into a deep, refreshing sleep; on being asked, when she awoke, how she was, she answered that she was very much better, and at the same time, she felt an irresistible longing within her to get up, and go and surprise her companions, who were in a room some way off. However, fearing it might be imprudent, she first tested her strength, and recited the Rosary. She felt herself becoming stronger whilst she was praying, and when she had finished, she ventured, with her beads in her hand, and without any assistance, to get out of bed. She was leaning against the bed, still hesitating whether she would have the power to walk, and deliberating what she should do, when the mid-day Angelus began to ring; springing up, she at once fell on her knees to honour the Mystery of the Incarnation. Then she rose to her feet, and feeling perfectly steady and well, dressed herself, after which she ran off to the room where her companions were assembled, and throwing open the door, she cried out joyfully, 'Pius IX. has cured me!' It can be imagined what surprise and admiration this unexpected apparition created, the most astonished of all being the Sister of Mercy, who had nursed the invalid; she wept from joy and emotion, asked a thousand questions, and kissed her tenderly. The good news soon spread all over the house, and everyone assembled in the chapel to sing a 'Te Deum,' in thanksgiving to God for this wonderful cure, obtained through the intercession of His Blessed Mother, and the merits of His holy servant, Pius IX. The same day, Carolina, in company with the Sister of Mercy, went to show herself to her family; from that time, all trace of the malady disappeared, and ever since, she has experienced very good health. All her friends, who had seen her in her former miserable state, were much astonished at her recovery, especially the doctor who had attended her, and had pronounced her to be incurable. He now loudly proclaims that her cure is miraculous, and is undoubtedly to be ascribed to the merits of the venerable servant of God, Pope Pius IX."

42. *To the Honour of Mary Immaculate.*

Three hundred years ago, when the general Council of Trent was being held, the Pope sent a Father James Laynez, a Jesuit, to join that venerable assembly, on account of his great learning and wisdom. The doctrine of Original Sin was then being treated of, and the question was proposed in this holy Council—which was so visibly inspired by the Holy Ghost— whether the most Blessed Virgin Mary had been conceived without the stain of Original Sin, or whether, after her conception, she had been sanctified, and freed from the stain common to all the children of Adam.

The humble Jesuit was asked his opinion on this matter, and being at that time in a very suffering state, he began by an apology for not being able to speak in a manner befitting so great and important a subject. He rose, and stood before the Council, pale and emaciated but a heavenly light shone in his eyes, when he began to speak of the Mystery of our Lady's Immaculate Conception. He spoke with such great fervour and depth of wisdom, that for three whole hours, he kept the Assembly spell-bound under the powerful influence of his arguments. When he ceased, the Fathers of the Council declared "that it was not their intention to include the Holy and Immaculate Mother of God, in the decision they had passed concerning Original Sin." Our Blessed Lady amply rewarded the humble defender of her glorious privilege for she not only obtained for Father Laynez an increase of bodily strength, but also a brilliant flow of convincing arguments; and besides the heavenly light that shone in his countenance, he received the gift of such marvelous eloquence, that on this solemn occasion, he spoke as he had never spoken before. Moreover, from that time, he was cured of the fever which had prostrated him, and never had a return of the same illness.

43. *The Best Physician.*

A Franciscan Father writes thus from China:—

"The following incident, which happened about three months ago, illustrates how richly the Mother of God rewards the faith and confidence of her devoted clients."

"X— —, the only son of pagan parents, was dangerously ill, medical aid had proved fruitless, and all hope of saving the child's life was already given up. The father, whose grief was driving him to distraction, had recourse to one last expedient; he called in the sorcerer and fortune teller of the district, and urged him to put forth all his skill and art to restore him his child. The sorcerer, having duly examined the patient, whose face was already livid and death-like, declared that the disease had reached such a height, that not even his remedies or charms could be of any avail; but he advised him to apply to the Christians, for they could certainly save his child, even in this hopeless state. The poor weeping mother, who was standing by, on hearing these words, hurried out to the next Christian settlement, where a zealous Priest was in charge of the Mission. She threw herself at his feet, beseeching him, with tears, to come and heal her dying son. The Priest, who was a devoted client of Mary, answered quite simply: 'It is not in my power to heal thy child, but the Mother of God, whom we Christians lovingly venerate, can do so, as she has done in many other cases. If, therefore, thou hast a strong and lively trust in her, and will promise to submit, together with thy son, to the yoke of Jesus Christ, then mayest thou surely hope to obtain the favour thou desirest and asketh for.' The sorrowing mother followed this advice, making a vow to our Blessed Lady, that she and her son would embrace the Christian religion, if he were rescued from death.

"Three days later, she came, filled with joy, to the good Priest, leading by the hand her little son, who was completely cured; throwing herself again at his feet, she thanked him for his good advice, and besought him to baptize her child, and to receive her among the number of catechumens. Soon after, the father, on whom this wonderful cure made such an impression, as to remove the scales of superstition from his eyes, also embraced the True Faith."

V.

44. Wonderful Power of the Prayer — "My Queen and my Mother!"

AT the time when the sermons of Father Zucchi, the Jesuit, were making innumerable conversions, a young man of noble birth, was so moved by his words, that he was induced to discover to him the sad state of his soul. This youth, by following the bent of his passions, had fallen into such a depth of misery, that he no longer had the courage to shake off the yoke of his sinful habits. The good priest, who possessed the compassionate heart of a Saint, was moved with pity on hearing the sad tale of his temptations, and said: 'Take courage, strive to do better in future, but if you should have the misfortune to fall again, remember you will ever find a true friend in me; so come at once that I may help you."

The young man followed the advice, but alas! without success, for he could not overcome the temptation. Then the kind and charitable Father said to him: "Consecrate yourself to the Mother of God; and every morning, on rising, say this little prayer in honour of her holy Virginity:—

" 'My Queen and my Mother! to thee I offer myself, and, to give thee a mark of my confidence, I place under thy protection during this day, my eyes, my ears, my mouth, my heart, and my whole person. Do thou, O my good Mother, preserve and defend me.'

"In the evening," continued the priest, "repeat the same prayer, and when you are tempted, say: 'O my Queen and my Mother, keep me and protect me!' "

The young man went away encouraged and happy to have found so easy a remedy. Soon after this, he had to leave Rome, but before starting, he went to his Confessor, to beg his blessing, and renew his promise.

Four years elapsed before he returned, and he then hastened to Father Zucchi, and made his Confession. The good priest himself says that he seemed to be "hearing the Confession of a Saint," and being much astonished, he asked his penitent what had brought about this great change. The latter answered: "I owe the grace of my conversion to those short prayers, for I have never failed to say them every day, and in her goodness, our Blessed Lady has heard my petition and helped me."

45. *A Legend of the Good Thief.*

The Roman Martyrology, on the 25th of March, makes mention of the Good Thief, who, according to tradition, is called Dismas, in the following words:

"At Jerusalem, on this day, is the Feast of the Good Thief, who acknowledged Christ on the Cross, and from Him deserved to hear the words: 'This day shalt thou be with me in Paradise.' The sudden change and conversion (for Dismas from a sinner became a penitent and Saint) has been rightly attributed to the prayers of our Blessed Lady. Mary, say the holy Fathers, had obtained the soul of the malefactor, as a recompense of her sorrows, and the price of her compassion. Saint Peter Damien assures us, that Mary prayed for the thief who was on the right side of the Cross, on which side she also stood, and exhorted him to hope in Jesus, and to do penance. Saint Anselm, in a treatise on the youth of Jesus, relates the following pathetic incident about the early years of Saint

Dismas, which we will give to our readers as a pious legend:—

" 'Dismas was living in a forest on the confines of Egypt, when Mary went thither with the Child Jesus, to escape the rage of Herod. He was a highwayman, and the son of the chief of a band of robbers. One day, as he lay in ambush, he saw a man, a young woman, and a little Child approaching, from whom he rightly expected no opposition. Therefore, he went towards them, with his comrades, with the intention to ill-treat them. But he was at once so charmed with the supernatural beauty and grace which shone on the countenance of Jesus, that instead of doing them harm, he gave them hospitality in the cave which he inhabited, and made ready for them everything of which they stood in need. Mary was grateful for the tenderness and care which the robber bestowed on her Beloved Son, and warmly thanking him, she assured him that he would be rewarded before his death. This promise was fulfilled later, when Dismas was crucified with the Saviour of the World, and obtained the grace of repentance in his last hour, openly confessing Jesus Christ's Divinity. When the Apostles had fled, he had the happiness to receive the first fruits of the Redeemer's Sacrifice, and soon after, entered the Heavenly Kingdom of his Saviour.'

"Saint Dismas is considered as the Patron of penitents, and is especially invoked for the conversion of hardened and obstinate sinners, and always with a favourable result. The Catholic Church has indeed sanctioned the veneration given to this Saint, by instituting a special Feast, with a most beautiful Office, in his honour, as also, a proper Mass. This Feast is allowed in many Dioceses and Religious Orders."

46. Mary hears the Prayer of a Jewess.

In the great fire which broke out in the "Ring Theatre," in Vienna, three children, whose mother was a Jewess, were in imminent danger. The mother had often heard people invoke our Lady when in peril, and in her distress, she cried out: "Mary help! thou canst help if thou wilt!" The prayer of the poor Jewess was not in vain, the children were saved, and she regarded their escape as miraculous. Full of gratitude, she caused six Masses to be offered in thanksgiving, at the same time relating the circumstances to the priest, who has sent it to us.

47. The Conversion of Alphonsus Ratisbonne.

The extraordinary conversion of Alphonsus Ratisbonne is well known to most Catholics, but so remarkable an instance of Mary's clemency, cannot be passed over in this record. Alphonsus was born May 1st, 1814, of rich Jewish parents, at Strasburg, and was educated at the Royal College of that city. His parents died while he was still young, and his uncle, a wealthy bachelor, then adopted him, and centred all his affections upon him. He gave him horses and carriages, and a free license to draw as much money as he desired from his firm, and finally he made him partner of his flourishing business. About that time, Ratisbonne was betrothed to a young relative, whose charms were too many to enumerate; however, as she was barely sixteen, the wedding was obliged to be postponed for a couple of years, and he sought to pass the time by travelling. His mind had been embittered toward Catholics by the conversion of his elder brother Theodore, in

1825, and when, soon after, his brother became a priest, he conceived an unmitigated hatred for the Church, which had caused a split in their hitherto united family.

Ratisbonne set out on his travelling tour in November, 1841, intending to go to Naples, and thence on to the East, but by an intervention of Providence, he was seized with a sudden desire to visit Rome, and arrived there January 6th, 1842. Shortly after, he became acquainted with Comte Theodore de Bussières, formerly a French Huguenot, who had been converted some time previously, and the two men soon struck up a friendship.

Meantime, Ratisbonne had been to visit the Ghetto, or Jewish quarter, in Rome, and the scene of misery which there met his eyes, so roused his indignation against the Christian populace, that no words can express the scorn and contempt he felt for the Christian Church. When next he visited his friend, he gave vent to his feelings on the subject, and at length M. de Bussières said to him: "Since you detest superstition, and profess such liberal doctrines, will you have the courage to submit to a very innocent trial, that of wearing a medal of our Lady, and saying a short prayer which I will write out for you. It may seem absurd to you, but it is a trial to which I attach great importance, and I ask it of you as a personal favour." At first, Ratisbonne refused, but presently consented to wear the medal, and to say the Memorare, treating the whole as an excellent joke. Yet for some reason, unknown to himself, the prayer kept recurring to his mind during the following days, and he found himself repeating the Memorare over and over again.

On January 16th, M. de. Bussières went to dine with Prince Borghese, and there met his friend, le Conte de La Ferronays, a man who, for some years, had edified Rome by his piety, and singular virtue. M. de Bussières was very full of the young Jew, and so interested M. de La Ferronays, that he promised to storm heaven for his conversion. The next day, he died quite suddenly, and it is commonly believed that he offered his life for Ratisbonne.

Two days later, as M. de Bussières was going to S. Andrea's, to make arrangements for the funeral of his friend, he met Ratisbonne in the street, and invited him to go for a drive, begging him to wait a few moments in the church, while he did his business. When he had finished, he came into the church, and to his astonishment, found the young Jew kneeling before the Lady Chapel, his face buried in his hands. He spoke to him, and touched him several times, but obtained no answer, till at length Ratisbonne raised his head, and he saw that he was weeping passionately, and kissing his medal as though beside himself. Then he exclaimed: "Oh, how that man must have prayed for me!" He alluded to M. de La Ferronays, whom he had never seen, nor did he know before that he had prayed for him.

When Ratisbonne had somewhat recovered from his emotion, he related, how, while waiting for his friend, the church seemed suddenly to disappear, only from the chapel, before which he stood, there issued a dazzling light, in the midst of which our Lady appeared, full of majesty and sweetness. He fell prostrate to the ground, and instantly, he felt perfectly convinced of the truth of Christianity, and seized with an intense longing for Baptism. In a moment, his prejudices melted, as snow before the sun, nor did a vestige remain.

Ratisbonne was, shortly after, solemnly baptized by

Cardinal Patrizzi, and finding that he could not induce his betrothed to follow his example, he broke off his engagement, and subsequently became a priest, devoting the remainder of his life to the conversion of his former brethren — the Jews.

48. *The Conversion of an Old Soldier.*

A soldier had lived forty years in the forgetfulness of God and his religious duties. At last, one day, following an almost irresistible inspiration, he hastened to find a priest in order to make his Confession. The Priest, greatly astonished, asked him if he had ever performed a good action. "Do you know the 'Our Father?' " "I have forgotten it." "Do you know the 'Hail Mary?' " "I have forgotten that also." "Then what prayer do you say?" "None." "Impossible! think for a moment, for no one returns to his duties after such a long time, without having been accustomed to make use of some pious practice." "I only know that I have often repeated the following lines, which I heard sung in my youth, with a certain feeling of devotion." —

> "I place all my hope,
> O Mary in thee,
> And trust in thy goodness,
> That thou wilt save me.
>
> .   .   .   .   .
>
> "And when Jesus shall call me,
> Thou wilt not refuse
> To bring me thyself
> The beautiful news!"

Thus had the poor sinner sometimes prayed, animated by a good but weak will, that he might break with sin, and return once more to his God. Mary, ever the Refuge of Sinners, our dear Lady of the Sacred Heart, the Hope of the hopeless, rewarded his confidence, and saved him, for like the merciful Heart of her Divine Jesus, she does not extinguish the flickering spark of a good will, but enkindles the light of grace within. Nor does she "crush the bruised reed," but makes it firm and strong.

49. Mary's Intercession Unfailing.

"It has never been heard of, that God has forsaken anyone who fled to Mary for protection." Our readers all know well these beautiful words of Saint Bernard; but we will relate a proof of this assertion in the following story:

"In the lovely Suabian land, there towers on a woodland height a little chapel, containing a picture, quite blackened by age, of the Mother of God. In all their intentions, both great and small, the pious inhabitants of the surrounding villages seek refuge with the Mother of Mercy in this little chapel, and the Queen of Heaven never forsakes them in the hour of their need.

"About two miles from this chapel is a pretty little villa, which was inhabited during the summer months by Herr Brenner, a rich banker of the capital, who was blessed with a large share of this world's goods. He had an only child, a bright and engaging girl of twelve, who was the pride and joy of his life. A Catholic in name only, Brenner would go to church, when it was either a matter of policy, or for appearance sake. He was not, indeed, an 'unbeliever,' but his lips curled disdainfully whenever he met a group of petitioners going to the chapel of our Lady.

"One day Brenner happened to meet the old village priest. They were both going the same way, and soon they were engaged in an animated conversation, which Brenner suddenly interrupted by asking abruptly: 'Father, has any miracle ever taken place in that old chapel?'

"The priest scanned his questioner from head to foot. Was it contempt, or real interest which called forth such a question? He quietly answered: 'Nothing wonderful has happened as far as I know, in the way you mean. But if the blind have not been made to see, nor the lame to walk, nevertheless the most remarkable miracles *do* take place, daily and quietly, for who can count the number of those who have regained their peace of soul through the Mother of God!'

"Arrived at a place where their ways diverged, and having mutually bowed, Brenner returned home. Yet the priest's words had touched a long silent chord in his heart. Once in his youth, he had also prayed to Mary with child-like confidence, but what a long time ago!

"The following night Brenner was suddenly awakened by a feeling of suffocation. He arose, and saw to his horror that the room was full of smoke. He rushed out, but was surrounded on all side by flames. The fire, which had originated in an unaccountable way, spread with amazing rapidity owing to a violent wind. The terrified servants rushed hither and thither with ever-increasing confusion. Brenner had but one thought—his only child. He rushed through the smoke and flames to Anna's bedroom, and on reaching it, he gave a wild cry, for his child lay on the floor quite senseless. He hastened out, carrying his precious burden, whither, he knew not, until at last he saw the chapel before him. Seeking for shelter, he entered the Sanctuary, and fell prostrate at the foot of the Altar.

Then he called to Anna by the tenderest names, and covered her pale face with caresses and tears, but the child did not give the least sign of life.

"Suddenly a terrible fear seized him. Perhaps Anna, his only child, his treasure, was dead! But no! it could not, must not be, for what should he do without her? His thoughts became confused, he was like one distracted. Then his eyes rested on the picture of the Mother of Mercy, who seemed to look at him with compassion. The words which the priest had said the previous day recurred to his mind, and following a sudden inspiration, he fell on his knees, crying out: 'Holy Mother of God, do not let my child die, and I promise you to practice my religion again, and to proclaim your praise all the days of my life.'

" 'Father, where am I?' Anna asked at this moment, in a scarcely audible voice. With a cry of joy Brenner clasped in his arms the child so wonderfully restored to him. With tears in his eyes, he exclaimed to the priest, who had hospitably offered him shelter in his house: 'Father, I now believe in Mary's miraculous power, for she has given me back my child.'

" 'Your daughter was not dead, but had only fainted through fear and the density of the smoke; nevertheless a great miracle has taken place, for the Mother of Mercy has wrought a change in your mind,' said the priest.

"The villa was soon rebuilt as prettily as ever, and the chapel also was renovated most beautifully. At a fixed hour every day, Brenner and his daughter kneel in deep devotion before the Altar of the Queen of Heaven, heartily thanking her for the wondrous miracle of his conversion."

50. The Soldier's Medal.

An old soldier, who had neglected his religious duties for a long time, fell ill. He showed the same indifference about religion even then, saying, "he wished to die without the Sacraments." The parish priest, filled with zeal for the salvation of this soul, thought of offering him a medal of Our Lady. The soldier readily consented to wear one, and put it round his neck. The next day, the priest went to visit him, and said: "I congratulate you on wearing this token, for it shows what great confidence you have in the mercy of the Divine Mother; and it is also a sign of predestination, for Mary is the Refuge of Sinners. Will you not kiss the medal?" The soldier did so without hesitation, and at that very moment his heart was changed. He began to weep, and seizing the priest's hand, begged to go to Confession. The few days of life which still remained to him were days of edification to all who saw him. He died, holding in his hand the medal which had obtained for him the grace of conversion.

51. "Memorare."

Whilst I was still a soldier and corporal in Stuttgart, I had a young surgeon named Ferdinand F — — for my intimate friend, who was preparing for the higher examinations. He was well versed in scientific knowledge, studied unceasingly, and was, moreover, a man of good morals. He was loved by all, but he had one great failing. Through reading free-thinking literature, and intercourse with irreligious people, his faith had suffered shipwreck. We often discussed this matter, whereby he showed that he had the most unmeaning, rationalistic views about God, and the other world. The sayings of freemasons about a Creator, eternity, and the universal religion of mankind, were the weapons he made use of, to deny the existence of another world, and every endeavour to bring him to a better frame of mind was fruitless.

In the beginning of the year 18——, he fell dangerously ill, and at his own request, he was nursed by a member of a Protestant sisterhood. I visited him daily, but he would hear nothing about Catholic Doctrine; on the contrary, he always had prayers read out of a Protestant book, from mere curiosity. I became very anxious on his account, and thought him hopelessly lost, when, his illness visibly increasing, I telegraphed to his aged mother, who lived in the South of France.

One day, I had to carry an order for the Minister of War, and passing the Catholic church on the way, I entered. Casting myself down before the Altar of our Blessed Lady, I said the Memorare for my friend's conversion.

At that time, I also stood in great need of conversion, for though my Faith had not suffered shipwreck, I had imbibed certain principles, through frequenting the barracks, which were anything but Catholic or moral. I acknowledged in my prayer to the Refuge of Sinners, that I, myself, needed a thorough conversion; but in spite of my unworthiness, she deigned to hear me, and took pity on my poor sick friend. When I returned from the office, at mid-day, I was hastily called to my friend in the hospital. I was astonished to find him completely changed. At ten o'clock in the morning, the very time I was praying for him, the Memorare had suddenly occurred to his mind, a prayer, which, in his happier days of childlike Faith, he had loved so much. He said it, and at that very moment, a ray of Divine grace penetrated his once pure heart. He now begged me, with many tears, to fetch a priest, and, overjoyed, I quickly hastened to obey his request. I found, as if sent by God, Father Andelfinger, of the Society of Jesus, who immediately came with me.

My friend made his Confession, and received the Last Sacraments with great devotion. He said the Memorare again and again, and was so happy to be a child of Mary once more. His mother soon arrived, and found him weak, but cheerful and happy, and filled with a holy peace. I shall never forget that death-bed, and how he repeated, constantly, that he was a Catholic in life and death; and retracted whatever he had said against the Church. Mary was his hope, and he breathed his last sigh into her hands, for when he had once more repeated the Memorare, and had said Amen, he died.

52. *"And yet, Mary Loves thee!"*

St. Bridget says: "As the magnet attracts steel to itself, so does the ever Blessed Virgin draw hearts to God."

The great servant of Mary, St. Francis Regis, knew this well, when he was called to the death-bed of an aged sinner, who would hear nothing of preparations for death. All admonitions were fruitless, all threats and persuasions of no avail. Death drew nearer and nearer, and no human help could save him; he felt that his end was nigh, nevertheless, he refused every spiritual consolation. Then the Saint came to his bedside, and taking out of his breviary a picture of our Lady, showed it to the old man, saying these words: "And yet, Mary loves you!" "What!" cried the sinner, as if awakening from a dream, and looking steadfastly at the picture, "then she does not know me." "And yet she loves you!" quietly rejoined St. Francis. "Then she does not know that I have denied my Faith, and have mocked my Religion." "She does know it." "That I have insulted her Son, and trampled His Blood under my feet." "She knows it." "And that these hands are stained with innocent blood." "She knows it." "Do you speak the truth, priest?" "Yes, for heaven and earth will pass away rather than one of God's words. This, God once said, and says still to you to-day, 'Son, behold thy Mother!' " "A Mother, who loves me?" whispered the sinner, "My Mother, mine!" and hot tears ran down his cheeks, tears of true repentance. He then acknowledged with the most sincere contrition, all the sins of his life by a holy Confession, and soon received the God of Everlasting Love, Who, a few days later, called his soul out of this world, after it had felt the powerful attraction of Mary.

53. Prayer Abandoned.

A Catholic youth, of a pious and wealthy family in "Der Eifel," endowed with excellent talents, lost his parents whilst still young. When he left school he resolved to study, so as to prepare for a higher station in life, and for this purpose he went to college. But, through intercourse with depraved students, he became by degrees frivolous, fond of pleasure, unbelieving and impious; and having departed from the teaching of his good parents and his parish priest, he at last became dissatisfied and unhappy. Meanwhile he pursued his studies at various colleges, and satisfied his masters with the progress he made in scientific knowledge. When he had finished his course at college, he did not quite know what profession to embrace. It did not enter his mind to take counsel with God, in order to find out the Divine Will in this matter. First he applied himself to medicine, but soon tired of it; then he took to the law, but he gave that up also. Finally, he resolved to take up theological studies, and devoted himself to them for some years, becoming tired of them when the novelty had worn off, and at last found that he had spent all his means after so many years of study, so that now he was at a loss to know what he should do. He felt really unhappy, and the sight of so many of his fellow students, who had already obtained various distinctions in the Church and State, discouraged him still more. Yet what afflicted him most was his interior disquietude, and the qualms of his conscience, which bitterly reproached him for his former irregularities. Life was a burden to him, and indeed he did not know what to do next. Unfortunately, in spite of all his learning and study, he had forgotten that though unhappy, he might still find consolation and peace in religion. He had acquired great knowledge, but the important science of saving his soul, and the art of working out his salvation, were things unknown to him; in short, he had forgotten *how to pray*. At length he returned home, and lived for some months with his family, leaving to chance his future destiny. With a certain feeling of shame, he avoided meeting his parish priest, for he felt loth to see him while in this miserable condition. He passed his time in every kind of amusement, but was always uneasy, nowhere finding consolation, for no pleasure cheered him, and his face betrayed the interior state of his soul.

In the spring of the year 18— —, in order to drive away the "ennui" he felt, he busied himself in the plantations belonging to his family, propping up trees, removing the moss, cutting off the superfluous shoots, and digging up the soil round about.

One day, he found a Rosary lying near a young tree; he picked it up, and, without thinking, put it into his pocket. When he went to his room at night, he struck a light; then an indescribable anxiety took possession of him, he remembered the Rosary, and he distinctly heard an interior voice saying to him: "Pray, Pray, Pray!" He took the Rosary from his pocket, looked at it sadly, and then called to mind how happy he had been in his childhood, when he delighted in saying the Rosary, and how wretched and unhappy he had become, since he had given up praying. He thought of his dear, dead parents, then he remembered the disorders of his youth. It made him sad at heart, and hot tears of repentance ran down his cheeks. Once more he seemed to hear a voice saying: "Pray, Pray, Pray!" and falling on his knees, he began the Rosary. At first, it was not very easy to think of the mysteries, but by degrees, it became less difficult. When he had finished his prayer, he felt a sweet peace arise in his soul, and he became as light-hearted and happy, as if he had been delivered from some great danger, or had recovered from a severe illness.

The next day, he hastened to the priest, told him what had happened, asked pardon for his cold demeanour towards him, and the bad example he had given to the whole parish, and promising to become another man, he begged the priest to help him to make a general confession. When he had fulfilled this duty, he was quite changed, edifying all the villagers by his fervour at the services, and in the evening, he joined in the Rosary out loud in church. After mature deliberation, and many prayers, he resolved to escape the dangers of the world, and enter a monastery, there to spend the remainder of his life in the practice of penance and piety. Here also, he edified all his religious brethren, by his obedience, penance, and devotion.

In His own time, God desired to gather the sheaf, now ripe for Eternity, into the heavenly barn, and sent the young monk a dangerous illness, which he bore most patiently, and prepared himself for death. He died after much suffering, holding in his hand the Rosary, which, under Divine Providence, had been the means of his conversion.

This also shows how readily Mary hastens to the help of repentant sinners, who seek her aid, and how victorious is her help. We do not know, dear reader, if you also need our Lady's assistance in this respect; but, doubtless, you know some soul, who, steeped in sin, needs a great grace, the grace of God, in order to obtain conversion. Well, recommend such a one in earnest, trustful prayer, to the most Blessed Virgin, that she may truly be a Mother of Mercy to them, a refuge, and a help.

54. Our Lady of Victory.

"Whilst I was stationed in Paris," relates a soldier, "a young man who had joined a company of our regiment the previous year, attracted my attention, as he seemed in a depressed state of mind. He was good, and by no means quarrelsome, but weak and desponding.

"There was no reason to think him a coward, for he was not in the least afraid of gunpowder. It is the same with many soldiers; they do not fear death on the battlefield, but they dare not show that they believe in God at the barracks.

"As I said before, this young man interested me; I noticed that he had really a Christian heart, and therefore I tried to encourage him. I tried to win him by kind words, and showed him that it would be as disgraceful to renounce his Faith as to desert his flag. However, I laboured in vain, for it was clearly proved in this case, that all attempt to convert anyone is useless, if our Divine Lord does not help with His grace.

"So I resolved to keep silence and to wait, and in the meantime I gave my comrade various proofs of a sincere friendship. But I could not help noticing that he sank lower and lower. At first he used to say his prayers by his bedside, but a bad companion, noticing this, ridiculed him, and from that time the holy Sign of the Cross was given up.

"Another time he entered a church to hear Mass. Several comrades having noticed it, laughed at him. After this he no longer went to church, but went to the tavern instead, where his friends were often the cause of his taking too much, till at last the poor fellow was carried to the police-station, where he had to remain till he was sober again.

"Thus, gradually, he became quite wretched. Yet I often said to myself, that he was good at the bottom, and I felt that his heart was not corrupted, and that God would save him.

"One afternoon I was going to the church of our Lady of Victory, where a Feast was being kept by the Confraternity for the Conversion of Sinners.

"I was passing through the gallery of the Palais Royal, when I suddenly met my friend, who was looking at a stall.

"I went up to him, and said: 'Well, what are you doing here?'

" 'I am bored,' he answered, 'I had a ticket for the theatre with one of my comrades, and he has not come.'

" 'Then come with me,' I said, laughing, 'I am also going to a drama, which you will enjoy.'

" 'And where is that, pray?'

" 'At Our Lady of Victories.'

" 'And whatever is that?' he asked.

" 'Come and you will soon see,' I replied.

" 'That is a church, is it not?'

" 'To be sure it is. Did you never go to church in your village? Why will you not also go in Paris?'

" 'No,' he answered, 'it is much too long a time since I went. I cannot even remember the 'Our Father.' No, I will not go with you.'

"I tried to bring him to a better frame of mind, and noticed, too, that he hesitated, but he could not bring himself to go with me.

"I left him standing there, and went away slowly, looking back now and then. At last I saw him following me from a distance, so I stopped before a stall in order to wait for him, and when he came up to me I said —

" 'Come now, do not be obstinate, you want to go with me, but dare not say so.' As he did not answer, I continued —

" 'Well, really! do you not see and hear by the name, Our Lady of Victory, that I speak of the soldiers' church?' I took him by the arm, and we continued on our way.

"The good fellow was very much astonished to see the choir filled with men, young and old. 'What!' he said quietly to me, 'do so many men go to church even in Paris?' 'Yes,' I answered, 'do you think that the good God has not created Parisians to serve Him as well as other men?'

"The church was crowded with worshippers, and everyone was praying; I did the same. Then my companion whispered to me, 'Who is that venerable looking old priest in the pulpit?'

" 'He is the Director of the Confraternity, and he is going to preach, so let us pay attention.'

"During the sermon I often glanced at my companion, who

seemed quite riveted. Every word appeared to go to his heart.

" 'Well,' I said after the sermon, 'did you look at the priest to whom you listened so attentively? He is an old soldier.'

" 'A soldier! Impossible!'

" 'It is quite true. He has exchanged his uniform for the cassock, and having served his country like a brave officer, he enrolled himself under the standard of his Creator. But just tell me, do you think Religion is only for women, and not for us?'

"My companion seemed quite touched, for our Lord was knocking at the door of his heart.

"Then the Litany of Loretto was begun. He knelt down, and when they came to the words 'Refugium peccatorum, ora pro nobis,' he could no longer contain himself, and his eyes filled with tears. My prayer was heard, he was converted. I said to myself, to-morrow, perhaps, he will be a hundred times better than I am, if that is not already the case.

"When the devotions were finished, everyone left the church, but my companion remained praying. At last, when I saw that we were the only two there, and that the lights had been put out, I said to him: 'We must go now.'

"He raised his head, and said in astonishment, 'Go already! Must we really?'

" 'We have been here nearly two hours,' I replied. But this is always the way. Prodigals are God's dearest children. We went out, and then my companion warmly embraced me, calling me his saviour and only friend.

" 'Well,' I said, 'did I deceive you when I promised you a happy afternoon?'

" 'Oh no!' he replied, 'I shall always remember it. You cannot understand what a deep impression the voice and words of that old priest made on me; I feel quite overwhelmed still.'

" 'I do not wonder,' I said, 'for I told you that he was an old soldier. It is not surprising that a soldier should recognize the voice of his captain.'

"Next day I took him to a Sodality for soldiers, which brings so many blessings to the army.

"My comrade found there what he wanted, an excellent priest—who devoted himself entirely to the welfare of soldiers—friends, instruction, good advice and good example. From that moment till he left, he never gave up. I visited him afterwards at his home, and he has remained a good Christian. He says that he still can hear the voice of his captain ringing in his ears, and he always replies, 'Here I am!' "

55. *The Midnight Summons.*

In the town of X——, a loud ringing was heard at the door of the sacristy of our Lady's Church, one Saturday about midnight. An old lady stood there, who begged that the priest would bring the Last Sacraments to a sick person without delay; she named the street and described the house, and when the priest was ready to start with the Blessed Sacrament, she preceded him to show the way. He was following her quite closely, when suddenly she vanished from his sight; he then noticed that he was standing on the threshold of the very house, which had been so minutely described to him. He rang the bell, but received no answer. Finally, after many repeated, but useless rings, an old gentleman looked out from the upper storey, and asked who was there? And why he came at such a late hour? The priest answered that he had brought the Last Sacraments to a person dangerously ill, to whom he had been hastily summoned. "There is no one sick in this house," replied the old gentleman, "but if you wish to wait until this heavy shower is over, come in, for you are welcome, I am sure, as I am always troubled with sleepless nights." The priest, who was drenched by the rain, was only too glad to find a shelter, and so he walked in.

As he entered the room, the first object which met his eyes, was a large picture of the Madonna, before which a small lamp was burning. "I have indeed come to a Christian home!" the priest exclaimed, in joyful surprise.

"I am a man of the world, and I encourage progress," drily answered the old gentleman, "I care little for images or pictures, but, for the sake of my dead mother, who held this picture in great veneration, I have kept it, and I have even retained the custom she had, of lighting a small lamp before it, every Saturday." During this conversation, they had entered another room, and over a writing-table, hung a picture of a lady, attired in an old-fashioned dress of years gone by. The gentleman, noticing that the priest was looking at it attentively, said, with much feeling, at the same time pointing to the picture, "That is my well-beloved mother. How often and fervently has she not prayed before that Madonna! Indeed, she used to say she prayed for me before it. In her dying hour, she gasped, 'My unhappy son! if, through the mercy of God, I attain to the joys of heaven, I will unceasingly beg the intercession of the Blessed Virgin, with her Divine Son, for your conversion!' Oh, how willingly would she have led me back to the Good Shepherd, but," he added, smiling sadly, "Confession did not suit me."

Then he went on to relate some of the incidents of his past life; he spoke openly of the adventures of his youth, and he also related other circumstances of his life, without, in any way, disguising or excusing his faults and failings.

"You say you are so much against Confession," the priest said, "and yet you have just discovered to me, the actions of your life, so that the state of your soul lies open to my spiritual eyes. I seem to know you so thoroughly, that I should like to give you Absolution at once."

"Oh, if you could but do that!" he exclaimed, with emotion. "It is more than thirty years since I received Holy Communion"; and then, looking tenderly and sorrowfully on his mother's portrait, he was moved with self-reproach. Suddenly, as if animated by a higher inspiration, he took hold of both the priest's hands, and said: "Father, at the remembrance of my pious and devoted mother, I take you at your word. I feel, now, in the dispositions to make a good Confession. Can you really give me Absolution? If so, I entreat you to give me Holy Communion at once."

When the aged penitent, having fallen on his knees before the priest, had made his Confession, with great sorrow and repentance, he recited aloud the Apostles' Creed, and then, reconciled with his God, overflowing with love and gratitude, he received Holy Communion. The good priest said a few words of advice and encouragement, after which he took his leave. His soul seemed to be flooded with a heavenly joy, and as he passed the dead lady's picture, her countenance wore an expression of such sweetness and joy, that he stopped to look at the portrait, at the same moment, it struck him that he had seen the face before.

On his homeward journey, he pondered over in his mind, the mercies of God, Who had thus led him to reconcile a strayed sheep, and in passing through the streets he had left an hour ago, the thought of the lady, who had acted as his guide, came back to him. He asked himself who she could have been, and why she had so suddenly disappeared from his sight; but the more he pondered over the whole affair, the more confused did his thoughts become. The old gentleman—the portrait—then, connecting the circumstances together, by degrees, he came to the conclusion that the old lady wore the same look as the one in the picture, which he had gazed upon with such interest, as the mother of his recent penitent.

His sleep was restless and disturbed; he dreamed of his penitent kneeling before him, begging with such earnestness, to receive the Holy Eucharist; and between waking and sleeping, he seemed to hear the death-bell tolling, so he prayed in semi-consciousness, for the unknown soul that was passing away, that God, in His goodness, would grant it mercy and forgiveness, and a happy passage to Eternity.

The next morning, the priest inquired if anything particular had happened during the night, and he was informed that the death-bell had really tolled, for the old gentleman, with whom he had stayed, had died quite suddenly of an apoplectic stroke.

Here is another striking proof, how the fervent devotion of a pious mother to the most Blessed Virgin, obtained for an unfaithful son the grace of his conversion, before death, in a most wonderful manner. May we not piously believe that this was Mary's acknowledgment of the little lamp burnt before her picture every Saturday, which practice had been so faithfully kept up in her honour?

56. The Monument in the Forest.

A young man who was studying at the University of X— —,

was taking a walk one afternoon in a neighbouring forest; being still unacquainted with the country, he lost his way, and in spite of all his endeavours, he could not succeed in finding the right path again. Each direction he attempted only landed him deeper in the thickest part of the forest, and led to no outlet. This was certainly an unpleasant state of affairs! Devoid of all fear, he never thought of turning to God by fervent prayer, and growing angry, he began to storm and swear. All at once he felt himself seized in a strong grasp, and a man with a swarthy visage demanded his purse and watch. In the struggle which ensued between the robber and his victim, the latter would have undoubtedly fallen, had not a third party suddenly come on the scene, he opportunely aimed his stick at the robber, who only escaped a heavy blow by a speedy flight.

"I owe my life to you!" began the rescued man, and warmly pressed his preserver's hand.

"I know not who you are," rejoined the other, "or which way you are bent, but if you like to partake of my hospitality for the night, and so give yourself time to recover from your fright, you will be very welcome. I am Father M— —, parish priest of the neighbouring village of Th— —."

The student willingly accepted the offer, and told the priest that he had been studying for some weeks in the High School at X— —, and that whilst taking a walk in the forest, which was still unknown to him, he had lost his way. They had not gone very far, when the student's eyes rested on a statue of our Lady, which stood quite near, the priest thereupon begged his companion to wait a few minutes, and he knelt down and remained for a short time in fervent prayer. When he rose from his knees the student said, "This statue, I believe, was erected in honour of the Immaculate Conception of the ever Blessed Virgin Mary, in pious remembrance of a Mrs. Margaret Waller, who, according to the inscription, was struck by lightning on this very spot, on the 23rd July, 1808. Perhaps this deceased lady was a near kinswoman of yours, Father?"

"No," answered the priest sadly, "I never knew this lady in her lifetime, but I often pray very fervently for her, for her sad death was the cause of my soul's conversion to a better life. I had finished my higher studies, although not at the University of the neighbouring town, and I was travelling as a gay, high-spirited student, in these parts, with a fellow student. We went through this forest on foot, and on the way we fell into a hot dispute over a trifling matter; curses and imprecations fell like rain from our lips. I could not tell you how frequently I uttered the imprecation, that lightning from heaven might kill my friend and myself. As we walked on we came across this statue of our Lady, I read aloud that inscription you see, and we both stood petrified. Mrs. Waller had been suddenly called before God's tribunal, perhaps in a state of grace—or perhaps in mortal sin! 'What would become of us, if Almighty God should take us at our word?' I said; and deeply moved, we at once made an end of our disagreement, and mutually promised a thorough reformation of our lives, most especially never again to utter a curse or blasphemy. I believe that my friend and I have both kept our word. We gave up our studies for the law, and began to prepare for the Priesthood. When my present parish was entrusted to me, I repaired our Lady's statue, and now I frequently say Paters and Aves before it, for the soul of her who was struck by lightning."

The young listener had become absorbed in deep thought, and after a pause he asked, "Then it was only your devotion that brought you to this lonely spot?"

"You have guessed rightly, my friend," rejoined the priest, "in the neighbourhood of this statue you will find no frequented paths, and I very rarely meet anyone in this part of the wood. I should not have come here to-day, had it not been the 23rd July, the anniversary of that unfortunate woman's death."

The young student was touched to the quick, and said, with tears in his eyes, "Although brought up in the Catholic Religion, for many years I have been almost a free-thinker, and have frequently denounced the grottos, niches, and holy statues which are met with in the streets and roads, as only an excuse for the people's stupidity and superstition. Now, by one of these monuments, Divine Providence has wonderfully preserved my life. I therefore promise, before this Statue of the Immaculate Conception, to consecrate myself to the service of my Divine Saviour and of His ever Blessed Mother. I beg of you, Father, to hear the repentant acknowledgment of my sins this very day."

The young man kept his word, and later on, as a priest, he worked indefatigably for the honour of God, to secure his own salvation, and to lead the souls entrusted to him, in the sure way to Heaven.

57. At Length!

The noble penitent, De Queriolet, who lived about the year 1620, was a Frenchman of high birth, and has become renowned by his penitential life, after a long career of sin. As a youth, he studied at Rennes, where he gave himself up to every excess, letting himself be dragged down into the lowest vices.

In order to satisfy his longing for enjoyment and pleasure more perfectly, he determined to steal a considerable sum of money from his father; but his plans were frustrated, and he was caught in the act. Thereupon, filled with rage and shame, he left his home, and resolved to fly to Turkey, and become a Mahometan. But it is worthy of reflexion, to notice how Divine Providence always thwarted his godless intention, by numerous obstacles; and De Queriolet, at length, returned to his native land, after many wanderings, during which, he fought several duels, and was wounded in more than one quarrel. He had not, however, returned improved, for he only led a life of greater guilt, and continued his course of sin and strife.

The threats of Divine Justice, pronounced against impenitent sinners in the Holy Scriptures, did not deter him from his crimes, but only filled his heart, with still greater hatred, against Almighty God.

One day, De Queriolet was returning home during a dreadful thunderstorm; the claps of thunder, as he himself relates, succeeded each other so quickly, and with such violence, that he could no longer control his horse. Scarcely had he hurried into his house, when a tree, just behind him, fell, struck by the lightning. Yet, in spite of this, one of the many signs of Divine Forbearance in his regard, the poor sinner remained stubborn and senseless, his heart hard as stone.

A dream once made some slight impression on him, for he seemed to see, in sleep, the abyss of hell smoking with fire and brimstone, and heard, at the same time, the howls, and gnashing of teeth of the damned, resounding, oh, so hopelessly! throughout eternity. His innumerable sins came vividly before his mind, and De Queriolet gazed on the place, which, in all probability, would, one day, be his everlasting prison. He awoke, filled with fear, and, aroused for a time to repentance, he sought to allay his fears in a Carthusian Monastery; but his resolutions were not lasting, and his passions, deeply rooted, got the upper hand. So he secretly left the monastery, and sank, deeper than ever, into the grossest vices and errors; whenever he could, he mocked God, the Church, the Divine Service, the Sacraments, and priests, with fiendish delight. But the sweet longanimity of Jesus, his Saviour, still bore with this hardened sinner, and the eye of the Good Shepherd was ever looking down on him from heaven, trying to allure him to His Sacred Heart.

At length, grace conquered; De Queriolet's good parents had prayed, for many long years, for the conversion of their unhappy son, and their wish was at last to be granted.

In 1654, De Queriolet came to Loudun, in France, merely from curiosity, to be present at a grand ceremony, celebrated in the Catholic Church there. He was struck with awe at the attention and reverence of the vast congregation; and if God had at one time made known to him the sad state of his soul, by a picture of hell, He now drew him more efficaciously by the beauty and splendour of the Divine Service. Higher and nobler thoughts penetrated into his soul, and he saw reflected, as in a bright mirror, the grossness of his many errors and wanderings, and the unmerited graces so lavishly bestowed on him by God. Bitter tears of sorrow and repentance filled his eyes, and by a worthy general Confession, he was at last reconciled to his God. He practiced the most severe penitential exercises till his death, his castle became an asylum for the poor and infirm, and he himself humbly served the suffering members of Christ with his own hands. Later, he entered a Carmelite Monastery, and, after his death, he was buried in the church near Auray, before our Lady's Altar, whom he had loved so fervently as the Refuge of Sinners.

VI.

58. Devotion to Mary Rewarded.

IN 1852, two travelers, a gentleman and his servant, arrived at Munich, and the latter there related to me, how, through the intercession of Mary, he had come into the service of a most excellent master, who treated him rather as a friend than a servant. He told me he had formerly been stationed with the French troops, in Rome, where he had experienced much suffering. While there, it was his daily practice, to go to the church of the "Trinita dei Monti," and pray before the picture of our Blessed Lady. On one occasion, weary with camp life, he entreated our Lady to give him the means to withdraw from the army, and to find him a quiet place, in the service of some gentleman, where he might end his days peacefully.

He rose from his knees much comforted, for he felt he could safely leave his future in Mary's hands. As he entered the barracks, he was accosted by his commanding officer, who gave him a note, saying: "Here! I have just received this from a gentleman; he wants a soldier-servant, who has no ties, and who has a good character. I believe the place would just suit you. If you like, you may go and offer yourself." The soldier felt that this must be the answer to his prayer, and went off at once.

On being ushered into the room of his future master, the gentleman exclaimed: "Why, you are the man I saw praying so devoutly at the 'Trinita dei Monti,' this morning. I will most willingly take you as my servant, and I feel sure you will be happy with me. I am childless, and my relations are wealthy, and have no need of me; therefore, if you will be my faithful companion while I live, you shall be my heir when I die." It is needless to add, that the soldier most gratefully accepted so generous an offer, and ever after, he never failed, daily, to thank our Lady, for having found him a master, and a friend.

59. *The Angelus.*

One day, two labourers were standing together in the market place at Hamburg, waiting about in the hope of employment, but it was already close on mid-day, and as yet no one had hired them.

Presently, the old sacristan hobbled out of the cathedral porch, and began to ascend the tower in order to ring the Angelus. As the first peal rang out, Klaus Karstens immediately doffed his cap, and kneeling down, began his Ave. But Kaspar Meter, his cousin, remained standing with his hat on, mumbling to himself: "I shan't trouble to take off my hat, besides, a tile might fall from that shaky old tower, when the bell is ringing, and make a hole in my head."

At that moment, a little old gentleman appeared on the scene, and, after narrowly scanning the two men, he said to Klaus: "Come with me, I will give you work and good pay." Klaus Karstens was only too glad to accept the offer, and the two set off together. As they went on their way, the old gentleman remarked: "I exact one condition from all my workmen; that they should never ask *Why*." "All right," answered Klaus, "I'm not given to a great deal of questioning." So without further talking, the two arrived at the entrance of a large sugar factory. When Karstens saw the great piles of wood, he said to himself: "Thank God, I shall never want for work now."

He had sawn and hewn wood for a whole year and more, when, one day, the head of the factory, the same gentleman who had taken him from the market place, said to him: "Klaus, you have a long way to go every morning and evening into the town; if you like, you can live in the summer-house, with your wife and child. I do not want any rent."

And when Klaus had worked for another year, and was living in the summer-house, the old gentleman came to him once more, and said: "Klaus, the overseer of my factory has turned out to be a thief, and has gone away without saying good-bye. Would you like to take his place?"

A year later, the old gentleman had a wall built between the drying-loft and the summer-house, in which Klaus lived; but no one dared ask: "Why have you done this?" And even when Klaus, the overseer, had to go home a round-about way, still he did not ask, even by a look, the why and wherefore of this action.

At length, the master of the sugar factory died, and in his will was written: "Item: I leave to Klaus Karstens, half my garden, and everything which is on that side of the wall, and the summer-house. I desire, also, that my brother should retain him as overseer, and have a door made in the wall. If he does not wish this, he must give Karstens three thousand marks, and let him live undisturbed. But should the latter ask (which I hardly expect he will) "*Why* this has happened to me," the answer is: "I chose Klaus as woodcutter, because I saw him praying. But had his companion prayed, and he kept on his hat, I would not have chosen him, but his cousin."

60. Mary's Picture.

Such great misfortunes, following so closely, one after another, had come upon a certain family, that the father's confidence in God and his fellow-creatures, had given place to despair, which is the worst thing that can befall a man; and taking a rope, he resolved to go and hang himself. Before going away, he avoided seeing either his wife or little children, lest, perhaps, such a touching sight should hinder his evil design. He chose a lonely place situated outside the town, and planted with willow trees, for the execution of his desperate intention. On his way, he saw a square piece of white paper lying on the ground; he picked it up and turned it over; it was a little picture of our Lady, under which were the words:

"O Mary! conceived without sin, pray for us who have recourse to thee."

"It is very wonderful," he thought, and he stood still, "that I should find this little picture, just now, pick it up, and read these words." He went a little further, looking at the words, "Pray for us who have recourse to thee." He stood still again; suddenly, he felt as if the love of life had returned, and he said: "Pray for us"—he retraced his steps, and continued—"who have recourse to thee." He threw away the rope, kissed the little picture of our Lady, and hastened back to his family. Embracing his wife and children, he asked their forgiveness, and then showed them the picture; they all knelt down, and said: "O Mary, Mother of God, pray for us who have recourse to thee!" After this, the man made known his sinful intention to the parish priest, and soon succeeded, with God's help, in freeing himself from all trouble. But he ever kept the little picture as a sacred treasure, for he said that it was through the instrumentality of this picture of the Mother of God, that he had been saved.

61. Mary Rewards Alms Given in her Honour.

Carlo Dolce was the youngest child of a poor workman in Sienna. His parents could only give him a slender education, but his mother took care to implant, in his heart, a true and tender love towards Mary.

So the child grew into a youth, and applied himself to drawing and painting, for which he showed a particular aptitude, thereby earning a scanty livelihood. When in Florence, as he was once walking through the streets of the great city, he met a beggar, who asked for an alms, in the name of the Mother of God. Deeply moved, Carlo felt in his pocket, and found just one piece of money. At first, he deliberated as to whether he should give it away, as it was his last coin, and all he had in the world. But the artist thought within himself: "He asked me in the name of Mary, and, as I can refuse her nothing, I will give it joyfully, even if I have to die of hunger." After this, he entered a church, which was near, and, kneeling down before an Altar of our Lady, wept tears of joy, that he could prove his love for Mary, by such a sacrifice. The ceiling of this church was being renovated by the best Italian painters. Their master, Dominichino, looking down from the scaffolding, saw the young Carlo; he was pleased with his devotion, and left his elevated position to speak to him. He questioned him, and finding he had a real gift for painting, he took him under his protection. Trouble and misery had now come to an end, and under this good master, Carlo soon grew so skilful in his art, that he was looked upon as the greatest painter of his time.

His chief joy, was to paint pictures of his great benefactress, and the love he had for her, caused him to depict her with so much grace and majesty, that his Madonnas have always been regarded as his masterpieces.

62. Consolatrix Afflictorum.

God allowed a heavy trial to come upon Saint Francis of Sales, whilst he was studying in Paris. It overwhelmed him with sadness and misery, for he thought he never should attain eternal happiness. This tormenting thought never left him, day or night, and it almost dragged him to the point of despair. His bodily health even became affected, and all his friends feared he would become an early victim to consumption. What made the evil more unbearable, was the fact that the poor, despondent, and dejected youth, dared not confide the cause of his heavy sorrow to anyone. At last, he thought he would betake himself to the church where he had made a vow of virginity. The first thing which met his eye, was a picture of the ever-blessed Virgin Mary. At the sight of it, his former confidence in the "Consoler of the Afflicted," was re-awakened in his breast. He fell on his knees, and earnestly implored this Divine Mother "to obtain for him, the grace to love God above all things, at least, on earth, because, after his death, should he be condemned to eternal punishment, he could no longer do so." At once, it seemed as if a heavy load were removed from his heart, for he felt so wonderfully relieved and consoled, that his previous confidence in God's mercy returned, and his mind and body regained their usual strength and vigour.

Saint Bonaventure teaches us, that while our Lord's Blessed Mother lived in this valley of tears, her heart was ever full of love and mercy towards those in distress. How much greater will be her tenderness, now that she so gloriously reigns in heaven! She can see human misery so much more clearly, and makes her mercy the more appreciated, the more she gives her assistance. She is also our Mother, and is it possible that a mother can forget her children?

63. *The Lighted Candle.*

There lived in Paris a poor old couple, who dwelt in a miserable garret, for which they had to pay twenty francs a year. They often lay down to sleep hungry, and many a time for their breakfast, they had only an old crust of bread, which had to be first soaked in water, before they could eat it. They were ashamed to make known their poverty, for in former years, they had been in good circumstances; but little by little, through no fault of their own, they had gone down in the world. Finally, they sold all their goods, until nothing was left to them.

It was Saturday, and they had not a single penny, or even a piece of bread. The wife was sickly, the husband lay ill in bed; the day passed in the most fearful anxiety, night came, and no food had passed their lips. So, sadly, they sat down together, and wept, and prayed. Sunday was still worse, and, in the evening, the fearful pangs of hunger forced the woman to leave her husband's side, and go out into the streets.

She meant to beg; but, as often as she tried to do so, shame closed her mouth, and she returned home, more exhausted and discouraged than when she went out. They had tasted no food for two days, and tears of anxiety and distress, rolled down their pale, sunken cheeks. "We shall die, my poor wife," said the old man, "God has forsaken us." His wife made no reply; but, after some time, she lifted her head, and said, as if with a sudden inspiration, "We will invoke the Blessed Virgin, she is the Consoler of the Afflicted, and the Refuge of the Sorrowful; she will help us. I have still a little bit of candle, which we will burn before her picture. I feel confident she will send us help." No sooner said than done. They found the candle, lighted it, and placed it before a small picture of Mary, which was still in their possession, because none would buy it. Then the two old people knelt down, and prayed with many tears.

Now there was living in another part of the same house a needlewoman, whose child was ill. When she got up in the night to tend her little invalid, she noticed that the two old people still had a light. She knew them slightly, and whenever she met either of them, she would salute them. "Perhaps something is the matter," she said to herself, and without more ado she dressed herself, took a lantern, and went to look after the old couple. When she opened the door, a pitiful sight met her gaze! There lay the unhappy pair, pale and trembling, before Mary's picture, having fallen on the ground through sheer exhaustion. She went up to them and kindly asked what was the matter. Amid many tears they told her, and the good woman disappeared again quicker than she had come. She went to her little room, got some bread, broth, and whatever else in the way of food she could lay her hands on, and then returned to the old folks, whom she warmly embraced and consoled.

The following day this kind neighbour told the parish priest and the superior of Saint Vincent's Society, who both went at once to the house and reproached the poor people gently for having so long concealed their distress. The help was lasting, and a few days later the old couple came in for a little fortune, left them by a distant relative. In after years, how often would they relate that they owed their deliverance to the Mother of God, and that but for the little candle, or rather for their great confidence in Mary, which inspired the happy thought of lighting it, their neighbour would not have come to their aid, and they would have succumbed under their privations.

64. *The Holy Name of Mary Untouched by Fire.*

In the Annals of the Propagation of Faith, the following is related by P. Kopper, a Jesuit Missionary of Western Bengal, in India:—

"The village of Manapadam, situated in a heathen district, possesses very few Catholics, but at least God is faithfully served here, and the Mother of God has a modest little chapel built in her honour. For a long time not a drop of rain had fallen in the country around, the drought spread to all parts, and the harvest was in the greatest danger. The Indians had made use of every superstitious practice, but all in vain, the heavens remained shut, and the earth barren. Then they resolved to make a final effort; one thing only perplexed them, they did not know to which of their gods they should make a final cry for help.

"So they took eleven palm-leaves, and wrote on each the name of one of their principal deities. Several Indians proposed to add a twelfth leaf, on which should be written the name of Mary, the Helper of the Christians; and the advice was followed.

"Then a large fire was kindled on the public square, into which, in the presence of all, the twelve palm-leaves were thrown, with the understanding that they would invoke that deity whose name should come out of the flames unscathed. Scarcely had the leaves fallen into the fire, than they were burnt and reduced to ashes. One only remained uninjured in the midst of the flames; it was that which bore the sweet name of "Mary."

"There was now, no possible doubt, that Mary must be invoked. The people hastened to her sanctuary, where each one, in his own way, called on Mary, saying as they went: 'The God of the Christians is the only true God, and His Mother has great power.'

"The benign Mother of Mercy did not seem displeased with this ignorant homage, for the Indians had hardly left the chapel, when the clouds gathered in the heavens, and a great downpour of rain watered the earth—the harvest was saved! But Mary did still more, for she allowed a ray of grace to penetrate these sterile hearts, and a great number of heathens, urged on by this miracle, were converted. The leaf, thus wonderfully preserved in the midst of flames, is now kept in Mary's chapel, at Manapadam."

65. A Wonderful Answer to a Child's Prayer through Devotion to our Lady of Dolours.

During the last battle between Poland and Russia, Count S— —, a noble Pole, who had taken up arms, was seized and condemned to death. On hearing this dreadful news, his wife hastened with her little son to the chapel, where, kneeling before a picture of our Lady of Dolours, she prayed aloud, "O Mother of Sorrows pray for us, protect and save us! Give back to a poor, unhappy woman, her husband; to a child and son, his father! Thou must take pity on our tears, thou, whom no one has ever invoked in vain! thou, who so much lovest thine own Divine Son! O sorrowful Mother, who hast suffered so much, have pity on us!" She remained praying some time with the child, then she left the chapel. It was as if some mysterious consoling inspiration had taken possession of her soul. She went at once with her son, under the protection of a faithful servant, to the prison where her husband was detained. She was able to bribe the guard and jailer by some gold pieces, and then she was taken to the dark cell. An hour later the Countess and her child again passed the guard, the former with her face covered, weeping, the boy also crying bitterly. They did not open the cell again until it was quite dark. Then the Inspector came and examined all closely. He gave a loud cry, and called the guards, saying, "Betrayed! Betrayed!" Instead of the Count they found a woman! The Countess had entreated her husband to go away in her place; full of confidence in the assistance of the Mother of Sorrows she had made this resolve, and possessed the courage and strength to carry it out. Her husband was now safe, and on his way to Paris.

A year and a half passed by; from day to day the poor Count vainly awaited the return of his wife, hoping in Mary's protection that she would be pardoned; the unhappy man could not even hear what had befallen her. The continually-repeated questions of his child—"Where was his mother all this long time?"—only increased the racking pain of his tormented heart. He had placed the boy in a school under religious teachers, and he was growing up in piety, knowledge, and good morals. The time of his First Communion was approaching, but the thought of his mother followed him continually. He said to his father, "She *must* come to my First

117

Communion, and she *will* come." Quite taken up with this idea, one day he suddenly interrupted his studies, made the Sign of the Cross, and wrote the following letter to the faithful old servant, who had accompanied the Countess to Warsaw, where he was still staying.

"Peter, will you please tell my mother, that in four weeks' time I am to have the happiness of making my First Communion, and that she is to return to Paris, and must be present. I am not writing to her, because Papa says they intercept all our letters; but I firmly rely on you using all possible precaution, that this news may reach her, and that you will tell her all I want.

I embrace you, you good, faithful old Peter, with all my heart.

Your STANISLAUS.

Tell my mother that I am living in Pensionnat X— — Rue U— —, Nr. — —."

The letter being finished, the child put a little picture of our Lady inside, that the missive might bring happiness, sealed it, and took it to the post. Meantime Count S— — had received a note, in a strange unknown hand, containing the following lines: "No more hope—departure for Siberia decided upon— Peter will make a last effort; but they say that any attempt to escape will be punished with her life."

The day of the First Communion was now at hand. Stanislaus had said nothing about his letter, either to his father or teachers, but he talked all the more about it to his loving Lord, Whom he was going to receive. He counted the days and hours, saying to himself, "I will make a Novena to the dear Mother of God, before my First Communion, and will so

118

arrange that it shall finish the very moment I receive absolution after my general Confession; I will pray so earnestly, so long, and so well that the ever-blessed Virgin will be compelled to give me back my mother."

It was the eve of the Great Day. According to a pious custom, the parents saw their children in the parlour, gave them their blessing; and the little ones could then ask pardon for all their faults and failings. Count S—— came also. Stanislaus clung round his neck, lovingly kissed him, then asked his pardon, and kneeling down received a blessing. Then he said: "I have your blessing now, but I also hope to receive my mother's." His father remained silent. "Do you not know then, that mamma is coming?" The Count answered by a deep sigh, tears filling his eyes. "She will come, she *must* be present at my First Communion. Listen, dear father. I have made a Novena to the Mother of God, which finishes about five o'clock. At four o'clock I shall be absolved, and then I shall be pure as an angel; I will beg our Blessed Lady to send my mother this evening, or at least to-morrow." The Count tried to smile, but could not; he left his son, for he could no longer control his feelings.

It was five o'clock, and Stanislaus was on his way to the porter, when one of the Religious met him, and said, "where are you going, my child?" "To see if no one has asked for me." "Your father was only here this morning." "Yes, but I am expecting another visitor—my mother." "Why, she is not even in Paris!" "But I am quite certain she will come." "No more distractions this evening, my dear boy," answered the Father, "the time for visitors is over, so go to your companions." The Novena was finished, and the child thought that the Queen of Heaven must send his mother immediately, so full of hope was he, and he had prayed with such confidence, and so earnestly. It was a great sacrifice, not to see the porter, but he bore it bravely, ever saying to himself: "When my mother comes, she will ask for me, and then they will send for me." Six o'clock struck, then seven! No one was announced. Supper was over, and all went to their bedrooms; poor Stanislaus felt discouraged.

Just at this time, a woman, care-worn and meanly-clad, her face drawn and disfigured, very miserable-looking and thin, came up to the porter saying she desired to see the young Count Stanislaus S— —. The brother did not know what to think of such a late visitor; besides, he mistrusted her, for she looked like a vagabond. So he stoutly refused to announce the visitor; but she did not desist, begging still more earnestly. At last, tired by her persistence, he let her go to the window to see the children as they were passing by. Stanislaus, who still counted on his mother's return, could not resist going a little out of the ranks, and examined the parlour with a quick glance. The Countess, for she it was, had only time to call out: "There, there!" when a loud cry was heard, and she fell to the ground. .   .   .   .   . She had arrived at the exact time appointed by her child.

By a special providence of God, she had been able, in an unguarded moment to escape, on her way to Siberia. Over mountains, through woods, marshes and valleys, she had made the long journey on foot, and at last reached Paris, begging her way as she walked, for she had no other means of help. But whither was she to turn her steps in this great city?

Fortunately, Stanislaus, in his letter, had thought of giving his address. She remembered the name of the street, and finally, after many enquiries, arrived at the school, where her child was.

The next morning the happy parents, re-united after such a long and painful separation, were present at their son's First Communion. It is certainly wonderful what power an earnest and persevering prayer has with God. But it is not less wonderful how our sorrowful Virgin Mother compassionates her suffering children, and helps them.

66. *An Incident in the Life of Marie Thérèse.*

Among the many noble buildings that surround Vienna, the Imperial Palace of Schönbrunn is the most conspicuous, and is considered one of the finest in the country. At the time of which we write, the Empress Marie Thérèse was spending the summer in this historic old castle. She loved Schönbrunn, chiefly on account of our Lady's Church at Hitzing, which stands close to the magnificent park surrounding the castle. In the early years of her reign, when she had fought for her inheritance with such heroism, she often sought refuge from her sorrow before the Tabernacle in that quiet little sanctuary, and would spend hours in prayer, imploring the protection of God for herself and her beloved country.

On one occasion, as the Empress was returning from her daily visit to this church, she noticed a lady veiled and in deep mourning, who seemed to be going in the direction of Mariahilf, a suburb named after the church at Hitzing. Her sympathy was roused by the sight of one evidently so recently left a widow, but other pressing matters soon put all else out of her head. Meantime the lady had reached Mariahilf, and turning down a narrow street entered a pawnbroker's shop. The owner was standing by a window, carefully examining a very handsome piece of jewellery, but on perceiving his customer, laid it down and came forward to attend to her. She ventured a few remarks about the weather, evidently loth to tell him the real object of her visit. At length she nervously asked him to prolong, if possible, the time he had already given her for redeeming the necklace, which he was examining on her entrance. She had been forced to pawn it, on account of her straitened circumstances, yet the hope of pecuniary relief at no very distant date, encouraged her to ask this favour, and save the jewel she valued more as the gift of her dead mother, than for its intrinsic worth. The pawnbroker at first refused, but after many entreaties and much demur, he was induced to prolong the time for payment another week, and with this concession she had to be content.

When she returned home, she found a gentleman awaiting her. He saluted her courteously, and said: "Madame, I have just returned from Neustadt, where, in compliance with your request, I made enquiries about your lawsuit. I regret very much that it is my painful duty to tell you that, although your lawyer brought the case to a successful issue, he absconded with all the money to which you laid claim, treating many others of his clients in the same shameful way. The police are on his track, but as he has escaped out of the country, they have little hopes of his capture."

The poor lady was quite overwhelmed by this unexpected blow, and sinking down on a sofa, she covered her face with her hands; "Oh, my children," she sobbed, "my children, we are ruined!"

*   *   *   *   *

The Baroness Breuing, who had thus been so cruelly deprived of her last hope of recovering the fortune she relied on, was left in a most distressing position.

She had been engaged in a lawsuit with one of her relatives, concerning her claim to an inheritance to which she was justly entitled, and now, as the gentleman had informed her, the lawyer had absconded with the money, whither, no one knew. She had no further prospects, and she dared not contemplate what must eventually become of herself and her two children. Worn out by grief and anguish, and weakened by privations, to which she was so little accustomed, her health utterly broke down, and she had to suffer a long and dangerous illness. The whole management of the house devolved in consequence, upon her daughter Elise, who was but nineteen years of age.

At first, by practicing strict economy, things went on pretty well, for they had a little reserve fund, which they had laid by for a rainy day. But the expenses incurred by the Baroness' illness, soon exhausted this slender store, and before long, everything available had been sold or pawned. Yet, in spite of the poverty to which they were reduced, Elise never lost her confidence in God, and she determined, if possible, to overcome every difficulty, and by her labour meet their pressing necessities. She spent every spare moment sewing and embroidering for those who would employ her, and did her very utmost to keep the wolf from the door, but diligent as she was, she found it impossible to meet all her expenses, and often her courage failed her.

On these occasions, she would leave her mother under the care of her little brother Conrad, and slip quietly away to the church at Hitzing. There, kneeling before the statue of our Blessed Lady, she would pour her grief into the heart of the Mother of Sorrows, and she never failed to come away strengthened and comforted.

It happened one afternoon, that Elise, quite unconscious that any eyes were upon her, was praying most fervently for light and help in her difficulties; tears ran down her cheeks, paled by continual night watching and hard work; she remained kneeling, until her soul felt once more at peace, then rising she hastened home with renewed hope.

But, unseen by the weeping Elise, the Empress had been praying in her little side chapel; she, too, had besought Mary's intercession with God, that He would scatter the enemies who pressed her on every side; she was weighed down by sorrow, and anxiety, and she felt that she could envy the poorest peasant in her kingdom. Whilst thus sorrowing over her own burdens, she perceived Elise, and was struck by her sweet expression, and the evident earnestness of her prayer, while the sight of that childish grief, roused all the sympathy of her generous nature, and she determined to find out whether it was in her power to assuage it. With this intent, she sent for the parish priest, and asked him if he knew anything of the young girl. The good priest knew Elise and her mother well, and was able to tell the Empress all the particulars of their sad circumstances.

Some hours later, a servant from the Palace arrived at Baroness Breuing's house; such a very unexpected visitor caused some surprise to the inmates, and their astonishment was increased, when they learnt that the Empress had sent him to fetch Elise to Schönbrunn, as she desired to speak with the young lady.

Wondering what the summons might mean, Elise kissed her mother, and followed the servant to the Palace. After a short delay, she was taken to the Imperial apartments, and ushered into the presence of the Empress. She stood, with beating heart, before her much loved Sovereign, for Marie Thérèse was idolized by all the subjects of her vast Empire.

"You are the daughter of Baroness Breuing?" said the Empress; Elise bowed in assent. "I have heard a great deal about you from the priest at Hitzing. He tells me that you support your invalid mother, by taking in needlework, and that you have a younger brother. The good Father also tells me that your mother has been robbed of a considerable fortune by an unprincipled lawyer. Is this so?"

"Yes, your Imperial Majesty," replied Elise, who stood with bowed head, and only ventured to glance up shyly.

"It seems to me," continued the Empress, "that you must find it very difficult to procure even the necessaries of life, still less the luxuries, which your mother's delicate state requires."

"O yes, your Imperial Majesty," rejoined Elise, encouraged by the gentle, affectionate tones, "things go very hardly with us, but I have not lost confidence in God, and with His assistance I hope to surmount every difficulty. When I left the church to-day, where I had been praying before our Lady's picture for succour and comfort, I felt an interior voice whispering to me, 'Mary will help you!' "

"Yes, Mary does help," replied the Empress, "and we should always call on her when we are oppressed with a heavy sorrow. Our Lord so ordained that I should be in the church at the same hour as you were, and He has chosen me as His instrument, through our Lady's intercession, to be of use to you. Therefore, I will place you with my maids of honour; your brother shall go to the Military Academy at Neustadt, where he will become a brave officer in the army; and I will give your mother a pension, by means of which she will be able to live comfortably, and will thus be always free from want and distress. My private physician shall attend her, and you need have no more anxiety on her account."

"O! how can I thank you?" exclaimed Elise with rapturous emotion and joy, as she fell on her knees and kissed the robe of her kind benefactress, "Rise!" said the Empress, "do not thank me, but Him from Whom all good gifts come. Walk always in the way of the Lord, and His blessing will ever be with you!"

Marie Thérèse then waved her hand as a sign of dismissal, and Elise, having made a profound bow to the Empress, hastened home through the park, her heart overflowing with joy, in order to impart the glad tidings of the Empress' generosity to her mother. On the way she passed the church at Hitzing, and as it was open, she entered, and knelt before Mary's little sanctuary, joyfully pouring out her thanks to the Mother of all in distress, who had this day shown such maternal love to the hitherto poverty-stricken family. On arriving home, she told her mother all that had happened; the latter, deeply moved, listened to her daughter's narration, and her lips uttered a fervent prayer that God would bless and reward her who had acted so generously towards them.

The Empress carried out all that she had promised, and by degrees the health of the Baroness greatly improved. Her first visit was to our Lady's sanctuary, and then she asked and obtained an audience with her generous benefactress, in order to thank her for her noble patronage and sympathetic kindness.

It is needless to say that she never heard a word of the stolen sum of money, but she recovered her treasured necklace, and, day by day, she knelt in humble gratitude before the picture of her heavenly Benefactress in the church at Hitzing.

And what became of Elise? Well, she married a rich and pious young nobleman, making a good wife, as she had made a good daughter. She attributed the blessings which attended her every step, to the intercession of our Blessed Lady, who had so amply rewarded her childlike confidence.

VII.

67. Just in Time.

THE holy Bishop Wittman, of Ratisbon, in his "Account of the burning of the Episcopal Seminary," relates the following wonderful incident of the year 1809, when Napoleon I. routed the Austrians after the siege of Eckmühl. The town itself had been courageously defended, but a strong old stone bridge, which joined the small town of Stadtamhof to Ratisbon, had been held in a particularly brave manner. The inhabitants had to retire before the French flag, leaving their dead in such numbers on the bridge, that a passage was almost impossible. Then the Austrians, having retreated to the Dreifaltigkeit mountain, situated behind Stadtamhof, set fire to the little town, in order to render the progress of the French artillery impossible. The houses on both sides of the principal street were soon in flames; but Mary, the Mother of all in distress, herself helped to put out the fire on the western side, as the following incident proves:—

"Paul Lauerer, of Stadtamhof, had fled with his family to Pielenhofen, two miles from Ratisbon, and his house had thus been left empty. Soon after midnight, he dreamt that he saw before him the picture of Mary, which was venerated in his house, and which had formerly belonged to the old Franciscan Church at Stadtamhof. The picture spoke to him thus: 'Paul, get up! for there is yet time to save your home.' He arose, and hastening to Stadtamhof, found a wooden passage at the back of the house in flames, but the roof and interior still uninjured.

He easily pulled down the burning wood, and succeeded in extinguishing the flames, which had already reached the door and wooden frame-work of a window. Thus it was that through Mary's intervention, Paul checked the progress of the fire on the western side of Stadtamhof."

68. Mary, Help of Christians.

There lived in a lonely mountainous district, a poor miner with his little family; he had only two children—Herman, a boy of fourteen, and Anna, who was nearly eight years of age. These people were poor, because they had to live on the scanty wages which the father earned with much difficulty, yet, poverty-stricken though they were, they possessed the inestimable treasure of a most lively faith and solid piety. They cherished in particular a loving devotion to our Blessed Lady, a devotion which had been fostered by a remarkable event.

The father had formerly been a soldier, and had taken part in the battle of Waterloo, the mere mention of which would rouse all his old enthusiasm. He was but a youth at the time, and had never before seen any active service, hence he felt appalled at the sight of his comrades being struck down right and left by the heavy firing of the enemy; terrified at the prospect of a death which seemed inevitable, he bethought himself of what his mother had taught him of our Lady's powerful protection in time of danger, and falling on his knees for a moment in the thick of the fray, he cried out: "Holy Mary, Mother of God, pray for us sinners now, and at the hour of our death:" he was only just in time, for at that very instant, a bullet whizzing over his head must have killed him on the spot, had he still been standing.

Bergmann never forgot his miraculous escape, which he attributed entirely to our Blessed Lady's protection, and out of gratitude for this special mark of her favour, he caused her to be loved and honoured in his little home; Herman and Anna, his two little children, quickly imbibed the pious sentiments of their parents; day by day they might have been seen kneeling together saying their Rosary, while their delight was to deck the picture of their Blessed Mother with the wild flowers they plucked on the mountain side.

Not far from Bergmann's cottage, stood an old chapel dedicated to our Lady. Formerly there had been a castle near it, belonging to a rich and powerful knight, but his family had gradually died out, and the once beautiful castle had fallen into decay, only a few old ruins marking the site. The chapel, however, had survived the destroying hand of time, and Bergmann and his family often resorted there to pray quietly before the venerable picture of our Lady, and obtain her help and intercession in all their troubles.

Little Anna used to watch the flocks on the mountain, and her brother accompanied his father every day to the mine, and did what work he could there. A miner's life, as everyone knows, is beset with many dangers, and this particular mine is peculiarly perilous. The workmen are let down into the heart of the mountain, and thus, cut off from the outer world, they break up the stone by the light of glimmering lamps, after having first blasted it with powder. The underground passages are strengthened by great wooden pillars, to prevent them from giving way, and burying the workmen in their fall. The most dreaded danger, however, is an explosion, which is caused by a large accumulation of gas becoming ignited; any carelessness therefore, on the part of the workmen with regard to fire, may cost the lives of all engaged in the mine.

One afternoon, it was the eve of the Immaculate Conception, Herman, who knew very little as yet, about the mine, fell into an underground passage, which had not been propped up with beams. His father, and another workman, who were at some distance, did not notice what had happened, and they were so intent on their work, that they did not miss the boy. Suddenly, the passage behind Herman gave way, extinguishing his lamp at the same moment. Poor child! there he stood in a dark hole, calling loudly and piteously for help, but in vain, for his cries of terror only echoed through the narrow walls of his rocky grave. At length, realizing that his shouts could not be heard, and knowing that at any moment, the remainder of the passage might fall in, and kill him, he tried to prepare himself for death, and, kneeling down, he made a sincere act of contrition for all his past sins, together with an act of resignation. He then took from his neck, a little medal of the Immaculate Conception, and pressed it lovingly to his lips, while the hot tears ran unchecked, down his cheeks. As he implored the protection of our Blessed Lady, hope seemed to revive within his breast, and he promised her, that if she would save him from the terrible death which awaited him, he would devote the life he owed to her, to the honour of God, and the advancement of His glory.

Herman had met with his accident early in the afternoon, and it was not till late in the evening, when it was time to return home, that the other workmen discovered that he was not among them. The poor father was beside himself with grief and fear, and conjectured at once, that his son must have fallen down the passage which had given way. The workmen began to remove the debris, with the greatest eagerness; they all loved the boy, and were most anxious to rescue him; yet each one felt

131

sure, in his heart, that he must have been crushed by the falling rocks. They continued their labour the whole night, all working with a will, though with extreme caution, for fear of a fresh accident, the poor father heading the searchers in a state of feverish anxiety and excitement.

Meantime, Herman, in his dreadful prison, prayed unceasingly to our Blessed Lady; trustfully and tenderly he invoked her, in the words he knew so well: "Remember, O most sweet Virgin Mary, that, never has it been heard of, that anyone who fled to thee for refuge, was left unaided. Assist me, I beseech thee, in this danger; stand by me now, and at the hour of my death."

Presently he heard the dull strokes of a hammer, he listened eagerly, fearing lest he should be deceived, but no, again and again they resounded, and then he heard men's voices, he sprang up, and with the little strength that was left him, he cried out for help. His shrill treble reached the miners' ears, and a loud cheer rose, while they redoubled their efforts. At length they cleared away the last barrier, and the exhausted child, still clinging to his medal, was soon lying in the strong arms of his thrice happy father.

Amid shouts of joy he was carried to the surface, where his mother and a large crowd awaited him. The poor mother had spent a fearful night, but now tears of gratitude were in her eyes, as she clasped her son to her breast.

The feast of the Immaculate Conception was celebrated with great rejoicings at the little church on the mountain, for all ascribed Herman's miraculous preservation and escape to the intercession of our Blessed Lady.

69. Our Little Boy.

"Near our town of Saint-Avold, there stands on a hill a beautiful chapel, which was destroyed during the Revolution of 1793, but was re-built some years later. On the feast of "Sancta Maria ad Nives," the old picture of the ever-blessed Virgin, with the Child Jesus in her arms, used to be carried in solemn procession from the town to this chapel, and ever since then it has been a renowned place of pilgrimage, known as "Zwisehenden drei Bergen" (between three mountains), where the beloved Mother of God is honoured under the title of "Mary, our help!" and is visited by many pilgrims from far and wide, especially on Saturdays. The Holy Sacrifice of the Mass is often either said or sung there, and numbers of sick people have obtained their restoration to health through their prayers and faith, and others helped in divers necessities, as is shown by the number of votive offerings in the chapel. But to speak of our own case—

We had a little boy who was nearly two years old, but who was not yet able to stand. We went several times with the child to a renowned physician, but he said that our little one's weakness lay in the joints of his limbs. He prescribed accordingly, but it was of no use. The poor child cried day and night from sheer pain, and he was always bathed in perspiration, so we felt that our only hope lay in "Mary's help." We then began a Novena, and it happened that on the sixth day, while my wife was preparing the dinner, the child lay on the floor close at hand. Suddenly the little one got up, and without any support ran to his mother. Our astonishment may be imagined, and we both realized at once that our Lady had worked a miracle for us. Our child was, indeed, perfectly

133

cured, and our confidence in Mary abundantly rewarded.

70. *A Life for a Life.*

The venerable servant of God, Bishop Vincent Strambi, who died January 1st, 1824, was throughout his life a most devoted client of our Blessed Lady. While still a child, he had offered to her his heart, with all its affections; he daily recited her Rosary, and would never omit it even when the pressure of business was greatest. He had also a practice of saying a "Hail Mary, whenever the clock struck, a practice he adhered to, no matter what distinguished company he might be in. In every misfortune he had recourse to Mary, and he was wont to console the afflicted with the words, "Have confidence, our Lady will help you, she will remember you and strengthen you." His last sacrifice was accepted through her intercession—it was the sacrifice of his life, for the Vicar of Christ.

On account of his great age and bodily infirmities, Bishop Strambi had obtained leave from Pope Leo XII. to resign his bishopric, a favour he had begged in vain from Pius VII. his predecessor. At the express wish of Pope Leo, the Bishop now took up his abode in the Vatican, and the Pontiff gave him his full confidence, and sought his advice in all matters of importance. Suddenly the Holy Father became very dangerously ill, and Monsignor Strambi was summoned to his bedside in the middle of the night. The Pope kissed him affectionately, and said in a weak voice: "Ah! Father Vincent, I had hoped to canonize you, but another must do that." The Bishop then prepared the illustrious invalid to receive Extreme Unction, and left him much comforted, having promised to say

Mass for his recovery.

Before going away he said, "Take courage, Holy Father, some one has offered his life for you." Monsignor Strambi went at once to his chapel, and with glowing fervour and confidence, united the sacrifice of his own life to that of the Spotless Lamb for the recovery of the Pontiff. His devotion was such that all present were moved to tears. As he was making his thanksgiving, one of the Pope's chamberlains came to tell him that the Holy Father had taken a turn for the better. "It is well," replied the Bishop, "our Lady has heard my prayer, and God has accepted the sacrifice."

Leo XII. speedily recovered, but Monsignor Strambi was seized with a stroke of apoplexy on December 28th, and died four days later, after receiving the Last Sacraments, with the greatest possible devotion.

71. A Tyrolese Tribute to the Blessed Virgin Mary.

A traveler passing through the Tyrol, cannot fail to be struck by the number of *ex votos* which surround the pictures of our Lady in her many shrines. They are mostly the gift of Archers, and form a touching proof of the love, devotion and confidence they repose in Mary.

It is chiefly to the protection of God's Blessed Mother that the Tyrolese owe the successful issue of the campaign in 1866, as one incident will sufficiently demonstrate: —

One of their best regiments was undoubtedly a detachment of the Volunteer Rifles, from Innsbruck, commanded by Captain Zimmeter. On setting out, this regiment had to pass the Cisack Valley, and so availed themselves of the opportunity to go in pilgrimage to Trens. There they all arranged themselves in front of the picture of the Mother of God, and recommended to her protection their wives and children, begging for success and a blessing on the campaign. These brave men then promised to have a special Thanksgiving Service in the Parish Church of Saint James, in Innsbruck, should their homecoming be rendered glorious by victory. As Mary always rewards trustful hearts, so did she this time, for her maternal hand visibly smoothed the way of this detachment, and delivered it again and again from imminent danger. The two following incidents are worthy proofs:—

On the 19th of July, a party of scouts was sent into Venetia, which country had been for some time garrisoned by General Cialdini. "At a bend in the road," says the writer from whom we quote, and who was then present, "the party was unexpectedly confronted by a squadron of the enemy's cavalry; we only noticed them when they were just about forty or fifty paces from us. The road was enclosed on both sides by a wall, and before we could have had time to scale it, we should have been made prisoners; but lo! a few steps from us we perceived a lane, which led up to a house, and through this we quickly reached a steep mountain slope. Had the enemy come on us a few minutes sooner, or later, the greater number of our patrol would have fallen into their hands. In the twinkling of an eye, we climbed the mountain, whither the horsemen could not easily follow us, and a short skirmish took place, which cost the enemy six men, whilst not a single one of ours was even wounded, and we reached our camp again without any misfortune."

"On the 25th of July, the regiment was engaged in a hot battle at Vigolo in Valforda, from eleven o'clock till four in the afternoon. The situation was so dangerous, that the General no longer hoped for a successful issue, and believed Trient could not be saved; so that the troops already began to march towards the German Tyrol. The volunteers of Sonnenburg were from four to five hours under fire, and during the first attack their brave Captain received a bullet in his arm. Another soldier would have undoubtedly been killed, if the enemy's ball had not rebounded on his gun, and so he escaped with only the loss of an eye. At last victory declared itself for the Tyrolese, and after long and obstinate fighting, the enemy was driven from the field. Hundreds of Italians fell in the battle, but only one of our men was killed, and very few wounded; indeed we came off so well, that we gratefully ascribed it to the protection of the blessed Mother of God."

This favour was worthily commemorated by the poet of the regiment, whose verses we venture to translate as follows: —

"When bullets were whizzing about us,
And danger and death all around,
'Twas Mary who raised us a bulwark,
And shelter 'neath her mantle we found.

"Every Tyrolese warrior knew well
That invisible strength was at hand,
For he put his reliance in Mary,
Who protected our brave little band!"

The escape of the patrol, the protection in the contest at Vigolo, the honour and distinction which fell to the lot of the regiment, and many other favours, were certainly owing chiefly to the Mother of Divine Grace, and to the devout reliance these brave soldiers placed in their heavenly Mediatrix. On the conclusion of hostilities, mindful of their promise, the greater part of the regiment assembled, first at Mary's shrine at Trens, to testify their gratitude for her loving protection, and afterwards at the solemn Thanksgiving Service, which was held at Innsbruck, in the Parish Church of St. James.

72. *A True Imitator of the Apostles.*

On the 11th of March, 1875, Bishop Justinian, the veteran Bishop of Chios, died at his residence, in the eighty-fourth year of his age, the sixty-first of his priesthood, and the fiftieth of his episcopal dignity. He sprang from a very ancient and remarkable family, who, centuries before, had conquered the Island of Chios, and given it over to the Byzantine Emperors.

But Bishop Justinian could boast of more than his noble birth and ancient lineage, his chief praise lay rather in his great virtue, in his large-hearted charity towards his fellow men, in his love of poverty and lowliness, and in his untiring energy and apostolic zeal.

When quite a young priest, he witnessed the destruction of Chios by the Turks, after the rising of 1821, one of the most dreadful calamities ever recorded. The Catholics of the Island, thirteen thousand in number, although innocent, shared the fate of the rebellious Greeks, and were so mercilessly slaughtered, that only three hundred survived. Justinian, the only remaining priest, assembled his scattered flock when peace was again restored, and endeavoured by every means in his power to console them for the irreparable losses they had sustained.

In course of time he was made Bishop, and, assisted by Divine Providence, he was enabled to build a magnificent Cathedral and several chapels. He himself relates how his efforts were furthered by miraculous intervention. He says:—

"At that most trying period, money was so scarce that I had no means of carrying on the building. In my distress, I had recourse to our Lady. One day I heard a knock at my door, and opening it, an unknown visitor entered and handed me a sealed packet, after which he instantly disappeared. I felt somewhat bewildered by the sudden apparition, but collecting myself, I opened the packet and found a picture of the Sacred Heart, with the inscription, 'Beati qui confidunt in Domino' (Blessed are they who hope in the Lord), and two thousand seven hundred and sixty pounds."

The zealous prelate had devoted himself, from the very beginning of his episcopacy, to the work of ransoming young Greek girls who had been carried into slavery by the Turks. There was one family of three sisters who had been thus captured, but in spite of his enquiries, he had been unable to trace them. At length, after recommending their sad fate very earnestly to Mary's protection, he saw a lady of dazzling beauty enter the church where he was praying, and coming up to him she said, "Those three sisters whom you are so anxious about, are in a Turkish harem at Tchesme, in Anatolia;" she then gave him the name of their master and the particulars of their imprisonment, and vanished. A week later the good Bishop's messengers arrived at the place specified, on the very day when the Turkish master of the young girls had died quite suddenly, thus making their ransom a very easy matter.

73. *Mary, Help!*

The following is a very simple story, one, we may say, which has been often told; it lays claim to no miraculous intervention, and yet, each time that our tender Mother has vouchsafed to show the same merciful pity, is a fresh motive of love and gratitude to all her devoted clients:—

"There lived at Liège, a family, who were in great distress; they had formerly been in better circumstances, but they had gradually been reduced to such a state of poverty, that the father was forced to do the ordinary work of a day labourer. Unaccustomed as he was to such employment, the hard work told upon his health, while the menial tasks he had to perform, were like gall to his natural pride. Added to this, his wife was prostrated by a serious illness, and his two eldest children fell sick.

"One evening he returned home, after a long day's toil, and, worn out as he was, he sat down beside his wife's bed, to watch by her through the night. He was so oppressed with grief and harassed by anxiety, that he seemed on the verge of despair; his wife, who was a pious Christian, endeavoured, in vain, to console him, then, his eldest daughter said to him: 'Dear father, say a 'Hail Mary,' and our Blessed Lady will help you.' 'I can't pray any more,' he answered bitterly, and so saying, he sprang up, and rushed into the dark night. For a long time he wandered aimlessly about, until, at last, a flood of tears relieved his aching heart, and falling on his knees, he cried: 'O Mary, have pity on me; O Mary, help!'; after which, feeling his confidence revive, he stretched out his hands towards heaven, and recited an Ave Maria.

"As he rose from his knees, he thought he saw something lying on the ground, and, stooping down, found a pocket-book full of bank notes. He was returning home, with the intention of restoring it to its owner, when he met a gentleman, who enquired whether he had seen a pocket-book. 'Here it is,' replied the poor man. The gentleman was full of gratitude, and gave him one of the bank notes, asking, at the same time, whether he was in want. With tears of joy, the happy man exclaimed: 'I was, a moment ago, but now I am so no longer.'

"Some days later, the gentleman came and made minute enquiries, as to the circumstances of the family, and gave them most generous and permanent assistance. Gladness now returned once more to the poor cottage; the mother speedily recovered, and the children grew strong again; distress and want were at an end, and, by degrees, the father regained his former position.

"He often recalled, with deepest gratitude, the help which our Blessed Lady had tendered to him in his hour of need, and would relate how he had been saved from despair through one 'Hail Mary.' "

74. *A Pilgrimage to Maria Einsiedeln, and its Consequences.*

There are still many sceptics, who often look on remarkable and miraculous answers to prayer, not as the genuine results of devotion to Mary, but as exaggerated and far fetched ideas. This weakens confidence, and want of confidence dries up the source of Divine mercy and Mary's compassion. Our Divine Lord has Himself said that "they who ask with confidence will obtain their request," and Saint James likewise says that "he who doubts is like a wave of the sea carried hither and thither, and that such a man cannot think he will receive anything from God."

Indeed, it is an indirect blasphemy and dishonour towards God, when any one does not firmly believe that He *can* and *will* help. For if what we ask for, is not contrary to the Divine Will (which is always presupposed in a good prayer), and if we make ourselves worthy to be heard by freedom from sin, or by a repentant heart, God will certainly hear us through Mary's intercession. Jesus Christ, the Eternal Truth, assures us that "whosoever doth the will of My Father," *i.e.* a just man as well as a repentant sinner—"Amen, I say to you, whatsoever he shall ask the Father in My Name, He will give it." God demands confidence, and Mary demands it also, if indeed we wish to be heard speedily. It follows that perseverance in confidence is required, as well as perseverance in prayer. So we must not desist in prayer or devotion to Mary.

The following true story which happened in Baden, we give to our readers to strengthen their trust in the Blessed Virgin Mary:—

"One lovely summer evening in the year 1840, a carriage was passing through one of the most beautiful valleys of the Black Forest. The road was bad, and the horses, already tired, had begun to slacken speed. The coachman, who had unfortunately got intoxicated at one of the inns they had stopped at, was now gradually falling asleep, so that he could hardly keep his place on the box. Just at this point the carriage, owing to his unsteady driving, gave a lurch and he was thrown to the ground. An elderly gentleman stepped out of the carriage and tried to help him to rise, but all in vain, for the man only groaned, and it was found that he had sprained his ankle severely. To make matters worse, the horses, left to themselves, made for the grass which was growing on the side of the road, and the carriage thus coming too near the ditch, was overturned. What was to be done? The old gentleman could not raise the carriage alone, and the coachman was unable to stand.

142

"A sturdy-looking man, who happened to be passing, came to the rescue, he managed to right the carriage, and got the coachman back on the box. The gentleman was very grateful, and warmly thanking the man, gave him a louis-d'or. He then continued his journey to a little town not far off, where he intended to put up for the night, Valentine—for that was the man's name—continuing his way in an opposite direction. Night had already set in when he reached his little home. The children were all asleep, but Catharine, his wife, was still up, for wearisome anxiety had kept her awake; the next day the rent had to be paid, and the two florins, which were all that Valentine possessed, were not sufficient to make up the amount. It was for that very reason, he had gone, towards evening, when his day's work was finished, to a little town close by in order to ask help from one of his relations. 'My cousin, as I expected, refused me under all sorts of false pretexts,' Valentine said to his wife, 'but if the old miser would not help me, the good God has assisted us most generously— Look here!' he added joyfully, and then he related his adventure in the forest. Thereupon both thanked God with their whole hearts, and lay down to rest with relieved minds.

"The following afternoon, there was great excitement in the village; a magistrate had entered Valentine's little cottage with a gendarme, then the latter went alone in the direction of a farmhouse near, and after a short time returned with Valentine; whereupon he and his wife were taken to the town, where the court was sitting. 'Whatever has happened?' the people said to one another, 'Valentine was looked upon by all of us as a hard-working honest man, he was liked in all the farms in the neighbourhood where he worked, and he laboured well and assiduously; such a man could never have committed a crime.'

143

"At first the villagers were favourably disposed towards him, until it became known in the course of the day, that a considerable sum of money had been stolen from a farmer the previous night. The farmer, for whom Valentine had worked the day before, was a sullen, suspicious man; on being asked in court if he suspected anyone of the theft, he replied that he trusted his own household, but added, that Valentine had been seen in the neighbourhood of his farm late on the night of the theft, whilst he himself was absent; he further remarked that some of the stolen money was in bank notes, but the greater part was in louis-d'or. After having heard this, the magistrate went to Valentine's house, and had it searched by the gendarme. The piece of money was soon found, Catharine loudly protested that she and her husband were innocent, and Valentine being called, related most minutely the adventure of the previous night—it was of no use, he and his wife had to appear before the court; Catharine was dismissed the same day to her home, but with regard to Valentine, the trial took its course, and the poor man was sentenced to three years' imprisonment.

"In the beginning of winter, before Valentine was taken to the county gaol to undergo his punishment, Catharine was allowed to visit him. But what a sad meeting! their tears flowed so fast that they could scarcely speak to each other. Valentine was almost beside himself with grief, at the life-long disgrace which would be his lot, and with anxiety about his family. Catharine was the first to compose herself, and said: 'God will help us, I will make a pilgrimage to 'Maria Einsiedeln,' in order to implore the powerful intercession of the Mother of God; she certainly will not abandon us, so do not be troubled on our account, the neighbours are kind, the greater number believe you innocent, and are angry with the old farmer, who now almost repents of his rash suspicions. Do not grieve too much, dear husband, for you will see our Blessed Mother in heaven will help us.'

"The poor woman, after all the suffering she had undergone during the trial, became very dangerously ill, soon after her return home. The neighbours looked after her and the children as much as lay in their power, and, being still young, by degrees she got over her illness. Before May came she was restored to her usual health, and did not delay setting out on her pilgrimage to 'Maria Einsiedeln.'

"One evening in the month of May, a well dressed young man was sitting on the trunk of a tree on the highroad in the neighbourhood of Lake Zurich, he was evidently a tourist, to judge from the knapsack by his side, and his gaze wandered admiringly over the beautiful landscape. At last his eyes rested on a woman, who had a boy and girl on either side of her, and a little child in her arms. She was resting by the roadside, not far from where the traveler was sitting, but she evidently did not notice him. She and her children were poor, but neatly dressed, and appeared very tired. They were crying with hunger, so their mother took a piece of black bread from a bag and gave it to them.

"The young man noticed that the children said a short prayer before beginning to eat. The little group interested him, so he approached them, and began a conversation with the woman in such a friendly and winning way, that Catharine — for it was she — soon told him her whole history. 'If things are as you say, my good woman, you will soon have cause to rejoice; meanwhile have confidence in God and His Blessed Mother,' he said; then bade her goodbye, at the same time giving her a generous present of money.

"Several weeks passed by, during which Catharine daily pondered over the words which the stranger had said to her. One evening as she was on the point of retiring to rest with her children, she heard footsteps outside her little house, which made her heart beat with joyful expectation. Scarcely had she with trembling hands unbolted the door, when Valentine, covered with perspiration and dust, was in her arms. 'O my Valentine!' she cried, with tears of joy, and 'Father, dear Father!' called both the elder children, springing out of bed and fondly clinging to him; this cry woke the baby, who also crawled out of bed, lisping, 'Father, dear Father,' thus adding his share to the universal rejoicings.

"When the first outburst of joy was over, the whole family knelt before the Crucifix, and fervently said three Paters and Aves. Catharine's next thought was to get some refreshment for her husband, who had travelled half the long journey from the county town on foot, so as to reach his dear ones that day. Beer was brought from the inn, bread, butter and cheese from the kitchen, and whilst Valentine was appeasing his hunger he related what follows:—

" 'Early this morning, about ten o'clock, I was called from my work into the room of the director of the prison, where I found the chief magistrate and a distinguished looking old gentleman, whom at first I did not recognize until he came up to me, and put out his hand to shake mine, saying: 'Yes, gentlemen, this is the honest man who for such a long time has had to suffer unjustly.' Then the chief magistrate spoke: 'Valentine G— —, Count B— — has corroborated your statement, you are now declared innocent, and from this moment you are free, an official document to this effect will at once be delivered to you.' Whilst it was being drawn up, the Count told me that a few days ago his nephew had come to him, after a holiday tour in Switzerland, and amongst other things told him of a certain family whose father was undergoing unjust imprisonment.'

" 'The young gentleman has then kept his word,' interrupted Catharine, 'may God bless him throughout his whole life.' 'Count B— —,' continued Valentine, 'at once went to the county town, and took the necessary steps for my release, the result of which is that I am again with you, thank God. But the good old gentleman did still more, for when, with many tears of gratitude to God, I had exchanged the convict's garb for my own clothes, the warder, smiling, tapped the breast-pocket of my coat, saying, 'by command of the Count, I have just put something there, spend it well, and may God keep and guard you.' I felt in the pocket and drew out a sealed letter, in which I found some friendly lines from the Count, together with these 500 florins. He had already put into my hand a gold piece before leaving, 'for travelling expenses,' he said.

"The following day, which was Sunday, the burgomaster having assembled the whole parish under the lime trees, read the official document, by which Valentine G— — was declared innocent, and restored to his former position. The venerable old parish priest had already told his flock the story of Valentine from the pulpit, ending his simple account with these consoling words, 'Mary always helps.' "

75. A Remarkable Devotion to the Blessed Virgin.

Some years ago, a very striking devotion might have been

witnessed in the ancient church of Saint Isidore, at Madrid. On a certain day, every year, the members of a noble family were accustomed to assemble round the Lady Altar, and to pray, for some time, in silence, with great fervour. Then the Countess recited aloud, an act of thanksgiving to our Blessed Lady, and the priest, who had prayed with them, bestowed a solemn blessing on the lady and her children. But the most remarkable part of this public devotion was, that during the whole time, a servant held an open umbrella, richly covered with gold and precious stones, over the worshippers.

Now, let us hear what circumstance is connected with this umbrella. During one of the last political revolutions in Spain, an attack was made on the summer residence of one of Queen Isabella's most faithful followers, a person of high rank. Only his daughter, a widowed Countess, and the servants, were in the castle at the time; when they heard of the enemy's arrival, precautions for defending themselves were immediately taken; but they had not the necessary means. The castle was soon taken, and the rough soldiers sought at once for the rich heiress, on whom they had special designs. Like birds of prey, they tried to seize the young Countess by main force; she fled from room to room, until she reached a remote chamber, which had not been used for a long time, where she hoped, at least, to remain undiscovered. But in vain, for she soon heard her pursuers in the adjoining room; she threw open the window, resolved rather to die by one leap to the ground, than lose her honour. She commended herself to our Lady's powerful protection, and then awaited the result. Meanwhile, her eyes rested on a long disused umbrella; she seized hold of it, and hastened to the window, at the very moment when the leader of the wicked band rushed into the room. Mad with rage, he sprang towards the Countess, but she warded him off with the old umbrella; for a moment, repulsed, he stepped back a few paces. The Countess took advantage of the moment, and once more calling on the Mother of God for protection, she leaped into the court-yard below.

With a cry of terror, the men rushed to the window, convinced that they would see their victim dashed to pieces on the paved court-yard, but the old umbrella had saved her from death and shame. In the fall, it blew open, and miraculously acting as a sail, wafted her gently to the ground. She immediately hastened to the gate, whilst her dumbfounded pursuers looked on, without attempting to follow her. In the meantime, the Countess, saved through Mary's protection, took refuge in a peasant's hut.

This is the circumstance connected with the umbrella, under which the Countess, together with her children, knelt every year, on the anniversary of her deliverance, to pour out their hearts, in grateful thanksgiving, for our Lady's loving protection.

76. Help in Distress.

In 1855, one evening towards the end of summer, the scholars of the Preparatory School of P—— had turned out after their studies to give themselves up to the noisy pleasures of youthful sport. Suddenly, from the tower of the neighbouring parish church, the solemn call to the Rosary devotions rang out, but only a few of the boys left their games to go to prayer. Among those who remained behind to play was one in whose soul the voice of conscience tried to conquer the love of hide-and-seek, but the latter won the day. In the next game this boy, whose name was John James, hid himself in a coach which was placed in the porch of the former Abbey buildings, now used as a coach-house, and here he made certain he would never be found. Scarcely had he hidden himself when he heard in the doorway the footsteps of the owner of the coach, who, as he passed by, called out roughly, "I tell you what, if I can only catch one of them this evening, I will beat him black and blue" (he was alluding to the pupils, who annoyed him by their games). Poor little John shook in his shoes with fright; the man was certainly one to be afraid of, for in former years he had been imprisoned for the murder of his father; the boy felt an indescribable dread creeping over him, and the neglect of his duty weighed heavily on his heart; he now cried piteously with the most ardent fervour to the dear Mother of God, whom he had always honoured, asking her help, and promising never to miss the Rosary devotions after study time again. Meanwhile the man came into the coach-house, searching every nook and corner. A gloomy silence reigned in the court of the old Monastery, for all the scholars stood in awe of the brutal fellow, and had taken to their heels. He now began to search the coach itself, but just as his hands almost touched the boy, who was cowering under the seat, he suddenly said, "That reminds me, the brake has still to be repaired," and taking off the chain he went away.

Still trembling with fear the little lad escaped from his perilous hiding place, and ran with all speed to the church, where he thanked his loving protectress; and from that day forward he never again missed the Rosary devotions.

77. How Granada was saved.

For many centuries, a large portion of Spain was under the dominion of the Moors, who were the followers of Mahomet. They had wrested it from the Christians by force and stratagem, and though every succeeding Spanish sovereign fought strenuously to expel them from the country, it was not until the 15th century, that Ferdinand and Isabella finally and effectually delivered Spain from a yoke which had become intolerable.

In 1490, the Spanish forces laid siege to Granada, the Moorish stronghold, and completely surrounded it, the infidels, however, resisted so obstinately, that the siege was prolonged for several years. Many daring deeds of bravery were performed during this interval, on both sides, but perhaps none more remarkable than the courageous act of piety of Fernando de Pulgar, a Christian knight.

One night, when the besieged were somewhat off their guard, Fernando, with a few soldiers, galloped up to a gate in the city wall of Granada, and attacked the Moorish garrison. Immediately these tried to repel them, and a hand to hand combat followed, which was bravely fought on both sides. But whilst his men were fighting, Fernando made a daring leap, on his war horse, through the ranks of the enemy, and passed the gate into the town. Although the enemy surrounded him on all sides, he rode at full speed to the great Mosque, which stood in the market place. In a moment he was off his horse, and kneeling down, he fastened to the door of the Mosque, with the point of his dagger, a slip of paper, bearing the words: "Ave Maria"—then mounted again in a trice, and galloped so fast through the streets that his horse sent sparks flying. The terrified Moors rushed out of their houses to seize him, but the brave horseman on his "flying steed" was already out of their reach. At last he regained the little gate, and another bold leap through the ranks of the enemy, brought him once more among his own men.

The infidels were beside themselves with rage and fright, when on the following day they found the name of Mary, the Christians' protectress, fastened to the mosque of their false prophet. They took it as an omen of a speedy downfall, and, indeed, a short time after this event, Granada was taken by the Christians; the mosque was razed to the ground, and on the place where it once stood was erected a marble statue of the Immaculate Conception.

78. A Petition Granted before our Lady's Picture.

In the Imperial City of Rottweil, in Swabia, a picture of our Lady of the Rosary had for a long time been venerated in the Dominican church. This devotion was increased when the ever-blessed Virgin, by means of the same picture, showed her interest in the fate of the town.

In the year 1633, when the French and Swedes invaded the city, the inhabitants, who were devotedly attached to the Emperor, resolved to resist bravely, although the town was not very large, and not particularly well fortified. The enemy being fortunately repulsed on their first attack, advanced again with several pieces of artillery, and bombarded the town on the weakest side, so that in a few days it was feared that not only the fortifications, but the very houses themselves would be razed to the ground. During these days of anxiety, the armed inhabitants fought the enemy from the walls, whilst the old men, women, and children knelt before the picture of our Lady in the church of the Rosary, imploring her protection and help. On the 10th of November, at two o'clock in the afternoon, those who were praying noticed a change in the features of the picture, which betokened pain and sadness. The alteration lasted for two hours, and not only the Catholics were witnesses, but also the Lutherans, who had been attracted by the cries of the people. The latter, being convinced, openly acknowledged there was no deception, and from this they allowed that the veneration of holy pictures was not incompatible with Divine worship. A few days later the wonder re-appeared, but this time joy and happiness were depicted on the countenance, and the sight filled all hearts with courage and hope. And they were not disappointed in their expectations, for on that very day, the 27th of November, the enemy was surprised by the Imperial and Bavarian troops and obliged to retreat, after having suffered much loss. The whole affair was investigated by a Commissioner sent by the Bishop of Constance, certified by his authority, and the written document published, with the signatures of more than twenty-four witnesses.

79. An Aeronaut's Adventure.

On the Feast of the Presentation of our Lady, 18—, the faithful belonging to the Church of Notre Dame des Victoires witnessed a touching scene.

The aeronaut Duruof and his wife—who, as the newspapers informed the public, had suffered such terrible dangers in a venturesome aerial expedition which had almost been the cause of their being lost at sea—had come on this eventful day to the sanctuary of the Immaculate Heart of Mary, to return thanks for their wonderful deliverance, and they had brought with them, to present at the shrine of our Lady of Victory, a magnificent offering, an artistically wrought golden sheaf of corn twining round a sickle.

It was at the time of the siege of Paris that Duruof, with the celebrated Nadar, had arranged for an expedition in a balloon. When all was in readiness, he advertised that they meant to cross the channel to England; but when the day fixed for their departure arrived, the winds proved so contrary that it seemed probable, if they attempted the ascent, they would be driven over the North Sea, and so perish.

General B— — and other officers, seeing this, persuaded the voyagers to postpone the attempt, and the crowd that had gathered together to watch them start began to disperse, but a few of the more reckless spirits began to grumble at their disappointment, and to make use of opprobrious epithets; Duruof, overhearing himself styled "coward," felt his pride touched, and without a word he retraced his steps, entered the balloon with his wife, and gave the sign to the men to cut the ropes.

The violence of the wind soon drove them, as was anticipated, over the sea, and for three days they were given up for lost, as it seemed hardly possible that such a frail structure could withstand the storm. But what is impossible in nature is possible to prayer, and the voyagers were at length rescued from their danger by a cruiser, not far from the coast of Norway. They attributed this mercy to Mary, the "Star of the Sea," whom they had invoked in their peril.

80. A Protestant's Appeal to Mary.

A German Jesuit Missionary relates in one of his letters, that in passing through Paris on his way to America, he met an officer belonging to a cavalry regiment, which had been ordered out to quell a rebellion in Paris. This man, who was a Protestant, but whose wife was a Catholic, greatly admired the love and reverence that Catholics shew to the Mother of God, said: "I love to hear my wife and children say every night at their evening prayers, 'Holy Mary, Mother of God, pray for us sinners now, and at the hour of our death,' and the efficacy of this petition," he continued, "I strangely experienced during the revolution of 1848, when General B — — rode up one day in evident excitement to my house exclaiming, 'Make all haste you can to leave, for the rebels are upon us.' I sat down, quickly made my will, hurriedly embraced my wife and children, and then marched out to meet the insurgents. I confess," he said, "it was a terrible moment; I had been in action in Algiers, but had experienced nothing there to compare with these riots in the streets of Paris; it seemed as if thousands of bullets were whizzing around me, and I never expected to escape that day with my life; but, in the midst of the din of the fighting, suddenly there came to my mind that prayer which I heard so often repeated at home, 'Holy Mary, Mother of God, pray for us now,' I raised this cry to heaven, and I could hardly realize my good luck, so speedy was the succour that followed my prayer, for I reached a place of safety, and escaped all further danger." Such was the true and simple statement of a Protestant officer, and we sincerely hope that this favour of Mary's protection was followed by his conversion to the Catholic faith.

81. *A Ward of the Mother of God.*

A rich widow had one son, on whom she bestowed the tenderest love, but, far from spoiling him by a weak and foolish indulgence, she did her best to train him in the paths of virtue; and, to further her endeavours, she placed him when a child under the protection of the Mother of God. When he was about to leave school, it was thought advisable for him to make his First Communion. He was fourteen years of age, and as he was also to begin to make his way in the world, his mother wished to strengthen him for this serious turning point of his life. After a long and fervent preparation, the day at last came, and on the same morning, his mother, in an impressive and earnest exhortation, besought her boy to be ever grateful for the great blessing he had received; and in order to animate him to be faithful to his resolutions, she made him promise to undertake for the honour of God and the glory of Mary, to assist every Saturday at Holy Mass, and during the great Sacrifice to pray for the soul of his deceased father, as also to pray for her wherever she should be. "This faithful hearing of Mass," she said, "will secure for you during your whole life the special protection of God, and His Blessed Mother." The boy could not resist the wish of so loving a mother, and he promised to carry out conscientiously this offering to the end of his life. The faithful fulfillment of his promise was, as we shall see, the means of his temporal as well as spiritual welfare. On the death of his mother, some years after, he solemnly renewed it, and, Saturday after Saturday, at six a.m., he was to be seen in a little corner of the church assisting with great devotion at Mass, and also joining in the hymns, sung in honour of our Lady.

One day it chanced—if we may be allowed the word—as in reality it was so arranged by Divine Providence—the priest began his Mass quite fifteen minutes late, owing to a sick call to which he had to attend, in addition to this, he was unusually long celebrating; it was an exceptionally cold morning, and the poor young man had less time than usual to spare; nevertheless he stayed to the end, in accordance with his promise, but he felt sadly tempted to leave at the usual hour, as the devil represented to him that, as he had gone in good time, he was certainly not to blame; but he withstood the temptation, and remained till the end; and it was this patient waiting for which he was rewarded, for while he was in church, some robbers had gone to his house with the evil intention of not only seizing all they could lay their hands on, but also of taking his life—but when they found the owner of the house absent, and all the places carefully locked up—for he had taken the keys with him—they changed their minds and went away without further molestation.

This was indeed a visible sign of the power of a good action, and we feel sure that if the members of any of the Sodalities or Confraternities of our Lady would take this to heart, and be as exact in performing their *first* promises as was this young man—they too, would, in the hour of need, experience the like assistance.

82. *Our Lady of Trens.*

It was on the 23rd of December, in the year 1881, that a farm servant was going with his sledge piled up with wood, down a precipitous path, on the mountainous side of the river Eisack. Between M— — and G— — at a sharp curve, both sledge and man fell over a cliff for some fifty feet, rolling over rocks and stones in a most dangerous manner. A fellow servant, who was following at a short distance, on seeing his companion disappear into the frightful abyss, could only ejaculate in his terror "our Blessed Lady of Trens, help us," and then ran back, for about a mile from the scene of the accident, to try to get assistance, at the same time feeling quite certain that on his return he should only find the mangled remains of his comrade. It was not without considerable danger that they reached the spot again; nothing was to be seen of the sledge, but, seated on a huge stone, was the unfortunate man, wiping the blood from his nose and mouth, and except that his face was bruised and cut, he was none the worse for his fall, although he declared, that he was not conscious of anything after he was thrown from the sledge. Attributing his preservation solely to the Mother of God, whose assistance had been invoked in the hour of danger, he went as soon as he was able to holy Communion, in thanksgiving, and never for the rest of his life did he forget what he owed to her intercessory power.

83. In a Well.

The following true story comes to us from Austria: E. H— — was a servant in a wealthy family, and as she was walking home one evening, after having finished some shopping for her mistress, she suddenly slipped, and some planks, which had been placed over a disused well giving way, the good woman was plunged, without a moment's notice, into the water below.

In her consternation, she could only exclaim: "Jesus, Mary, Joseph," but this prayer was effectual, for some one, in passing, heard her cry of distress, and on coming to the spot, was horrified at the utter hopelessness of the situation, but, kneeling down, she appealed first to Mary, in these words: "Oh, dearest Mother, Queen of Angels, thou art all powerful with God, send one of His heavenly messengers now, that this poor woman may not perish." After these few, but earnest words, she rose, and running as fast as she could, she soon returned with some neighbours, who brought with them, a long rope ladder, but, alas! it was too short, and did not even reach the water. What was to be done? "Mary, Mother of God, you must help us," cried the distracted woman, when suddenly, the man who had let down the rope, felt something heavy hanging to it, they drew it up, and, safe enough, unharmed—except for a thorough wetting—was E. H——, though almost stupefied by fear. When somewhat recovered, and strengthened with restoratives, she told them how, when beneath the water, and, giving herself up for lost, she felt herself lifted up by invisible hands; but, being of an incredulous nature, she doubted its being the effect of any supernatural agency, whereupon she began to sink again; the feeling of faith then revived, and once more, she perceived herself lifted up above the water, and kept in that position some time. She could not touch the bottom of the well, owing to its depth of water, neither could she hold on to the sides, for they were smooth and slippery; after a while, she saw the rope suspended over her head, but quite out of reach; again those invisible hands came to her aid, and, once more, raised her so as to enable her to lay hold of the rope, which she did "convulsively," as she expressed it, and thus she was saved from a dreadful death. Whether they were the gentle hands of the Immaculate Queen of Angels, or the wings of the angels sent by Mary, that sustained the woman in her perilous position, we know not, but we do know that the cry of the heart is a prayer in the ears of our heavenly Father, and He never lets those who trust Him—be confounded.

84. *"Ave Maris Stella."*

Some years ago, twenty-two Protestant young men left their own country to go in search of gold in California, never for a moment expecting that, before they reached their destination, a treasure far more precious than gold or silver was to come into their possession. On the same ship, but with quite a different end in view, was a simple servant of Christ, a fervent missionary, who had left all he held most dear that he might gain souls and bring them in safety to a secure harbour.

The weather was most unfavourable during the whole voyage; they had experienced two bad storms already, when a third, far exceeding in violence the preceding ones, burst upon them; a furious gale lashed the ship mercilessly on the seething billows, and in the intense darkness of the night they were quite unconscious of a new danger, until a terrific shock told them they had struck on a rock. Enormous waves broke over the vessel with a piteous moaning sound, and the captain, brave as he was, saw it was almost hopeless to save himself or the passengers, for the sea seemed like a wild beast waiting to receive its prey; at this critical moment, the hitherto silent missionary raised his voice, and in perfectly calm and tranquil tones (which contrasted strangely with the uproar around), said, "Brethren, have confidence, I implore you, this day is the Feast of our Blessed Lady's Purification, and I feel sure that if we only invoke her aid now with a strong faith, she will not only protect us, but bring us in safety to our journey's end, only, as there are many Protestants amongst us, I ask will they, too, unite with us in putting their trust in the Mother of God?" Without hesitation every one on board, Protestant or not, acquiesced in the old man's request, and in a wonderfully short time the storm began to abate. The crew were now able to work the ship, and all once more began to breathe freely, being no longer in any anxiety about their fate.

The gratitude of the travelers was unbounded, especially that of the company of Protestant young men, who were so deeply moved at their miraculous deliverance, that, without a single exception, they presented themselves before the missionary, and asked him, as a favour, to tell them all that he could concerning the Mother of God. Gladly did he accede to their request, for the gentle old priest was never tired of proclaiming the virtues of his Queen, and his simple instructions bore abundant fruit, for ere they reached their journey's end, there took place on board that ship one of the most touching ceremonies of the Catholic Church—viz., the reception of converts into the one true fold.

They erected a modest altar on deck, before which all the passengers and crew made a public act of thanksgiving, and our Protestant friends, laying aside all former prejudices, the doubts and storms of their minds were tranquilised by the saving waters of Baptism, which brought that calm that only can be found in the bosom of the Catholic Church.

85. *Beneath the Waves.*

It was in the spring of 1855, that a little fishing smack was overtaken by a storm, not far from Marseilles.

The son of the owner, a lad of fifteen, suddenly lost his balance and fell overboard, the sailors at once did their best to rescue him, but though the boat, impelled by the wind and stormy waves, came near enough to enable them to throw him a rope, the youth's strength seemed so exhausted that every time it came within his grasp, he would sink back unable to retain his hold. For an hour he thus battled, and fought against the waters, but all in vain; at last, in an agony of mind, he called out, "Our Lady of Perpetual Succour, dearest Mother, do not permit that I should perish." It seemed as if this would be the last cry he would ever utter, for he immediately sank again, when almost as suddenly he felt himself gently drawn to the surface, and near to the boat; the sailors delighted to find there was a little hope left, once more threw out the rope, but the poor boy's fingers were so cramped with the cold, that they could no longer hold it, happily however, it came into contact with his mouth, and by a violent effort he seized it with his teeth, and thus, more dead than alive, he was dragged safely into the boat. In due time he recovered his former health, youth and a good constitution being in his favour, and he made it his first duty to go on a pilgrimage of thanksgiving to the chapel of our Lady of Perpetual Succour. He prostrated before the altar, and exclaimed aloud: "Oh! my Mother, what had I done to merit such a grace?" and it seemed to him that Mary's sweet voice answered, saying: "You wear my Scapular, and you invoked me in your distress, this was sufficient to bring me to your assistance." May we not also ask ourselves a similar question? What claim have we on Mary's protection? Do our lukewarm prayers, and half-hearted services deserve any special remembrance or reward from our Blessed Lady? "Recordare, Virgo Mater Dei, dum steteris in conspectu

162

Domini, ut loquaris pro nobis bona."

86. *"Sancta Maria."*

The following incident is a striking example of how naturally and spontaneously the people of Switzerland turn to the Mother of God, whenever they are brought face to face with danger. When the Saint Gothard railway was in course of construction, some men were sent to blast a rock in a very high and dangerous spot. The most expert and bravest of them had arranged his plans so that by means of a rope slung over a projecting rock, he would be able to swing himself out of the way as soon as he had set light to the powder; but to his dismay, he found the rope begin to slip as soon as he laid hold of it, slipping and slipping until he actually was hanging over the auger hole a few yards beneath. Do what he could, it was quite impossible for him to extricate himself from this position, and his comrades, who were watching below, were far out of reach, so were powerless to help him.

Imagine, if you can, the situation of this poor man—hanging midway 'twixt sky and earth, the smoke of the burning touch-string gradually surrounding his face, and penetrating his eyes and mouth; but only for a moment, for a piercing cry of "Sancta Maria," followed by an awful explosion, told that the work had been done, and the rock was blasted.

*   *   *   *   *

The bystanders waited in breathless suspense till the dense clouds of smoke had cleared away, when, to their utter astonishment, they beheld the brave fellow, still clinging resolutely to his rope, untouched by the descending debris—unscathed by the gunpowder. Now that all danger was over, he glided down as swiftly as he could, and rejoined his companions, who greeted him most heartily. The intervention of our Blessed Lady, in answer to his appeal, was taken as a matter of course, and we cannot help admiring their simple faith.

87. One "Ave Maria."

It is forty years or so, since a terrible gas explosion occurred in an immense manufactory in Berlin, six men were killed, and seventeen severely injured. In reviewing these disasters, it is pleasant, indeed, to be able to unite recollections of the Divine goodness and mercy, to the remembrance of those appalling scenes, which are the effect of the justice of God.

It was in the evening of this eventful day, that a young servant girl came to the church, and presented at the Altar of Mary, a beautiful nosegay of the choicest flowers. She seemed quite overcome with emotion, and tears were streaming down her cheeks. At the end of the service, for it was the month of May, and devotions were being offered up, each evening, in honour of the Mother of God, some neighbours went up to her, and enquired, kindly, the cause of her trouble. "It is not trouble," said she, "but I am moved with intense gratitude for a wonderful thing which has happened to me to-day: I was sent by my master, to the soap manufactory this morning, with the purpose of remaining all day; on passing the church, it entered my mind, that, as in all probability, I should be too busy to return in time to attend the May devotions, I had better slip in, and say one 'Hail Mary,' in order that I might not let the day pass without some remembrance of our Blessed Lady. I acted upon this inspiration, and when I had finished my little prayer,

I started for my day's work; but, oh! just as I was approaching, that terrible explosion took place, which you have all heard of, and, if I had not stopped on my way to say that 'Hail Mary,' I, too, should have been one of the victims," and her tears began to flow afresh. "What would my poor mother have done, if I had died?" she continued, smiling amidst her tears; "I, indeed, have reason to come here to-night, and give my Mother Mary this bouquet." They all agreed in this, and went away marveling at the benevolence of the Mother of Mercy, who, for the sake of one "Hail Mary," saved the life of a poor servant girl.

88. Our Lady of the Sacred Heart.

An appalling hurricane swept over the town of Aquileia in 1883, beginning in the middle of the night of the 29th of June, and continuing for forty-eight hours. It wrought sad havoc in every quarter, but in a poor dwelling, about one hundred yards from the sanctuary of our Lady of the Sacred Heart, it was the means of arousing the devotion and gratitude of the people to the Mother of God.

In this particular dwelling several families resided together, numbering in all fourteen persons. The walls, which were in a very shaky condition, soon succumbed to the violence of the storm, one side of the house being struck by the lightning, fell in completely just in the very room where four little children were peacefully sleeping.

Confusion reigned everywhere, and those sleeping on the ground-floor were so beside themselves with fright, that they rushed out of the house, regardless of their scanty attire.

When the fury of the storm had spent itself, the terror of the people began to calm down; and on returning to their dwelling, they all on a sudden bethought themselves of the unconscious children, and hurrying to the tiny bedroom, found them still sleeping amidst the ruins—stones, bricks, mortar, all scattered around the bed, but the children were untouched and unharmed. It was truly so marvelous an escape that they all exclaimed with one voice, "It is our Lady of the Sacred Heart who has protected us, we belong to her, as we live in the quarter dedicated to her!"

Late as the hour was, the fourteen persons who had thus been so wonderfully delivered from danger, called together some of their neighbours, and went in a body to the church, bareheaded and barefooted, but finding it locked, they knelt on the pavement outside, and returned thanks to their heavenly Benefactress. A few hours later, a Mass of thanksgiving was celebrated, and the people who flocked to attend it were so numerous, that they could hardly find standing room, and the priest was obliged to leave the church doors open throughout the day in order to satisfy their ardent desire of offering their grateful prayers and gifts to their Mediatrix. Those who were able, brought presents, but those who were poor, and who had nothing else to offer, laid at her feet their garments and personal belongings, which to the Madonna was more pleasing than all the gold in the world—because it was all they had.

A collection was made which enabled them to celebrate a triduo with befitting solemnity, and a general Communion terminated these grateful acknowledgments of Mary's bounty.

89. An Extract from a Letter of a Redemptorist Missionary, South America.

"On the 10th of June, I and a brother priest left Riobamba, spending the night on the summit of the Cordilleras, in a very miserable hut, and like poor people, we slept on the bare floor; however, we had mounted our horses by six o'clock the next morning, and placing ourselves under the protection of our Lady of Perpetual Succour, we began our descent of the first range of mountains. We had reached a very steep slope, and I was riding in front—the path being so narrow that it would not admit of riding two abreast—when suddenly I was startled by an awful shriek from behind; looking back, I saw to my horror that Father Jenger had been thrown from his horse; the animal had fallen, and in trying to regain its footing, had slipped a second time, falling on the chest of the good priest; at last, however, it succeeded in standing upright, but in its struggles pushed poor Father Jenger over the edge of the path, and he went rolling down the mountain, until at last, coming in contact with a bush, his descent was arrested.

"He remained quietly there till I was able to reach him and help him out of his precarious position. I found him looking pale as death, but when I asked him whether he was hurt, he got up, shook himself, drew a long breath, and said, 'No, I do not feel the slightest pain anywhere, our Blessed Lady has saved my life.' I quite agreed with him, as never before had I witnessed such a narrow escape, or experienced so forcibly the power of Mary's protection.

"FELIX GRESAR, C.SS.R."

90. Our Lady of Perpetual Succour.

My object in relating the following proof of Mary's perpetual succour, which I myself experienced, is both to testify my gratitude, and to incite others to have recourse to her in all their needs:—

At a certain period of my life I was in very great trouble; constant illness in my family, loss of money, and many other trying circumstances had given me much cause for anxiety; further, these pecuniary troubles had involved me deeper and deeper in debt, and yet at this very time I was called upon to pay a large sum of money, which it was not in my power to raise. I knew not which way to turn for help, or even for advice; the dreaded first of June, the day fixed for the payment of the required sum, was close at hand, and yet I could do nothing; it was like a spectre haunting me by night and day, so much did the thought torment my excited brain—for unless my merciful Father interposed, I should lose my situation, and thereby the only means of supporting my family. Would He fail me now? No, surely not. I made up my mind to begin a Novena to our Lady of Perpetual Succour on the 23rd of May, relying on her power with her Divine Son—indeed I felt so sure of the intervention of our Blessed Lady, that a voice seemed to whisper within me, that I was already heard.

On the fourth day of the Novena, I sat at my desk musing and turning over a page of advertisements in the newspaper, in an absent kind of way, when my eye rested on a certain name, quite unknown to me, and yet I felt so strangely moved, that I was compelled to look at it again and again, until I heard once more that interior whisper urging me to apply, with the assurance that from this quarter I should get some help, I do not know exactly how I came to follow this inspiration, for it was not until my letter had gone to the post office, that I realized the boldness of this step, in writing to a perfect stranger.

As my wife had been very ill quite lately, I kept this transaction to myself, for fear of worrying her unnecessarily; what was my surprise then, when on the following morning, she told me that a stranger had called, and after enquiring about our circumstances, had left word that he desired me to go and see him. I made no delay, and by six o'clock was on my way, with a heart beating even faster than my steps. When I arrived, I was so agitated and embarrassed, that all the carefully-turned phrases I had prepared on my way vanished from my mind, but the kind manner of the strange gentleman soon reassured me. I found he was the owner of a large brewery, and very rich; he questioned me first as to the reason of my applying to him. I frankly told him I could give no reason. It made no difference, however, and he insisted upon my giving him a list of all the sums of money I wished to discharge. All this took about ten minutes; at last he rose, and his kind face wore an expression of deep thought. It was a moment of most intense suspense, and in the fullness of my heart I turned my whole soul to Heaven and breathed these few words, "Holy Mary, help me," and she did. "Strange, strange," murmured the gentleman, more in a kind of soliloquy than to me, "strange, I do not know why it is, but some interior power seems to compel me to help you, something I cannot account for, presses me to assist you."

Oh! how easily I could have explained the reason to him. I felt as if I could have dropped on my knees on the spot, so great was my gratitude to the sweet Mother of God.

"Come to me to-morrow," said he, turning to me, and speaking in an extremely cordial manner, "come to-morrow, and I will give you a sufficiently large sum of money, to meet your creditors, you may pay me back by degrees, or not, as you find you are able, and if you are not able, never mind, I will think no more about it," then, in a most friendly manner, we parted.

How I found my way home that night I cannot tell, I believe I several times knocked up against people, whom, in the exuberance of my joy, I had not noticed, but this I do know, that, before we lay down to rest that night, my wife and I had promised a life-long offering of thanksgiving to our Lady of Perpetual Succour. The stranger's promise was not an empty one. On the sixth day of the Novena, I was able to meet the dreaded first of June with a light heart, for my purse was full, and I was now able to apply myself, with new vigour, to my daily duties. Thus, from my own experience, I can truthfully assure my readers, that it has never been heard of, that anyone having recourse to the Mother of God, has been left unaided.

91. *The Miraculous Rose-Tree of Hildesheim.*

One day the Emperor Louis, surnamed the Pious, was hunting a magnificent snow-white hart. Mounted on the swiftest of horses, and followed by his best hounds, he pursued the beautiful animal, and very soon he had left his suite far behind him, in his eagerness for the chase. At length they reached a river, the hart rushed straight into the stream, as its only means of safety, and the Emperor followed without a moment's hesitation, but, although he himself reached the opposite shore, he lost both his horse and hounds in the

170

attempt. Quite exhausted, he sank under a tree, unable to proceed any farther, and keenly disappointed that the hart had escaped.

Separated from his retinue, he remained alone and forsaken in this great forest, but he recommended himself to the care of the Virgin Mother of God, and taking a little casket of relics, which hung round his neck, he placed it on a wild rose-bush, by which he was sitting. Tired out with his exertions, he fell into a deep sleep—but when he awoke, he was amazed to find the piece of ground just in front of him, and the spot that surrounded the rose-tree, all covered with snow, whilst the rest of the forest was verdant and clothed with the beauty of summer; he noticed also that his reliquary was quite frozen to the bush, and yet the roses on it were in full blossom, and even appeared more beautiful than before. He was not slow to perceive the meaning of this miracle, and at once promised to build a church in this place marked out by heaven. Scarcely had he made the vow, when a welcome sound reached his ears; the notes of the bugle and the baying of the hounds, at no great distance. Joyful indeed were the hunters to find their sovereign unharmed, whom they had scarcely expected to find alive after his adventure in the river. The good Emperor, on his return home, at once began to fulfil his promise, and the noble cathedral at Hildesheim, with its handsome dome, now stands on the hallowed spot, to commemorate to future generations, this miraculous incident; the rose-bush was planted close to the choir, and fills the little cemetery and surrounding cloisters with the fragrance of its flowers.

92. An Elephant's Revenge.

The following event was related by a Christian in the East Indies, to the Missionary, Father Oliver: —

"That I am alive at this moment," he said, "is owing entirely to the protection of the Blessed Virgin. Some time ago I went, with several others to fell wood in a neighbouring forest; as we intended to stay some considerable time, we erected a small hut, and covered it with branches. One night as we were all together in our little house, we heard a great noise, proceeding from the direction of the wood, and we did not for a moment doubt that this betokened the approach of an elephant. As we hardly considered it safe to remain where we were, we agreed to separate, and that each one should endeavour to provide for his own safety. Scarcely had I left the hut, when an elephant — for our surmise had been only too correct — coming up with me, seized me by my hair, and lifted me five or six feet from the ground, and then carried me some distance. In this frightful situation, the horror of which I cannot give you the remotest idea, I placed myself under the protection of our Lady, adjuring her to intercede with her Divine Son for my life. I had only time for this short prayer, as I became unconscious, through very fear.

"Having carried me some way, the animal dug a kind of ditch with his foot, into which he dropped me, heaping over me a mound of earth, he then left me, and trotted back towards the wood. Recovering from my first swoon, I managed, by dint of great exertion, to extricate myself from my strange grave, but no sooner had I emerged, and was proceeding to a safe retreat, when the wily beast returned, evidently suspecting some foul play on my part, and seizing me by the foot, he threw me savagely on the ground. Not far from where I lay, was a sandy bank, and here the elephant now scooped out another hole, rolling me into it, and covering me with such a mass of sand, that I was unable to stir. Being quite satisfied with his work this time, he now left me, and the whole of that night, I remained in that painful situation; unceasingly, I prayed to Mary, the Mother of the destitute, to send me timely assistance, for I knew that if I did not die of starvation, I should probably become the prey of some wild beast. At last, morning dawned, and I thought I heard the voices of several persons, lamenting and moaning, and above them all, I clearly discerned the voice of my beloved mother, evidently directing a search; she called again and again, but I had no strength to answer, still, I felt confident, now that she was aware of my danger, that she would not cease her quest till she found me, dead or alive; and Almighty God so directed her steps, that she came close to the bank of sand where I lay half buried. After a while, she distinguished a slight sound, and when she saw a mound of sand, newly piled up, the thought flashed across her mind that I might be beneath, but how I came there, she knew not. Calling to my late companions, who accompanied her, they hastened to examine the pile, and found me lying half dead. Yes, as I said at the beginning, it was owing to the Mother of God, that I was thus preserved, and I feel as grateful now, to her, as I did on that day, when she rescued me from such a miserable fate."

93. An Inundation.

The newspapers recorded at the time at which it occurred, the dreadful devastation caused by the overflowing of the river

Garonne, in the South-West of France. It well deserved the name they gave it of the "Deluge," flooding, as it did, without anyone being prepared, an immense tract of the flourishing country around, submerging populous towns and villages, and, in that one night of its unrestrained career, causing the death of 3,000 persons. The loss of property alone, has been calculated at over seven millions of francs; seldom had the world witnessed such a catastrophe. In looking back upon this scene of misery, it is a relief to dwell on those acts of heroism and self-sacrifice which were performed at the time; but more pleasing still were the examples of loving confidence in Mary, and it is one of these touching incidents we wish to recall: —

"In a house at Toulouse some twenty people had congregated together, on the first alarm of the impending danger, in order to say the Rosary, to avert, if possible, the ravages of the flood. The waters now began to enter their house, and they had to take refuge in a room in the top story. The head of the party—a devout lady, as brave as she was good—offered to give a Scapular to anyone there present who had not one. Many accepted her thoughtful kindness—but one, with a kind of callousness, only too common, refused, saying it was a 'useless precaution.' When the force of the inundation had destroyed the house, it was noticed that the only person who lost his life was the unfortunate one who had refused the Scapular. Thus did our Blessed Lady show her disapprobation of those who did not value her livery—and we hope this true episode will prevent our readers from ignoring or refusing any gift, the object of which is to evoke the protection of Mary."

94. "Angelus Domini."

It was midday, when two little brothers were playing together by the river side, not far from the gigantic mill that stood on its banks. The eldest, who was only eight, was very proud of his responsible post of looking after his younger brother, but carefully as he watched him, he was unable to prevent him slipping away out of his sight from time to time, and in one of these wanderings, a sudden splash told him that the little lad had fallen into the river. Without a moment's delay, the brave boy plunged in after him, for he well knew the danger which threatened him. The overpowering velocity of the water was carrying the child towards the machinery of the mill, which was working full speed, and should he be caught in the wheel, death would be instantaneous. With all the strength he could muster our hero swam on, propelled by the force of the stream. At length he reached the little fellow, who was half stunned with fear, but it seemed as if it were only that they might die together, for no sooner had he grasped his brother firmly by his hand than they were borne with terrific speed towards the dreaded wheel, and any moment they might have been caught up by one of the spokes. No one could hear their cries for help, and the poor boys seemed forsaken by God and man; but no! the clock strikes the hour of twelve, all hands stop work, the mill stands still, and one of the men, with head uncovered, coming out to say the Angelus in the open air, spies at once the two little black specks in their proximity to the mill-wheel, and before long they were once more in safety by their mother's side. Thus was the devotion to the "Angelus," in a little village of Lower Austria, visibly rewarded in the year 1883.

95. An Episode of an Indian Sedition, 1740.

In the early part of the last century, a wild and barbarous tribe of mountaineers, consisting of a thousand men, made a sudden descent on Kharnatra, on the coast of Choromandel. Wherever they appeared they caused the greatest consternation, and even when the greater number had satisfied their greed and thirst for plunder, and had returned, laden with the goods of their neighbours, they left behind them several bands of robbers, who pillaged or destroyed all that was left.

One day, one of these devastating parties fell upon a Christian village, which was privileged to possess a Catholic church, and what is called a "mission-house." The men, on the approach of the robbers, effected their escape, but the women and children took refuge in the church, recommending themselves to the protection of the Blessed Virgin; not feeling secure enough, however, they betook themselves to the mission-house, and shutting themselves up in a passage, adjoining the private room of their pastor, they began the recital of the Rosary.

After the bandits had pillaged the whole village, they forced open the church, and proceeded to the house, destroying all on their route, but strange to say, they never noticed the passage, in which the trembling people were hiding, and telling their beads, and thus they escaped all molestation.

During the same period, a young girl was so alarmed at the appearance of the marauders, that she endeavoured to hide herself in a dense thicket, one of the men, noticing her flight, tracked her to her hiding place; to escape was now impossible, and her only security was in a heavenly protectress. She turned with a simple faith to her, who is so full of tenderness and charity, to Mary, the Mother of God; and just at that moment her persecutor dropped down dead—bitten by a poisonous snake. This was without doubt a clear interposition of Divine Providence.

96. The Bouquet.

In 1857, a ship bound from Marseilles to India, was at anchor in the harbour. Two figures were standing together on the deck, just before the vessel set sail—a young sailor, who was about to make his first voyage, and his mother. She held a bouquet in her hand, which had been specially blessed that morning, at an altar dedicated to the Blessed Virgin; "Take it, Jean," she was saying, "and let it every day remind you to say at least one 'Hail Mary,' which shall be to you a pledge of her protection;" then, embracing her son, she left the vessel to return, as so many mothers have had to do, to their daily round of duties, while their hearts are far away, following the destinies of their beloved absent ones.

The young man laid the bouquet reverently between the crucifix—also the gift of his mother—and her portrait, and every morning he would take his three treasures out of his trunk and try to learn their lessons. The crucifix would preach to him of the love of God, the bouquet reminded him that he had been bequeathed to Mary, and the portrait recalled the face of his beloved mother. The voyage was a particularly tempestuous one, and many were the times the sailors gave themselves up for lost, but in these perilous moments, Jean would take from his trunk his precious bouquet, and pray quietly and devoutly to Mary.

*　　　*　　　*　　　*　　　*

A year had passed since the separation of mother and son, when one day a woman was to be seen kneeling before the image of the Immaculate Queen of Heaven, and assisting at Mass, with more than usual devotion; when it was over, she went and laid at the feet of the statue a beautiful fresh bouquet of lovely flowers. Yes, it was the mother who had come to return thanks, together with her son, for his preservation; but he bore in his hand a bouquet of faded flowers, which he presented as his token of thanksgiving. Twelve sailors accompanied them, for they had come to acknowledge, that it was the constancy of their comrade, to his mother's parting advice of persevering prayer to the Queen of sailors, that had brought them in safety through such frequent and violent storms.

Let us, too, remember that the perfume of our flowers will reach the Throne of Mercy, if they are safely deposited in Mary's hands, and that these perfumes signify the fidelity with which we offer up our daily prayers, crosses, or mortifications, of which our little bouquets must be composed.

97. A Providential Escape.

An Apostolic Missionary, in North Japan, has sent us the following story, which was related to him by Father Alexander Berliez, a brother missioner: —

"Some time ago, the Christians of this district devised a plan for erecting a house for the benefit of the poor. For several days, they had been at work, and had made good progress with the building, when, suddenly, without any warning, the ceiling of the ground-floor gave way. Fourteen persons were working in the house at the time, eight being down stairs, and six in the upper storey; five of these latter fell through the opening in the ceiling, with a terrific crash, which brought the neighbours hurrying to the scene of the disaster, expecting to find their friends buried beneath the ruins. However, when the cloud of dust had cleared a little, they beheld, to their astonishment, that the five men were not only alive, but had not even received a scratch. They still felt some alarm as to the fate of the women and children, who had been working in the lower rooms, but their fears were soon allayed on this score, as they presently emerged, unscathed, from the back of the house. By a special interposition of Divine Providence, they had left the building a moment before the accident occurred, to do some work in an opposite direction, otherwise, they must, inevitably, have been killed. There was still one fear left, a little child of three years old, had been left in its cot, fast asleep. Only a short time before, it had been lisping, in a delightful manner, the first words of the 'Our Father,' and now, they scarcely dared to hope ever to hear its voice again, for it was buried beneath a great pile of rubbish. The men began at once, to work through the mass of bricks and mortar, all scattered about, until they reached the place where the child lay, and there they found it sleeping, as quietly as if no accident had happened, for a large block of wood had so fallen, as to support the beams, and thus prevent them from crushing the child, and in this manner, its life had been saved. In short, not one of those fourteen persons had suffered any hurt. The good Christians attributed this to a miracle on their behalf, and even the heathens were forced to acknowledge that some invisible power had befriended them.

"In the morning, just as I was starting to give a French

lesson, I saw these good people flocking to our church to return thanks for their deliverance, and they gave me full details of all that had happened, but, wishing to convince myself of the truth of their story, I went in the evening to survey the scene of the accident, and found it was as they had said; whereupon I invited them all to come next day to a Mass of thanksgiving, which they eagerly agreed to do. After the Gospel, I said a few words to them on the powerful protection of Mary, to whom they owed their lives, and exhorted them to be faithful in their devotion to her, as a lasting profession of gratitude."

98. *The White Roses.*

In a beautiful and spacious villa, on the banks of the Rhine, there dwelt a noble family named Elmau. They were exceedingly rich in the goods of this world, and possessed besides, those essential qualities which constitute real and lasting happiness. Herr von Elmau and his wife had but one child, Rosa, a sweet, bright, lovable little girl, whose simple gentle ways endeared her to all. Needless to say, she was the apple of her parents' eyes, yet they were too wise to spoil her, and trained her most carefully, in order to fit her for the position she would have to take in the world. But their chief care was to foster in her young heart a tender and loving devotion to our Blessed Lady, and to this, Rosa's gentle nature quickly responded, her greatest delight being to show her heavenly Mother every mark of childlike affection, by adorning her pictures and statues with the choice flowers with which their garden abounded. When Rosa was old enough she was sent to a convent school, and the nuns, perceiving her special devotion to the Mother of God, gave her the care of the Lady

Altar.

It happened on one occasion, that she was returning to school after the holidays, escorted by her father; they were seated alone in a first-class carriage, Rosa, as usual, chattering merrily, and making remarks about all they passed. Suddenly she bounded to her feet, like a little bit of quicksilver, and pointing to a beautiful garden exclaimed, "Oh, do look at those lovely white roses, just fancy, at this time of the year! I must have some for our Blessed Lady. Dearest father," she continued, coaxingly, "mayn't we get out at the next station and pick some of them, and then go on by the next train, it is not far to the convent now, only three more stations."

Herr von Elmau smiled at her enthusiasm, as he replied: "My dear child, you do not know what you are asking; that garden belongs to a wealthy nobleman, who cultivates those roses you covet as his special hobby, he certainly would not deprive himself of them for a little girl he has never seen, besides it is more than an hour's walk to his house." "Oh! the distance doesn't matter," implored the child, "and the gentleman could not refuse to give me the flowers for our Lady." However, Herr von Elmau did not mean to humour this strange whim, so he merely laughed and tried to change the subject; but the child would not be put off, and throwing her arms round her father's neck, she besought him to grant her this last favour before she returned to school.

Herr von Elmau could not resist her pleading any longer, and at length, with some misgiving, he acceded to her request. They alighted at the next station, and after a long, hot walk, they arrived at the residence of the owner of the beautiful garden. He received them most cordially, insisted on their taking some refreshment, and was so kind and genial, that the little girl had no difficulty in telling him her desire. He immediately sent for his gardener, and told him to pick a large bouquet for her, and her delight was unbounded when he returned with a basket full of the coveted treasures. After a pleasant visit, father and daughter took leave of their new friend, and started once more for the station.

When they reached the platform, they found everyone in a state of great excitement, and on enquiring the cause, they learned from the stationmaster that the train from which Rosa and her father had alighted, had met with a terrible accident, that many of the passengers had been either killed or severely wounded, and that the very carriage in which they had been travelling had been smashed into atoms.

It was evident, both to Herr von Elmau and his little girl, that it was to our Blessed Lady that they owed their miraculous escape, and it was with intense emotion, and a deep sense of thankfulness, that, a few hours later, they laid the bouquet of white roses, which had been the indirect means of saving their lives, at the feet of the statue of Mary, in the little Convent chapel at B——.

99. *"Mary" and the Student.*

In the summer of 1865, two students from the Gymnasium at Mährisch Trüban, went for an excursion up a mountain-pass, their object being to find some rare plants, specimens of which they required for their botanical pursuits; for several hours they searched in vain, when at length they reached a large quarry, the sides consisting of loose rubble-stones, in the middle of which they spied a magnificent sample of the wished for plant. They consulted together how to get possession of it;

at first they tried to dislodge it from its rocky bed by means of throwing stones at it, hoping thus to loosen it, soon, however, they gave this up as useless, and one of them, in desperation, determined not to be baulked of his prize, began to climb down the side of the rocky wall; in his temerity, he never thought of the danger to which he was exposing himself, and forgot the precaution of taking off his boots, which facilitates this kind of climbing. Hardly had he begun the descent, than the loose stones gave way under his feet, and he found himself slipping gradually, but surely, down the side, towards the edge of the precipice; vainly he clutched at every object as he passed, it only loosened in his grasp, rolling before him into the abyss below. He was petrified with terror, and a thousand dreadful thoughts succeeded one another in his excited brain; he plainly saw that he could not save himself, yet he could not face death. In this extremity he had a sudden inspiration, and he cried from the depth of his soul, "Oh, Mary, my Mother, help me!" Yet our Blessed Lady appeared to turn a deaf ear to the poor youth's cry of anguish, for instead of his course being arrested, he began to slip with greater rapidity to the edge, one foot was already hanging over—another moment he would have been dashed to pieces on the rocks beneath. In this supreme moment he was unable to utter a word, but a heartfelt prayer arose to heaven, imploring Mary's help to save him, not from temporal death, but from the everlasting abyss of hell. Immediately, his other foot struck against a projection in the rock, thus checking his descent, and supporting him, until his companion was able to bring him assistance from some labourers working near.

After a slight delay, which seemed an eternity to the poor prisoner hanging between heaven and earth, a rope ladder was let down over the precipice, by means of which he was rescued from his terrible position. The anguish he experienced during this interval of suspense, is best described in his own words. He says:

"Only now, can I fully realize the horror of my situation. Below me a frightful precipice and sharp pointed rocks on every side, which had already torn and wounded me in my descent, and there was I, leaning for support against a thin ledge, which jutted out from the cliff, and which was the only thing between me and instant death. While I was awaiting my companion's return, who had called out to me encouragingly from above, I was able to view the situation, and I felt that if the ledge gave way before assistance arrived, I was lost. The thought made me quite dizzy, my eyes grew dim, my whole body was bathed in a cold sweat, my only comfort being the constant repetition of my little prayer, 'Mary, help me!' It was with difficulty that I kept myself from jumping over the precipice in the agony of mind and body I was experiencing, and I owe it to my Angel Guardian that I was able to keep my head. When, at length, I saw the rope ladder slowly descending, I trembled in every limb, and even then, had it not been for my trust in Mary, I should not have had strength to lay hold of it. Once again I cried 'Mary, help me!' and my trust was not in vain.

"I have always been inclined to be very incredulous with regard to anything supernatural, but I have no hesitation in affirming that I owe my preservation entirely to our Blessed Lady, since all human succour was out of the question. It was Mary I appealed to, and it is to her, I repeat, that I owe my life. 'Praised be Jesus and Mary.' "

100. The Pilgrimage to Clausen.

During the war of 1870, the following narrative appeared in one of the Catholic Missionary papers: —

"On my way home I met with a small party of travelers; very soon we were engaged in an interesting conversation, the topic naturally turning on the present war. One of the company, a young girl of about twenty-five, edified us by narrating the details of a miraculous interposition of the Blessed Virgin on her behalf. I will give, as nearly as I can remember, the story in her own words: —

" 'I was a servant in a large mansion, situated just outside Metz, and shortly before the war broke out, I was sent by my mistress on several important messages into the town, as she liked me to do all her commissions for her. However, after a while, the whole country swarmed with French troops, and one day our household was put into the greatest confusion, by the arrival of a number of soldiers, who surrounded the castle and grounds; without giving any reason, I was taken prisoner, the rest of the household being left unmolested. I was at once led before the Mayor, to be tried by court-martial, on the charge of being a spy, a sentinel declaring he had seen me going backwards and forwards to Metz, and afterwards communicating with the Prussians. It was in vain I denied, protested, and implored to be let free, assuring them of my innocence, my master and mistress also corroborated my statements, and interceded on my behalf, but all to no purpose. I was sentenced, and the following day was to lose my life. I hardly knew what to do with myself, so great was my terror and agitation, I tried to pray, but the near approach of death seemed to paralyse my whole being; I then began to make plans for escaping, but I saw very soon, that this was impossible. In this hopeless condition, I had recourse to the Mother of Dolours, and besought her to assuage my fears, if she could not obtain my release; by degrees, my fears lessened, and, before the eventful morning, I was calm and resigned, and ready to meet death, sustained by the thought of the Queen of Sorrows.

" 'Quite early, on the day appointed, I heard footsteps coming towards my prison cell, and I naturally expected it would be the priest, come to prepare me for death, but no! it was a messenger announcing that I was free. Overwhelmed with surprise and delight I hastened home, not even waiting to make enquiries as to the reason, but afterwards we learned that my accuser had confessed that though he had seen me in Metz, he could not say that I was the same person he saw conversing with the Prussian sentinel.

" 'How it came to pass, that this man, at first so positive in his assertion, admitted that he was a liar, seems to me something very remarkable, as it could have been no easy task for him, considering the penalty he would have to undergo, but it convinced me, more than ever, that my appeal and trust in the Mother of Sorrows, was the real cause of my restoration to liberty. I am now going on a pilgrimage to the famous shrine of our Lady of Dolours, at Clausen, in the diocese of Trèves, in order to thank her for the great favour she has bestowed on me.' "

101. The Ringing of the Angelus.

Three times a day, the solemn sound of the Angelus, echoing throughout Christendom, recalls to all faithful

Catholics the thought of God's holy Mother, and the great mystery of the Incarnation; for we may say with truth, that the Angelus is a compendium of the grandest mysteries of our Faith, and that it re-awakens in our hearts a sense of wonder and gratitude, for that infinite act of Divine Love, which was announced by the angel to the Virgin at Nazareth.

In Catholic countries, where the simplicity and devotion of former times may yet be seen, the people naturally uncover their heads and kneel down at the first sound of the Angelus. In Italy, in France, in Spain, in Ireland, this pious custom has always been preserved, and the following story is only one of the many proofs, of how much our Lady values it: —

"After the defeat of Don Carlos, the famous Pretender to the Spanish Throne, many of his followers were taken prisoners, among others Don Zavala, the most faithful of all his adherents. In course of time Don Zavala was brought before a court-martial to be tried for high treason, and after a very short sitting he was sentenced to death. He heard his fate with the utmost calm, and merely asked when the sentence would be carried out. 'This evening, half an hour before the Angelus,' was the reply. Don Zavala bowed his assent, and having asked for a Confessor, spent the interval in preparing for death. In the evening the guard arrived to lead him to the place of execution; he was quiet and composed, and passed apparently unmoved through the crowd of spectators who had assembled to see the famous Carlist die. Meantime the soldiers arranged themselves in single file, awaiting the order to fire.

" 'Present arms,' cried the officer. Immediately every gun was raised. There was a moment of awful silence, the onlookers held their breath, when suddenly the Angelus bell rang out loud and clear. Instinctively, every man dropped on his knees with head uncovered. Don Zavala also knelt, and commended himself once again to the Mother of the God who had redeemed him. Doubtless too, many a one in the kneeling crowd offered their prayer for him who in another minute would be standing before a heavenly tribunal. But it was not to be, Providence had otherwise ordained; for, as the last sound of the bell died away, an emissary rode up at full gallop, waving the white flag. The air was at once rent with shouts of delight, bursting from the immense multitude; party spirit, the desire of revenge, rancour, all these had been quelled by that unanimous recital of the Angelus. Zavala was pardoned; who his deliverer was he knew not, but he attributed the mercy bestowed on him to the intercession of Mary, the channel through whom life had been given to the whole human race."

VIII.

102. A Conversion through the Intervention of Mary.

BRUCA, the daughter of a rich Turkish merchant in Tripoli, had been made a slave in her early youth. In the year 1765 she was living in a very good Christian family in Malta, who did everything in their power to induce her to become a Christian, but in vain. The devil had fixed the idea in her mind, that eternal blessedness is dependent only on the good works we do; therefore she answered each time any of the Christians who spoke to her on the subject, "that she had been born a Turk, and a Turk she would live and die, that her happiness in the next world only depended on her good works, and that she would pray to God for grace always to be able to perform them." Upon these she set her hope and confidence, and in this belief she did not wish to be disturbed. All were soon convinced that such stubbornness could only be conquered by a special grace. Her master, who had given up hope of obtaining anything by persuasion, advised her at least to recommend herself daily to the Mother of God, in order to obtain light and strength to discern the real truth.

The Turks have a great veneration for Mary, and honour her as the Mother of a great Prophet, therefore Bruca willingly promised what she had been asked, and faithfully kept to it.

Not long afterwards, one night, when she had gone to bed, the whole room was suddenly lighted up by an indescribably bright light, and she saw a most beautiful Lady, whom she recognized as Mary, come towards her. She touched Bruca and said: "Become a Christian, and take the name of Marianne!" Then the vision disappeared, and Bruca was at once entirely changed, and firmly resolved to become a Christian, and be baptized without delay. She rose, called her master, related to him with great delight her vision, and asked him to let her be baptized at once. He was astonished at this sudden change, and yet the girl's wonderful narration seemed perfectly true. He praised God a thousand times for His great mercy, and told Bruca that she had to learn first of all the tenets of our holy religion, before she could receive baptism; all this would require time, attention, and perseverance. At present she might thank our Divine Lord, and His holy Mother for their great mercy, and ask, through the intercession of this same Blessed Mother, that He would give her still greater light to learn the Catholic truth, and confirm her in her holy resolve, thus fitting her for baptism, which would at last bring her to a blessed life hereafter.

Bruca was pacified by all these arguments, and spent the rest of the night in fervent prayer; during the next three weeks she was instructed in the Christian Doctrine, and persevered in her resolution, and her desire for baptism. But after this, doubts arose in her mind concerning the vision, and temptations about the necessity of baptism; she fell into her former error about good works, and obstinately refused to be baptized. She was even more stubborn than before, and continued thus till the February of 1778.

In September of the preceding year, Bruca had been bought by Signor Carl Giorgi, of Rome, and in the following month, she entered the service of her new master. The family and many other persons endeavoured to convert her, but they too were unsuccessful, for she only became more and more hardened and inaccessible to all human persuasion; this lasted till the evening of the 21st of February, 1778.

It was Saturday, and Bruca, having gone to bed very late, soon fell asleep. She had not been asleep long, when she heard someone calling her by her name. She woke up, and saw the whole room filled with bright and beautiful light, and near her bed stood a youth, clothed in shining white garments. At first she was overcome with a holy fear, but by degrees she became calm, and felt her courage return, at the same time being filled with sweet and joyful confidence.

Humbly and reverently she asked the youth who he was, and what he wanted with her. He answered: "I am Aloysius Gonzaga," and when he had said this, he pointed out to her in the distance, a most beautiful Lady, and added: "Look there! that is Mary, the Mother of God; but as you are not a Christian, she will not come near you." At these words, Bruca felt her heart penetrated with such new, efficacious consolation, that in her joy, she could not utter a single word; but she was completely changed, and was now firmly resolved to become a Christian. Then the vision disappeared.

In the morning, Bruca related to her master and mistress what had happened during the night, and assured them she would become a Christian and be baptized. They were very much surprised at such a sudden change; and although they did not doubt the facts that Bruca related, as she was very truthful and sincere, nevertheless they sent her on the same morning (it being a Sunday), to the Church of the Roman College; and, as soon as she entered, she noticed a picture which she recognized at once, exclaiming, joyfully, to the servant who had come with her: "That is the youth who appeared to me last night, and spoke to me!"

On the 2nd of March, Signor Giorgi took Bruca to a convent, where she was carefully instructed in all that was necessary for a good preparation for the grace of baptism. She was full of fervour and ardent desire for this great privilege, and at length, on the 9th of June the same year, she was solemnly baptized by Cardinal Mark Antonius Colonna, Vicar of Rome, in the Church of the Collegium Romanum, taking the name of Marianne Aloysia de Giorgi. Her godparents were Signor Dominicus Giorgi, and the Countess Scotti, children of the above-mentioned Signor Carl Giorgi.

103. *The Power of a "Hail Mary."*

Under this title the *Catholic Times* published some time ago, the following true story, told by a Lancashire priest: —

"One day an honest workman came to the presbytery, and asked to speak with me at once. He said that he was not a Catholic, but he would be very grateful if I would kindly visit his wife, who was in a decline, and he believed that she had not very long to live. I asked him if she were a Catholic. 'No,' he answered, 'but she insists on seeing you, and will not hear of a clergyman of any other religion.' I then enquired where he lived, and found that it was in the most miserable part of the town.

"On reaching the house, I was welcomed most eagerly by the poor woman. She at once declared that she was convinced of the Catholic truth, and begged me to instruct her in the doctrines of our religion. I was astonished at all this, for I learnt that not one of her relations or neighbours were Catholics; so I asked her somewhat anxiously if she really knew I was a Catholic priest. She answered in the affirmative, and added that she perfectly understood what she was saying, and what she was about. Under these circumstances, I at once began my instruction, and was surprised to find how quick the poor woman was; she was very eager and interested about all I had to teach her, and showed a very retentive memory. The thought of Confession and Communion did not trouble her, and as death did not seem so very near, I had time for a thorough preparation. After six weeks she made her first Confession, and when death was approaching she received the Last Sacraments with great devotion, dying a very happy and edifying death shortly after.

"Before her death, she made her husband solemnly promise to become a Catholic, and to send their two children to the Catholic school, and to have them brought up in the Faith. After his wife's death, he faithfully carried out this promise. He declared that he owed his conversion mainly to the extraordinary patience and cheerfulness which his wife showed during her painful illness. I myself have not the slightest doubt of the sincerity of her conversion, and I am firmly convinced that at her death she was a Catholic from the bottom of her heart.

"Astonished at the exceptional graces the poor woman had obtained, I was naturally curious to find out by what means she had merited such favours. I asked her if, before her illness, she had ever entered a Catholic church. Having received an answer in the negative, I continued: 'Have you ever spoken to a Catholic priest?' 'No,' she answered. Then I asked her if she knew the 'Our Father'—she knew nothing of it—nor did she know the Apostles' Creed. 'Have you ever said any other prayer?' First, she answered in the negative; then, as I asked if she never prayed before going to bed, she answered, smiling, and hesitatingly, as if not quite sure, if what she did say, deserved the name of prayer: 'When I was a little girl, I often played with some Catholic children, and I caught a few words from them, which I have repeated every night, before going to bed.' Then she recited the words: 'Hail Mary,' etc: the secret was at last discovered. In the hour of death, Mary, her Heavenly Mother, had claimed her for her own.

104. *Mary, the Channel of Grace.*

A priest, a friend of mine, wrote to me that, not long ago, he had come across a case, which showed how many and great graces, are obtained through the intercession of the Blessed Mother of God:—

"A schoolmaster in our parish," he writes, "had a Protestant mother, who was more than seventy years of age. She had married a Catholic, and her son had been brought up in his father's religion; after her husband's death, her son begged her to live with him. He had, naturally, longed, for some time, that his beloved mother might have the grace to become a Catholic, but, from a shy reserve, he dared not reveal this ardent wish to her, lest he should disquiet her mind. She was nearly blind, and, having recently broken her leg, she was always obliged to remain in her room. Her son had been, lately, in W——, following the exercises of a retreat, which was being given there. On his return home, he came to call upon me, and joyfully told me, that his life-long prayer had, at length, been answered, and that the longing desire of his heart was about to be realized, for his dear old mother had decided to become a Catholic, and as he said this, the good man's eyes filled with tears. Then he related to me, how, at the end of his retreat, he had made a pilgrimage to the shrine of our Lady at B— —, and implored of her, to obtain for him, the conversion for which he yearned.

"As he was praying, his mother suddenly called her daughter-in-law, and told her that she had an extraordinary feeling of uneasiness about her salvation, which she could not in any way account for, since she had never before experienced any doubts but that she now felt so convinced that the Catholic church was the only true one, that she could not any longer remain a Protestant. When her son returned home, on the following day, she communicated to him the glad tidings, and he recognized that our Lady had bestowed this signal grace at the very moment when he was invoking her so ardently on his mother's behalf.

"Soon afterwards I paid a visit to the old lady, whose only anxiety was that I would refuse to receive her into the church. After a few words of kindly greeting, she began, 'Oh! father, I am so old and feeble, and useless and a burden to everyone, there is scarcely anything I can do, laid up as I am,' and with tears she added, 'My son can go to W— —, and is able to make a beautiful retreat, my daughter-in-law can receive the Sacraments and hear Mass; and I—!' 'You are right, good mother,' I said, 'but now that you have once made the resolution to become a Catholic, you have gained a great grace, and it is your son who has obtained it for you, through the intercession of the Blessed Mother of God.' After a few more encouraging words I left her, promising to come again soon; she was very happy, now that the first step had been taken.

"In about two months the good lady was sufficiently prepared, and with deep emotion she went through the usual ceremonies of reception into the church, a few days later, receiving the Sacraments with great devotion. The ceremony took place in her own house, on account of her age and infirmities, but nearly the whole parish assisted at it, and rejoiced over this happy event.

"Praise and thanks to Jesus and Mary!"

105. Conversion of a Rabbi at Maestricht.

When someone was reading to Blessed Catherine Emmerich, the incident of the conversion of a certain Rabbi, at Maestricht, she exclaimed: "I am acquainted with this man, for I have sometimes seen him. Once I saw him whilst he was on a journey, some of his fellow-travellers, who were pious people, happened to be speaking about the Mother of God, and of a certain miraculous shrine (I think it was that of our Lady of Good Counsel), which they had just visited, and of the miracles they had seen there. The Jew said: 'Mother of God? Mother of God? God has no Mother,' and he scoffed at this belief. As I have had from my childhood great compassion for Jews, and as I have been shown in vision many subjects for prayer, this one also was presented to my mind, and I prayed earnestly for this Rabbi, frequently seeing him afterwards, but I noticed especially that he could not get rid of the thought of Mary. I often saw Mary approach him, holding out to him the Infant Jesus, as if she would say: 'This is the Messiah.' But I do not know if he really saw them, or if it were only his interior thoughts which were shown to me. Certainly, he himself considered these thoughts as temptations, and fought against them, endeavouring among other evil things to be always present at Processions of the Blessed Sacrament, in order to have opportunities of shewing irreverence, and uttering blasphemies concerning the Real Presence. Once during a Corpus Christi Procession, I saw him involuntarily fall on his knees. I do not know if it was only a sudden emotion which he experienced within himself, or if he saw what I saw, namely, the Mother of God holding out to him the Child Jesus, from the Blessed Sacrament. I saw in the end, that he became a Christian, and I am certain that if anyone questioned him, he would be obliged to own that the thought of Mary pursued him unceasingly. But till now I had heard nothing of this conversion, and thought it was only a dream."

106. Sanach, the Mussulman.

P. Francisco Rosignoli, who died in the year 1775, was an ardent lover of the Blessed Virgin, and obtained many favours from her. He was an indefatigable labourer in our Lord's vineyard, and the founder of the "Della Floriana," a house for making retreats, at Malta, where many conversions took place. But the most remarkable of all was that of a Mahommedan, named Sanach, who was executed on account of a conspiracy against the Knights of Malta and their Grand Master. He had arranged with some other Mussulmen, that the Turk who was accustomed to shave the Grand Master, should cut his throat, and having given a pre-arranged signal that the deed was accomplished, the rest should fall upon the other Knights, and kill them. But, through the intervention of the Blessed Virgin and Saint John the Baptist, the special Patrons of the Order, a rumour of the conspiracy got noised abroad amongst the Knights, and all the conspirators were taken prisoners, and brought before the tribunal. Sanach, the leader of the band, although a Mussulman, was a devout client of the Blessed

Virgin, whom he called the Mother of the Great Prophet, Jesus Christ; and whenever he came to Trepani, he always gave a little offering to her shrine, which is venerated there.

One night, when he was asleep, the Mother of God appeared to him in his dream, and said: "Listen, Sanach, I will not refuse your presents, but you are such a great sinner, that a day will come when you will be executed on account of your evil deeds. When that time *does* come, send for Father Rosignoli "Della Floriana," and do whatsoever he bids you." Mary then gave him signs by which to recognize the priest.

When all had confessed to their share in the conspiracy, and had been sentenced to death, Sanach remembered his dream, and sent for the Father, as he had been directed. A Capuchin, from a Monastery hard by, came, but Sanach did not find in him the signs which Mary had given him, and refused to speak with him, saying he wished to see Father "Della Floriana." They guessed that he meant Father Rosignoli, and brought him to him. He at once recognized the priest, who had been pointed out to him, and placed himself entirely in his hands. Father Rosignoli instructed him and all the others, twenty-five in number, in the Catholic religion. Although they knew very little of the Maltese language, still by the help of grace, they learnt in a short time all that was necessary, and to their great delight they were baptized. Before execution, they received Holy Communion; and with the assistance of Father Rosignoli, who made them often pronounce the holy names of Jesus and Mary, they met their death in a manner which edified all the inhabitants of Malta.

107. Dr. Hugo Lämmer and the "Ave Maria."

On the 21st of November, 1858, the learned Protestant theologian, Dr. Hugo Lämmer, of Brannsberg, embraced the Catholic Faith. Soon afterwards he became a priest, and in 1883 was made canon and professor of theology in Breslau. The cause of his conversion may be related briefly, as follows:—

By most arduous study, he had instructed himself thoroughly in Catholic doctrine, but a treatise on the "Hail Mary," by Alban Stolz, in a book entitled *Calendar for Time and Eternity*, had impressed him more than anything he had previously read. In it, he came across a passage to the effect that, if a Protestant was really in good earnest to discern Divine Truth, he should endeavour to invoke the Blessed Virgin by the daily recital of the "Hail Mary." "It may be," continues this author, "that a spark of veneration for Mary remains in you, inherited from your ancestors, who, centuries before your birth, faithfully and continually invoked the aid of the Mother of God. If you would only have the courage to think a little of this, it would seem to you that you heard the echo of an old hymn, which had been sung to you in your childhood. Be strong in mind, and as Samson tore the bonds of the Philistines, so do you tear away the bonds of prejudice by which you have been so long enthralled. Christian intelligence, if set free, seeks after the truth, and insensibly venerates Mary; therefore take heart, and bravely begin this very day to recite an 'Ave Maria.' Try it only for a month; after that time you will find that you have learned to love it, and will never relinquish this daily practice till the hour of your death."

Lämmer resolved to follow this advice, and the Mother of

God, who never forsakes anyone who has recourse to her, bestowed her maternal care on him also.

"I began," Doctor Lämmer himself relates, "to recite the sweet 'Ave Maria,' and to implore Mary's powerful intercession for my speedy entrance into the true Church. The sting of intellectual conceit had become extracted, and in my solitary dwelling, on my knees before the crucifix, I fought, with many tears, these interior battles. Prayer banished all scruples, and when, later, I knocked at the door of the True Church, I could say with the greatest conviction 'Credo' to every tenet of the Catholic religion."

108. Our Lady Hearkens to the Prayer of some Protestants.

A terrible accident happened in the year 1860, at a coal mine, in Lothringen. Eleven men were working in a portion of the mine, some 800 feet below the surface of the earth, when the scaffolding gave way, falling however, in such a peculiar manner, as to leave the men uninjured, though naturally, a good deal shaken and alarmed. They began at once, to endeavour to extricate themselves from the wreckage, when, suddenly the gas exploded with a terrific report. Every man must necessarily have been killed, had not an invisible hand protected them, in answer to their cry for mercy, for at the very moment which all thought would have been their last, the miners had dropped on their knees, invoking the holy names of Jesus, Mary, and Joseph, after which they began the "Hail Mary."

Among the workmen were two Protestants, who joined most heartily, in the recitation of the "Ave Maria," and one of them suggested that they should promise a Votive Mass of

Thanksgiving, if our Lady would save their lives, and rescue them from their perilous position.

For two days and nights, they laboured unceasingly, and, at length, succeeded in clearing a passage through the mass of timber and stone which had fallen. They were thus enabled to reach the shaft in safety. Thanks to their confidence in the Blessed Virgin, they stood, once more, safe and unharmed, in God's glorious daylight, amidst their anxious relatives and friends.

This account was related by one of the men who had been in the accident.

109. *A Story of Pope Pius IX.*

A few days after the return of Pius IX. from Gaeta to the Eternal City, Colonel G——, a retired officer, visited the Vatican, with his wife and children, and was allowed to see the private apartments of His Holiness. His wife was a Protestant, and clung most tenaciously to her own religious opinions, in spite of her husband's cherished desire, that they should be united in the one true Faith.

She seemed much impressed by all she saw, and with pardonable curiosity, examined every object of interest. Amongst the other things, she noticed in the private chapel, a *prie-dieu*, covered with scarlet velvet. She paused for a moment, saying to herself, "Here it is that the head of the Catholic church daily implores the blessing of heaven on the whole world, why should not I kneel here too, and ask for happiness and blessings for myself and my children?" She knelt as she felt compelled to do, and burying her face in her hands remained absorbed in prayer for a few minutes, recommending those dear to her to the Mother of God. On lifting her eyes she saw above the Altar the figure of a Lady, surrounded by a dazzling splendour, holding by the hand her own two children, and in front of the altar she distinctly recognized Pius IX as it were facing her. Perplexed and deeply moved by the vision, Mme. G— — hastened to assure herself that her two little boys were still at her side, and was much relieved to find them all unconscious of anything extraordinary, but the excitement caused to her nerves by this occurrence was such as to alarm her husband, to whom she said nothing of the real cause, only feigning a slight indisposition; for days, however, she thought of nothing else than this extraordinary vision.

Shortly after the events above recorded, Mme. G— — was seated in the Lateran awaiting the solemn entry of the Pope, which had been fixed for the 12th of April; the very first glimpse she caught of His Holiness, produced in her a strange sensation, for she recognised at once the same figure she had seen in the private Chapel of the Vatican, and moreover, even now, she perceived over the head of the holy Pontiff the same figure of the Virgin Mary exactly in a similar attitude of blessing. Although quite overcome, she managed to conceal her emotion, and remained outwardly composed to the end of the ceremony.

The day at last came round when she, with the rest of the officers' wives, were to have an audience with the holy Father; they were placed in two rows, the Pope passed down bestowing his blessing on either side, when he came to Mme. G— — he stopped, caressed her children, asked their names, and presented each of them with a Rosary; overjoyed by this mark of paternal kindness, she could not speak, and at this moment she again beheld the vision of the Blessed Virgin over the figure of the holy Pontiff. From this time Mme. G—— felt compelled to become a Catholic, and after spending two wakeful anxious nights, and offering up many prayers for light and guidance, she told her husband all that she had gone through. After a month of fervent preparation she was received into the church, and confirmed by the Cardinal Vicar. At the conclusion of the ceremony, Colonel G—— took from his neck the Cross of Saint Gregory, with which the Holy Father had decorated him, and laying it upon the altar, said: "The favour we have received to-day is so great, that I feel I can best show my gratitude, by offering to Mary the badge of honour which I prize more than anything in the world, and I do it most willingly, in thanksgiving for all our Lady has done for us."

110. Don Emmanuel.

Don Ramirez, a Spanish nobleman, lived at Toledo, with his wife, Dona Mercedes, they were exceedingly rich, and belonged to a very ancient and distinguished family—but above all, they were most pious Christians, and the love of God was deeply planted in their hearts.

For many years they had no children, but at length, in answer to their prayers, a son was born to them, whom they called Emmanuel; his mother dedicated him from his baptism to the Blessed Virgin, praying, as she lifted her child to her image, "Sweet Mother of Grace, to thee I give up my child, never permit that his soul should perish." The prayer was heard, but not before the boy had caused deep grief and anxiety to his parents, for although highly gifted in mind and body, he grew up in the utter disregard of his duties to God, his neighbour, and himself, till at last he threw off any pretence of religion, and avowed his disbelief in God or Eternity. His poor mother, who could make no impression on him, sorrowfully turned to the Mother of Sorrows, constantly reminding her that she had dedicated this child to her care.

After a time spent in the free exercise of his evil ways, Manuel fell dangerously ill, and was brought to the point of death. In this extremity he began to reflect on the past, and promised, if life were spared him, to mend his ways; but alas! his resolutions were founded on fear, not upon the knowledge and love of God. As his health returned and he regained his strength, he fell back into his corrupt manner of living. Soon after this, his parents died, and other misfortunes followed, including the loss of all his property, but these trials had no effect, save to harden him, and he now began to indulge in the passion of gambling, which brought him to such straits that he was obliged to seek refuge in America.

Hardly however, had the vessel in which he embarked set sail, than it caught fire. All on board perished miserably in the flames or waves, except Manuel, who was so fortunate as to lay hold of a plank; clinging to it, he battled with the waters for a whole day and night. His strength was well nigh exhausted, when a passing ship rescued him from his perilous position, but his terror was indescribable when he discovered that he was on board a Privateer, and in all probability he would be deprived of his liberty for the rest of his life. At this prospect, thoughts of despair swept over his soul, and he buried his face in his hands, groaning aloud. At this moment he felt the pressure of a kind hand on his shoulder, and heard the well-known accents of his native land speaking words of comfort.

Looking up, he saw the emaciated figure of an old man, clothed in a long brown habit; it was a missionary who had been for a long time in captivity, and who, seeing the young man in such distress, wished to comfort him. He soon discovered that his soul was in a worse condition than his body. However, seeing that the time had not yet come for speaking on spiritual matters, he contented himself with trying to make his present circumstances more bearable. Manuel was not unmindful of the good priest's exertions on his behalf, he respected and esteemed him, and that year, which they passed together, so fraught with hardships and difficulties, bore its fruit in due time, the calm and gentle tranquility with which Father Fidelis bore his trials and severe sufferings, influenced the young man, and in the long hours which he had for reflexion, the admonitions of his loving mother came back to him.

One day he related to the holy priest the history of his ill-spent life. When he had finished, Father Fidelis exclaimed: "Truly, my son, the Mother of Mercy has, indeed, shown her care of you in a special manner, and it is very clear all these misfortunes that have befallen you, have only been the means in the hands of the good God to draw you to Himself." Manuel was at last softened, and grace triumphed, melting, with its gentle rays, that wall of ice which had surrounded his heart for so long. He was reconciled to God, and in expiation for his sins, he bore the remaining years of his captivity with patience and resignation. He remained three more years a captive, after the death of good old Father Fidelis, at the end of which time he was released, and returned to Europe, becoming a lay-brother in the holy Order of St. Francis, praising and blessing God to the end of his life, for "His tender mercies," which he had experienced, with the Psalmist, to be "above all His works."

111. A Goldsmith of Berlin.

Bernard of Luxemburg, who lived about the year 1490, relates the following story, which in 1661, was published in the "Treasury of the Holy Rosary." There we read that: — "In the town of Berlin, in the Margraviate of Brandenburg, there lived an apprentice to a goldsmith, who for six years had neglected the Sacraments. He was a thief, and also in other ways a great sinner. One Sunday, as he came near the Dominican church, he was on the point of passing it as usual, when he felt himself suddenly, so irresistibly drawn into the sacred edifice, that, without knowing why, he was compelled to enter, and remained for the whole service, which was then taking place. The sermon had just begun, and treated of the great benefits conferred through the holy Rosary. At first only the enthusiasm of the orator captivated him, but soon the subject of the sermon engrossed his attention. The impression it made on him was so powerful that he became quite attracted by the preacher's account of the Rosary, and he at once made a firm resolution to say it henceforth every day, until his death.

"During one of the following nights, he had a frightful dream. A crowd of devils fell upon him, with the intention of dragging him, body and soul, into hell. He struggled against them with all his strength, but in vain. The devils had him already in their clutches, and it seemed to him that there was not a spark of hope left. Already he saw the gaping jaws of hell open before him — one moment, and his eternal fate would be irrevocably sealed. Once more he lifted up his eyes to heaven, and behold!—before him stood an exceedingly beautiful and heavenly Virgin, with a lovely child in her arms. Hardly had he seen her than he, in his desperate condition, grasped her mantle, and held it firm with such strength that the infernal spirits were no longer able to move him from the spot. The Holy Virgin fixed upon him a glance of intense earnestness, saying severely: 'Thou art not worthy to touch my holy garment, away with you to the devils, to whom you justly belong.' But the more the Virgin showed herself displeased, the more firmly did he cling to her, and because he recognized her as the most Blessed Mother of God, he implored her for help and deliverance, and so ardently and impressively did he beg, with so many tears and groans did he plead, that the loving Mother of Grace yielded, letting mercy over-rule justice. With a compassionate look she said: 'If thou wilt faithfully serve my Divine Son and me to the last hour of thy life, and wilt continue to say daily the Rosary devoutly, I will deliver thee from this frightful danger.' The young man without hesitation promised, and by the command of the Blessed Virgin, the evil spirits vanished at once.

"Then the unhappy man awoke from his terrible dream, and when he came to himself, he felt as if all his members were bruised and crushed. His whole body was bathed in a cold sweat, and tears were pouring down his cheeks. After a little reflection, he recognized the frightful condition of his soul, and the necessity of a thorough reformation. Finding he could rest no longer on his bed, he jumped up, and, overwhelmed by deep emotion and remorse, fell on his knees, and began to prepare himself for a general Confession. At the first dawn of day he hastened to the church, and after he had been reconciled to his God and Saviour by the Sacrament of

Penance, he knocked the same morning at the gates of a religious house, and was received into the number of the brethren, and in that holy community, he served God, and the holy Virgin, with admirable fervour to the hour of his death, thus showing his gratitude to her, who had been such a true Mother to him, in the time of his greatest distress and peril."

112. A Wonderful Conversion.

When I was staying in London, with a friend of mine, the following event took place: One Sunday evening, a rumour got about that the renowned Oratorian—Father Faber—was going to preach at Saint Anne's Church, on account of which, three young Protestant gentlemen went, through curiosity, to assist at Vespers. But without any of them being aware of it, the resident priest preached as usual, and afterwards gave Benediction. Suddenly one of the three, Dr. S——, fell on his knees, and began to weep and sob. His friends were alarmed, and thinking that he was ill, asked what was the matter. "Oh, I believe in Transubstantiation," was his answer. When he left the church, he met with another acquaintance, Mr. H. A——, and said to him: "Henry, if it were not for Confession and the worship of the Virgin Mary, I would become a Catholic this very day." Mr. H. A—— repeated this to us, and we at once resolved to make a Novena to our Blessed Lady. We gave our friend a medal of the Immaculate Conception, begging him to give it to Dr. S——, who, taking it, smilingly promised to say the little aspiration attached to it. Three days after we heard the joyful news that the young man had made his confession, abjured his Anglican errors, and was received into the Catholic church; he afterwards became the most fervent Catholic in the whole parish.

113. *Conversion of a Young Protestant Lady.*

A young lady, belonging to an ancient family, but one exceedingly prejudiced against Catholics, happened one day to pass a Catholic church. Impelled by curiosity she entered, and was much struck by a picture of the Madonna, holding the Divine Child in her arms. She noticed that the church was very poor, and the hangings behind the picture a good deal the worse for wear; at the same time she felt inspired to make a present to the Mother of God, of some new silk curtains in place of the old and dirty ones.

She carried out her resolution, and our Lady bestowed on her in return the grace of conversion. All her former prejudices vanished, and she became a most fervent Catholic, and a devout client of Mary.

114. *"Edelweiss," or the Chamois Hunter.*

In my various travels through the beautiful Tyrol, a country so thoroughly Catholic, I have constantly come across proofs of the devotion of the Tyrolese towards the Blessed Mother of God. In this age of scepticism, it is certainly most refreshing to find remnants of the old simple faith of the middle ages among those peasants; their mountains seem to have screened them from the icy blast of materialism and unbelief.

The hero of the little story I am about to relate was a chamois hunter; he had been carefully trained by a pious mother, but despite all her endeavours, his wild and impetuous nature soon asserted itself, and throwing off all restraint, he gave himself up to a life of adventure and licence.

On the Feast of our Lady's Assumption, there is a very ancient custom, both in the Tyrol and in the Bavarian highlands, of having certain plants blessed, as a protection against lightning. The thunderstorms in those parts are often terrific and fraught with great danger, especially to the mountaineers, and as a preservative they wear these blessed plants in their hats, and when a storm comes on, they throw a few leaves into the fire, and implore our Lady to protect them by virtue of the little plants blessed in her honour. The plant most commonly blessed is the "Edelweiss," a small white flower, which grows on very high mountains where no other kind of vegetation can live—it is always rare, and often those in quest of it have to run some risk, on account of the inaccessible places in which it is usually found.

One evening, shortly before the 15th of August, an exceptionally severe storm swept over the Alps, all nature seemed convulsed, and the mountains echoed again and again the awful claps of thunder, which shook them to their very base. Two cowherds, seeing the approach of the storm, had hastened to drive their cows into a shelter under a crag, and when it burst they shut themselves up in a little hut, and there, kneeling before a rude cross which hung upon the wall, they commended themselves to the loving protection of their heavenly Mother, now and again throwing a blossom of the Edelweiss into the fire they had kindled.

They had begun to recite the Rosary together, when suddenly the door flew open, letting in a deluge of wind and rain, and the giant form of a much dreaded and notorious brigand—the hero of our story—stood upon the threshold. He entered without any ceremony, slammed the door with a curse,

210

and sat down in front of the fire. The herdsmen stared in terror at their unwelcome visitor, and dared not utter a word, expecting to be throttled on the slightest provocation. The brigand sat quiet for some time, drying his saturated clothes, then turning, he snatched the Edelweiss from one of the cowherds' caps and fastened it in his own.

At length the storm subsided, the sun shone out again bright and hot, and the thick black clouds dispersed. The brigand then rose, and without a word of thanks for the shelter afforded him, abruptly left the hut. The two men were only too delighted to get rid of him so easily, and though they regretted the loss of their Edelweiss which was their last sprig, they consoled themselves with the thought that our Lady's Assumption was at hand, and they could get some more blessed. With this intent, they determined to set out on an expedition on the morrow, in search of the coveted plant.

Meanwhile the brigand went off with his stolen bouquet, and, climbing over crag and rock, spent the night on a mountain height. Scarcely had daylight dawned, when he was already on the alert, looking out for chamois. He had to wait some hours, but his patience was rewarded as a beautiful animal came within range. He crouched down behind a huge boulder, took aim and fired. The chamois fell, and the hunter hastened to dispatch it, but just as he reached it, it leapt up, and fled — it was wounded, but not mortally. Our hero at once gave chase, leaping from rock to rock, now sliding down chasms, now jumping over creeks, till at last, his headlong course was stopped by a broad and impassible crevasse. However, he would not be beaten, and clinging, with hands and feet to the projecting rocks, he tried to slide down into the abyss below. But he had overstepped his power, and he recognised too late, that he had got himself into such a position, that he could neither advance nor recede. Seized with terror, he began to shout loudly for help, but his hoarse cries only echoed and re-echoed against the sides of the chasm, and he felt, in his heart, that he was out of reach of human assistance.

Thus clinging to a crag, unable to turn or ease his posture, the unhappy man remained to face death, which seemed inevitable; his cries and curses alone relieved the awful silence, until from sheer exhaustion, he was forced to desist. The hours wore slowly on, evening approached, and still the brigand clung to the ledge, his limbs were fast becoming numb with the intense cold, his head began to turn from weakness and suspense, and he dreaded lest, any moment, he might lose his balance, and be dashed into the precipice.

With a desperate effort, he managed to get into a sitting position, hoping thus to avert his fate a little longer. The agony he endured is not to be described, as he sat, his feet hanging over the chasm, darkness surrounding him on every side, and the cold intense, now the sun had set. In the middle of the night a thunder-storm came on, which only served to increase the horrors of his plight; the rain fell in torrents, and the lightning appeared to his confused brain, like diabolical forms mocking at his distress. He became more and more terrified, a cold sweat came over him, and he fancied that hell lay beneath, waiting for its prey. "Holy Mary, Mother of God, pray for us sinners now!" he cried in his despair; at that moment a gust of wind carried off his hat and hurled it into the abyss below — "and at the hour of our death." His appeal to Mary was not in vain, and she obtained from her Divine Son the grace of contrition for that poor hardened sinner. His proud heart was touched at last, tears came into his eyes, as he thought of his mother, and how she had first taught him to repeat the "Hail Mary," he remembered how she had striven to avert his downward course, and how ill he had repaid her; then, one by one, his many crimes reverted to his mind, together with his utter forgetfulness of God, even the little bunch of Edelweiss, which he had lost together with his hat, recurred to his memory, and reminded him how, in sheer wantonness, a short time ago he had taken that blessed sprig; and it seemed to him as if the Mother of God had deprived him of the object of his crime, to the commission of which he attributed his present perils. A light broke in upon his soul, grace knocked loudly at his heart,—he wept, he prayed. At length morning dawned, and still deliverance seemed as hopelessly distant as ever; but for the first time since his early childhood, he began the day with prayer. He tried to resign himself to what seemed certain death, and began to prepare to acknowledge before God the sins of his whole life, the sight of which caused anguish to his soul. For a moment the devils regained their power over him, and once more despair took possession of him, but the remembrance of the Mother of God restored peace to his mind, and with perfect calm he made an act of contrition. His physical sufferings increased as the sun rose higher in the heavens, its powerful rays exhausting his little remaining strength; all the surrounding objects were becoming indistinct to his vision, and unconsciousness was fast stealing over him, still he kept repeating "now and at the hour of our death."

At last he fancied he caught the faint sound of voices, but he tried in vain to answer the call, for his speech had failed him; presently he fancied he saw a dark object descending towards him, and in another moment, a man, with a rope tied round his waist, was hanging by his side, it was the younger of the two cowherds who had given him shelter. He held another rope in his hand, which he fastened securely round the exhausted brigand, he then shouted to his brother to hoist, and once more the poor man found himself on "terra firma."

The two cowherds had set out on their expedition in search of Edelweiss, and after a fruitless hunt, had at last found the brigand's hat, with their lost treasure fastened to it. They guessed at once that he had met with some accident, and scarcely expected to find him alive, great then was their relief when they espied him on his perilous perch; they went at once to the nearest hut, to fetch ropes, and were thus enabled to rescue him from imminent death. When the poor man had somewhat recovered by the aid of restoratives, he knelt down, and thanked our Blessed Lady both for his safety and conversion; the two brothers were overjoyed at the sudden change in one who had been the terror of the neighbourhood, and they offered to take him to their hut and give him hospitality. He expressed his gratitude for their great charity in helping one who had served them so ill, but refused their generous offer, preferring to go his own way. When they had parted, the chamois hunter sought out a little shrine dedicated to our Lady, which was situated in the valley beneath. There, prostrating himself before the altar, he solemnly vowed to amend his life, and become a worthy son of Holy Church. And he kept his word.

In after years he would often spend an evening with the two men who had so generously saved him from death, and many a time they would talk together of the eventful thunderstorm and the stolen sprig of Edelweiss.

115. Only one "Ave Maria."

During the terrible period of the French Revolution, when all France seemed to run with blood, the fury of those satanic men, who were its instigators, was chiefly directed against the church and her ministers. Hundreds of priests mounted the scaffold, not to assist poor criminals in their passage to eternity, but to be the victims of an infatuated mob. One of these venerable martyrs was the Reverend Père Raclot. On his way to execution, a woman who took a fiendish delight in scoffing at priests, approached to where he stood, and openly insulted him in most blasphemous and detestable words. Père Raclot looked at her with an expression of indescribable tenderness and compassion, and said: "Pray for me." "What," she cried, "Pray for you!" "Yes, my good woman, say a 'Hail Mary' for my poor soul, which is about to appear before my Saviour and my Judge." "Very well," she replied somewhat softened, "I will say it." Scarcely had she uttered the well-known prayer, than she felt herself completely transformed, and with folded hands and bent head she followed the priest, weeping and praying, to the guillotine.

The death of that saintly man was for her the beginning of a new life, she entirely abandoned her scandalous excesses, and dedicated herself to works of piety and charity. Every year she made a pilgrimage to Einsiedeln, in expiation of her former crimes, and though she had wealth, and could have procured herself every comfort, she always made the journey on foot, begging her way as she went.

116. The Martyr's Palm as a Reward.

We read in the lives of many of the Saints that our Blessed Lady, as a reward of their piety and devotion, would appear to them, holding her Divine Son in her arms. We find examples of such apparitions in the lives of SS. Cajetan, Felix, Stanislaus, Hermann Joseph, and many others too numerous to mention. It may be, however, that the following little story, which occurs in the life of Blessed Livinus, will be new to most of our readers: —

Blessed Livinus, a most devout client of our Lady, lived in Cairo, and there exercised his sacred ministry. He occupied his leisure hours in writing a book in honour of the Infant Jesus and His Blessed Mother; this however, on some groundless pretext, he discontinued. He had several times been favoured with visions of our Lady bearing the Child Jesus in her arms, but when he interrupted his little labour of love, the Blessed Virgin again appeared to him, but—alone. Livinus was bitterly disappointed, and exclaimed: "O, Holy Mother, where is your Divine Son, my sweet Lord?" And our Blessed Lady replied: "He will not come to you, because you have abandoned the work you began in His honour, yet if you resume it, my Jesus will not only visit you again, but will also bestow upon you a martyr's crown as a reward for your labours."

Livinus did not need any further incitement; he recommenced his little book without delay, and having finished it, he eagerly awaited the longed for crown.

At last, in 1345, he was put to death by the infidels, and went to join the white-robed army of martyrs in the heavenly Jerusalem.

Let this little story serve as an earnest admonition to those of

Mary's clients who have grown forgetful and negligent, let them remember the many promises they have made, and take themselves to task for their tardy fulfillment of good resolutions. And let it be an incentive to one and all, to labour as much as lies in their power for the glory of Jesus Christ, and the honour of Mary Immaculate.

IX.

MARY, THE MERCIFUL MOTHER OF THE DYING.

117. From the "Revelations of Sister Catharine Emmerich."

IN one of the revelations of Sister Catharine Emmerich, we have the following account of the death of one who had been a notorious sinner. We give it to our readers in an English form, hoping to enliven their faith and trust in the intercession of our Blessed Lady, and to stimulate them to intercede more frequently, for those thousands of poor souls who are daily passing from our midst, and are sadly in need of that "prayer of Faith," which shall save the sick man.

She says: "I saw a poor man die, full of contrition for the past, and I could see the holy Virgin, with her Divine Child, standing by his bedside. His whole history was then revealed to me; he was born of noble parents, in France, and was dedicated at his birth, to our Blessed Lady. His parents were executed at the time of the French Revolution; after their death, he got a commission in the army, but for some unexplained reason he deserted. Throughout this time, his devotion to Mary remained unchanged, and she protected him against the many temptations to which camp life is subject.

"Unfortunately, after leaving the army, he fell in with a bad set, and eventually joined a band of highway robbers, becoming altogether reckless and dissolute. In spite, however, of his godless state, he still adhered to one pious practice, and respectfully saluted any picture or statue, of our Lady which he might chance to meet, and often when so doing, his conscience would smite him with feelings of remorse.

"At length, he was seized by the police, cast into prison, and condemned to die, but he managed to effect his escape, and continued his wild life for several years. He was again arrested, for some theft, and confined in jail. After his liberation, he was somewhat subdued, and enlisted as a private, but he could not brook the restraint of military discipline, and deserted a second time. Then he married, and tried to settle down, getting work wherever he could. It was now our Blessed Lady's hour, and on account of his devotion towards her, she deigned to reveal to him, that the time had come when he must repent, and do penance for the past, or he would perish eternally. He took the warning so lovingly imparted, and, by means of assiduous austerities, fasting, watching, disciplines, and the like, he atoned for his previous crimes, and I saw him in a vision last night die, peacefully and joyfully, and Mary, claiming him for her own, presented him to her Son."

118. The Mercy of God.

The well known and renowned Archbishop Polding was once on one of his long missionary journeys, which brought him to a region almost destitute of inhabitants, in the interior of Australia. On his way, feeling very ill, he luckily was able to find a hospitable reception in the house of a poor widow, who nursed him with every possible care and kindness. Before leaving, he promised his benefactress, in return for her attention to him, that he would come and attend her last hours himself, and administer the Last Sacraments, if she would send him word, even if he had to travel a considerable distance to do so.

Some time after this, one night in autumn, a letter arrived reminding the Archbishop of his promise, stating that the kind widow was near her death. Without any hesitation, in spite of the rough season, the holy prelate set out to keep his promise. He had to travel for some days before reaching his destination, and on his arrival, tired and exhausted, he was surprised to find no one at home; while he was musing as to what course was best to pursue, his attention was arrested by a sound, evidently caused by some one occupied in felling trees. He went in the direction whence the sound proceeded, hoping to come across some one who could give him information, and was delighted to find a sturdy Irishman, who told him that the good lady, although very ill, fearing that the Archbishop would not be in time, had had herself carried elsewhere for spiritual help.

The Archbishop knew it was useless to attempt to overtake her, even did he know which direction to follow, so he sat on the stump of a tree and began to converse with the woodcutter. After a few remarks, Archbishop Polding said, as if by sudden inspiration, "Now, my good friend, although I came here on quite a different mission, I need not waste my journey, do you kneel down here, and let me hear your Confession."

The Irishman at first was quite taken aback, and refused, alleging that he was totally unprepared, that it was so long since he had confessed, and the usual round of excuses. By degrees the Archbishop persuaded him that the reasons he had given for not making his Confession, were the very reasons why he should do so at once, and that there probably would not be such an easy chance for him again. So the man knelt down, made a hearty accusation, and showed every sign of repentance, promising to receive Holy Communion on the following Sunday. The Archbishop then gave him his blessing, and prepared to start on his homeward journey. He had not gone far on the way, when he heard a crash and a groan; returning with all speed, he found his penitent already dead, struck down by a fallen branch.

Merciful indeed was the Good Shepherd, to bring hither, from such a distance, the channels of His grace, and to turn the tide of events in such a way as to cause them to flow, where they were most needed.

But it was to the compassion of Mary that Archbishop Polding ascribed this wonderful, if not miraculous, occurrence, for he found on the body of the woodcutter, the Scapular of Mount Carmel.

119. *Confidence in Mary.*

A Bishop, in the wildest part of Scotland, was making a visitation of his diocese on foot, he was travelling through a most mountainous district, and did not notice how fast the day was declining; night overtook him, and he found he had gone quite out of his beat, in fact had lost his way; he walked on until he came to a house, which proved to belong to some honest country folk, who willingly gave him shelter, not in the least suspecting who their guest was. The Bishop, on his part, did not know whether his hospitable entertainers were Catholics or not, for he saw no sign to betoken any religion, but noticing the kind and refined way in which they set about preparing the frugal repast, he surmised that they had been well brought up.

During the meal they conversed with the reserve natural to persons who are thorough strangers, but still he was quick to detect that, in spite of their affability, they were evidently suffering from the pressure of some affliction or anxiety. His kind heart was moved to compassion, and at last he ventured to say: "You have indeed shown charity to an utter stranger, and I see you are an upright and generous family, but something seems to tell me you are in distress, will you not tell me, in case I should have the happiness of assisting you, and by this means make some little return for the trouble of my intrusion?"

The lady, who was a widow, seemed quite relieved at being given the opportunity of unburdening her mind, and she then told him how, in the adjoining room, her old father lay in a dying state, and, although he was quite aware of his condition, he refused to prepare himself for death. The Bishop was much moved, and asked at once if he might go to him; this was gladly permitted, for the poor lady was greatly harassed, and would have been glad of anyone to influence her father. As soon as the Bishop entered the apartment, he saw that the old man was indeed in a dying state, and after a few kind words, to lead up to the object of his visit, he broached the subject of death, but the moment he alluded to this possibility, the good man seemed to regain strength, and with wonderful energy he exclaimed, "No, I shall not die yet," to every reason brought forward by his visitor he would only reply, "Not yet, it is impossible." Finding that he was so confident, the Bishop began to suspect that there was some deeper meaning in his persistence than mere obduracy; so, after a moment's thought, he put the question to him: "What reason have you for maintaining you will not die?" At these words the dying man was deeply moved, and giving the Bishop a piercing glance, said, "Sir, are you a Catholic?" "Yes," he quietly responded, but gave no further information. "Then," said the old man, "I will tell you why I shall not die," and, gathering up all his strength, he sat up in bed and said confidently: "I am a Catholic, and, from the day I made my first Communion till now, I have never omitted any day to ask the Blessed Virgin for the grace not to die without the assistance of a priest; do you believe, sir, that she will refuse me? no, I shall not die yet;" with this he leaned back again on his pillows much exhausted.

The Bishop was visibly touched, and replied, "My son, your prayers have been heard, not only has your good Mother sent you a priest, but your Bishop has been sent to console and strengthen you." With this he unfastened his cloak, and displayed to the good old Christian man his pectoral cross.

Overjoyed, the poor man could hardly contain himself, and he called out: "O Mary, my Mother, I thank you a thousand times," and, turning to the Bishop, he added, "Yes, I shall die now, and am ready to make my Confession to you." Like holy Simeon, he could ejaculate, "Now dost Thou dismiss Thy servant, O Lord, in peace, because mine eyes have seen Thy Salvation."

120. *The Old, Old Story.*

It came from the Tyrol—from the mother's own lips—the oft-repeated tale of the evil courses of a son, and its consequent miseries, but, as in her history there was the pleasing feature of a "happy end," too generally wanting in the biographies of sinners, she desired me to publish the incidents, as the means of instilling, into the hearts of many Christian mothers, that confidence and reliance in the Mother of Sorrows, which will sustain them in their trials, if their faith fail not, and show them that the havoc caused by the evil one in the hearts and souls of their children can be extinguished by her, who was decreed to crush the serpent's head.

Knowing the family, I can vouch for the accuracy of the assertions. She told her story simply, after the following fashion:—

"My son, even from his youth, was of a light and frivolous nature, very obstinate, with an ungovernable temper, and as his years increased his evil nature seemed to gain ground. He was easily drawn into bad companionship, and took delight in all the cheap and useless reading that came in his way; this kind of literature, which tarnishes the souls of all our growing youths before they have stability of mind enough to hold fast to the firm principles of faith, soon told its sad tale, and deprived my boy of all religious feeling. He gave up going to church, never approached the Sacraments, squandered his money, and would remain away from home for days and nights.

"Our Lord was pleased to visit him with a great affliction, and indeed, for one of his character, it was a serious trial—he was attacked with constant vomiting of blood, which not only gave him considerable pain, but prostrated him for hours together. At these times, he would promise me to mend his ways, but no sooner was he well again, than he returned to his evil pursuits, and no warning of the doctor, who represented to him that he was aggravating his complaint, nor persuasion of mine, could make him settle down.

"Seeing that his disease was fast telling on his constitution, and yet no improvement becoming visible in his disposition, I became more and more afflicted, for it was useless to take so much care of his body, and suffer the loss of his soul, and so, in deep sorrow, taking my daughter with me, I started on a pilgrimage to our Lady of Dolours in Weissenstein, some twenty miles from where we lived; I felt unusually sad and dispirited on the way, but when we arrived at the Shrine, we poured out our tale of misery, and implored of our Lady of Sorrows, to move the heart of our prodigal, and give him light to see the great peril he was in of losing his soul eternally. In the morning, we assisted at Mass, and received Holy Communion, after which, I enrolled my poor son in the Apostleship of Prayer. Strengthened in mind, and more hopeful for the future, we retraced our steps homewards. On our return, we found John had already gone to bed, apparently, much as usual, but at midnight, he was seized with a most violent attack of hemorrhage. I immediately sent for the doctor, who did not seem to think very seriously of it, but another, and still more exhausting attack, followed, and the priest was hastily summoned. He at once anointed the poor boy, but delayed to hear his Confession, on account of the incessant sickness. I was silently praying by his bedside, and when he appeared a little quieter, I gently suggested to him to ask our Lady to give him grace to make a good Confession. With this, he opened his eyes, and replied: 'Yes, our Blessed Mother is helping me, send in the priest to me again.' With every sign of true contrition, our son made his Confession; when it was over, he beckoned to his father and myself, and, most humbly asked forgiveness for the sorrow and anxiety he had caused us. Our sobs choked our utterance, but we kissed the pale hand stretched out on the bed, and he sank back on the pillows, content to feel that all was forgiven and forgotten.

"Contrary to our expectation, he lingered on in a suffering state for five more weeks, during which time he bore his pains with heroic patience, receiving the Sacraments continually, and never tiring of asking his father and me to forgive him. I told him I meant to make another pilgrimage to our Lady of Dolours, to thank her for his conversion; he was very much pleased, and asked me to go soon, in order that I might bring him a picture from her Sanctuary, at which we had obtained such a great grace for him. I brought it to him the day following, he kissed it reverently, saying: 'Oh mother, that wall opposite seems quite white to me now, up to this I have always seen all my sins written on it in black letters,' and indeed he was 'quite white,' and he died like a child, peacefully, without any struggle, in a few days after kissing our Lady's picture for the last time."

121. *The Death of a Saint.*

We have given to our readers several instances of the deaths of sinners and of converts, all trophies of our Lady's victories over souls; but it may be refreshing to turn for awhile to witness the last moments of a saint, a devout client of Mary. For what saint is there in whose life there is not some trait which marks his tender love for Mary.

Alexius Falconieri, the last to die of the "Seven Holy Founders," of the Servite Order, was one hundred and ten, when, in the words of Father Niccolo Mati, who was present at the time, "Jesus called him to His Paradise" after seventy-seven years of faithful service. Our brethren hastened to surround his deathbed; and truly it was a joy to all to see how he welcomed death. He saw doves flying about him, these must have been Angels under that form, for certainly no birds could have got in by natural means; and all on a sudden he called out joyously: 'Kneel down all of you—do you not see Jesus? Happy are those who serve Him faithfully with great humility and purity, for a glorious crown awaits them;' then he repeated, as was his custom, one hundred 'Ave Marias,' and when he had said the last of these he died. 'See you now,' he had said, almost at his last hour, 'we shall all have a share in this crown, if we practice purity and religious humility, and if we endeavour to imitate the most pure and humble Mother of God, our heavenly patroness.' "

122. *"An Enfant de Marie."*

A true and pathetic little story of a child of only twelve years of age, will edify our readers, and moreover, assist the little ones of the flock, who have consecrated themselves to our Blessed Lady, to strive more earnestly to keep themselves holy and innocent, as become members of the retinue of the Queen of Heaven:—

During the recital of the Rosary in the chapel belonging to a Training School, the nuns and children were disturbed by Mary R—— fainting. She was at once carried out, and remained about three hours in a swoon. When she came round, the Superior asked her jokingly, "What she had been doing all the time?" But Mary looked very grave and answered solemnly: "I am going to die soon; fearing I should become corrupted if I stayed in the world, as I see there is no good in it, I begged our dear Lord fervently, to take me away some days ago, but He would not answer my prayer, and I felt that Jesus is such a Supreme and Great God, and I am only such a little tiny nothing, that He had not heard me, so it suddenly came into my mind that I ought to have gone to our

227

Blessed Mother, for then she could ask Him, and it would be quite easy for her to tell Him what I wanted. So this afternoon, while we were saying the Rosary, I asked St. Joseph and St. Vincent de Paul to join our Blessed Lady in obtaining for me the grace to die soon, and now I am quite happy, for I feel they have heard me."

The Superior was deeply affected at this simple recital, and felt that the child was right in her presentiment. From that day she visibly declined, and bore her weakness with great tranquility and patience. One day she asked the Superior if the Divine Child might not be brought to her. They guessed what she meant, and the priest coming, gave her the Holy Viaticum. A few hours after this she expired. Her prayer had been granted, through the pleading of her Heavenly Mother, who now presented her pure young soul to her "Great and Supreme Jesus."

123. "Mary, Mother of Mercy, Pray for Us."

Father Gelasius, a priest in Lower Styria, tells us of a young man who left his bed in the middle of the night, and walked eighteen miles, in order to make his peace with God, his conscience being awakened by the sudden recollection of his evil life, and the unfitness of his present state to appear before his Judge should he die at that moment.

Why these thoughts came that night more than any other time was, no doubt, due to the Mother of Mercy, who is ever on the watch for a favourable moment to soften and influence the hearts of sinners. She knows the designs of her Son, and when she sees the span of life is nearly run out, she drops, as it were, a little word of warning into our ear, or touches with her gentle hand, a vulnerable spot in our souls. In innumerable cases it is this "unknown something" which brings sinners on their knees to the tribunal of penance, being nothing else than the intervention of Mary; and so it was with this young man.

Strong and well, he left his house to carry out his good intention of making a general Confession at the Franciscan church, where he arrived about eleven o'clock, tired with his eighteen miles' pilgrimage, but still as firm in his resolution as he was contrite of heart. The good friar gave him Holy Communion just after twelve, and the brave penitent remained another hour making his thanksgiving, little thinking it was to be his preparation for another journey. Leaving the church, he had got as far as the apothecary's shop, when, feeling faint, he entered to get something to revive him. No sooner had he sat down, than his head sank upon his breast, and he yielded up his soul to Him Who, a short time before, had entered within his breast as a Saviour and a Guest. It was on the sweet Feast of the Holy Name of Jesus, and we have not the least doubt that in that hour "Jesus" showed Himself to be a Saviour.

124. A Beautiful Death.

"God's ways are not our ways," is a well-known adage— clergy and laity alike use it whenever any heavier trial than usual falls upon any member of the human family, but is it a strictly submissive maxim; for did we make *our* ways God's ways, and run alongside His adorable Will, we should more easily fathom those mysterious "ways" that seem to run counter to ours. Yes, as soon as we have bent the knee, and bowed the head under the mighty hand of God, then it is, and not till then, that we can distinguish how "mightily God reaches from end to end, and orders all things sweetly" for our good. These thoughts were called forth on hearing of a young man stricken down with cancer, just when he was beginning to support his family, and whose apparently strong and active constitution had promised great things for the future. It was long before he could reconcile himself to his fate, especially when he saw his former companions and colleagues advancing in their business, and bringing home their weeks' earnings with pride and delight to their parents. Envy and impatience held sway over him for some time, but at length, helped by the good priest, who visited him day by day, he was brought to a more contented frame of mind.

The bitterness and harshness disappeared, and his lot, he found, was proportioned to his strength; he therefore resigned himself to bear all with manly courage, and a quiet content succeeded his former restlessness, learning that it is far more noble to bear the sacred cross of suffering gladly, than to succeed in any course of life.

In one thing, however, he had ever surpassed his comrades, and that was in love and veneration for the Mother of God; he had a tender, enthusiastic admiration for her, and his confidence was unbounded; to speak of her was enough to animate his whole frame, and he would smile sweetly, in the midst of his sufferings, whenever her name was mentioned.

At length, the day came round when the annual pilgrimage to Kevelaer, in honour of our Lady was to start, and the priest, resolving to go, came to see his patient before setting out, in order to ascertain if he was fit to be left, and, if so, to take his message to the shrine. He brought him Holy Communion, and bade him keep up his heart till he came back, bringing with him fresh graces from his benefactress. The young man, taking the priest's hand in his, thanked him for all his kindness in the warmest terms. "Father," he said, "I have only one request to make, and that is that you will remember me in the Holy Mass at her sanctuary, for while your procession is winding round the trees by her chapel, I shall have finished my earthly pilgrimage, and shall have seen the Mother of God herself."

Deeply moved, the priest promised all he asked, but did not think the end was so near; he left him, feeling quite certain of finding him alive on his return; but it was not so, for at the very hour when the procession was re-entering the chapel, the sufferer passed away to the "Temple of the Living God, the Heavenly Jerusalem,"—the City of Peace.

"Requiescat in pace."

125. *At the Last Hour.*

In the February of 1857, a rich gentleman, who was distinguished for his mental and worldly advantages, fell ill. Unfortunately he belonged to that class of persons who make it their boast to ignore altogether the dictates of conscience, preferring to drown its voice in scenes of dissipation or pleasure. But all these endeavours are vain, when struck down by an Almighty hand, and brought face to face with the truth,—which in health is too easily and entirely put on one side—that everything which has an end is but hollow and does not meet the requirements of the soul.

Mr. B— — had in his service two devoted servants, who led a very different life from their master, being pious and faithful to every Christian duty, both to God and their employer.

In spite of his unholy life, they were devotedly attached to him, and when they were informed by the doctor of his dangerous state, one of them hazarded his master's displeasure and went for a priest, warning him, however, of possible difficulties in the forthcoming interview, telling him something of his master's former life, and their dread of his dying unshriven.

The Reverend Gentleman was greeted with the ungracious question of "what do you want here? I never sent for you."

"True," the priest gently replied, "but I heard you were ill, and as visiting the sick is always a work of mercy, and a sacred duty with the clergy, I came to cheer you up a bit."

Somewhat mollified, and not objecting to be diverted from his own train of thoughts, he invited his visitor to be seated. At first, all went smoothly, as long as the topic was only on his health or indifferent subjects, but the moment the Last Sacraments were mentioned, the invalid became excited, and angrily informed the priest that he had long ago given up his religion, and never meant to change again.

With the experience which long dealing with souls had taught him, he saw persuasion or arguments were useless in this case, so, dropping the subject, he turned his conversation with an unruffled countenance, into another channel; and after a while departed, saying a few brief words of encouragement to the disappointed servants, advising them to continue their prayers and direct them especially to our Blessed Lady, for he said, smiling sadly, "This kind is not cast out, but by prayer and fasting."

For five days they continued in earnest prayer, carefully avoiding all allusion to religion to the dying man, leaving the safety of his soul entirely in the hands of the Blessed Virgin. At the end of that time the priest received another message, brought in a very different manner from the former; no fear now, as to how he might be received, for the poor old gentleman was at length softened, and the chains which he had worn so long, and which the tempter had represented to him as too heavy to be cast off, gave way, through the secret, silent influence of prayer. He told the delighted priest how, up to the previous night, he had rebelled against acknowledging his errors, but that night had been almost intolerable to him, groaning under the burden of his sinful life, and nothing could appease his troubled conscience till he had sent for the priest. The good Father finished the work grace had begun, and a Confession, full, complete, and contrite, was the recompense of his zeal. He told him later, how on that painful and eventful night, the Blessed Virgin, carrying the Infant Jesus in her arms, had appeared to him, looking at him in so sad a manner that it pierced his very soul, the Divine Child also wore a very grave and pained expression; he trembled all over, and tried to persuade himself it was only an empty dream, or the result of his weak state; but it was of no use, the apparition was too vivid, and he felt compelled to admit that our Blessed Lady had given him visible marks of her love and care.

The priest informed him how assiduously his servants had prayed for him, and how to them, after God and our Lady, he owed his conversion. He then received all the rites of Holy Church, and twenty-four hours later, the tolling of the bell announced another passing into life, another "rich man," who had overcome the "hardness of entering into the Kingdom of Heaven."

X.

PRIVILEGED PLACES AND THEIR MIRACLES.

126. Cure of an Invalid through the Intercession of the Mother of God, at Philippsdorf, in Bohemia.

CAROLINE HOLFELD, who lived in Georgswalde, near Philippsdorf, was about thirty-one years of age. She had suffered for many years, from epileptic fits, which sometimes were so violent, that she lost consciousness for hours — once, a fit even lasted for fourteen hours. Seeing human means were all in vain, she betook herself to Philippsdorf, to implore the help of our Blessed Lady.

She had made the pilgrimage for nine successive days. On the last day of the Novena, she had another fit, which was the last, for from that time, she was not troubled by any return; but alas! the fits were succeeded by violent hemorrhages; twice every day she lost great quantities of blood. For eight whole weeks she was under the doctor, but without any improvement. She then entirely refused all remedies, and sought relief, where alone it was to be truly found — from heaven itself. Her exterior sufferings had increased, and were further intensified by great interior afflictions.

Once, it seemed to her as if her husband, who had died the previous year, appeared to her in her sleep, in such a sad and sorrowful state, that it plunged her into great grief; he was apparently in want of prayers to alleviate his sufferings. She thereupon resolved to say every day, the Rosary of the Immaculate Conception for his soul. After this she felt her mind relieved.

As her long illness had pretty well exhausted her slight means, a benevolent and pious lady, touched by great compassion, took her into one of her houses, which she intended to give up for a hospital, and had already furnished for this purpose. Here also, in spite of doctors and medicine, and most careful nursing, her condition remained the same and to every one it seemed most probable, that death would soon put an end to her miseries, for they had discovered she was suffering from an abscess in the stomach. Under these circumstances, the poor woman grew weaker every day, and caused great anxiety to those around her. When the danger became imminent, she resolved to try once again, what a Novena to our Blessed Lady of Philippsdorf, would do for her.

She began her devotions on the 28th of November, 1872. The next Saturday, at three p.m., her husband again appeared to her, but this time he seemed very happy; and he told her he had good reason to be so, and exhorted her to have courage, saying: "To-morrow, thy hour will also come, do thy duty well." When she awoke, she reflected on these words, and came to the conclusion, that they were a summons to prepare for death. In consequence of this, great sorrow and anxiety filled her heart, so much so, that she almost looked like a dying person, and every one feared that her presentiment would be correct. The invalid, who hitherto had been able to take a little food, could not be persuaded to touch any that day, and only swallowed a little water, which had come from our Lady's shrine at Philippsdorf, in order to show her special confidence in the Mother of God. To be thoroughly prepared for her journey into eternity, she received, once more, the holy Sacraments, and so awaited the next night. Towards evening, she asked her nurse to say the Rosary for her, and told her of the intention for which she had always said it. The nurse promised, and said that she would, at the same time, say it in honour of Saint Joseph, that he might obtain for her a happy death. About nine o'clock, p.m., they persuaded the poor sufferer to take a cup of warm coffee, but it only caused her violent sickness, and gave her agonizing pain. At last, she fell asleep, and, shortly after midnight, she had a remarkable dream.

She saw the Mother of God standing not far from her, in a white garment, with a long white veil, under which her hair was flowing down her back. Her features were most kind and beautiful. She stepped forward, bent graciously down to her, and said: "Thy illness is cured." But benevolent as she knew the Mother of God to be, the invalid scarcely dared to hope that she would so suddenly restore her to health. Her countenance betrayed this distrust, upon which our Blessed Lady brought from under her garment a paper, which looked like a folded and sealed letter, and put it on the bed before the sick person, saying: "Here you have a proof of what I am doing for you." For some moments the invalid looked at the paper, but did not dare to touch it; at last she took and examined it, and found that the seal was a little round picture of "Mary, Help of Christians." And when she turned it over, she read these words: "Thy Mother Mary will help thee." Whilst she examined the letter, she heard a noise, as if a lady was walking through the room in silken garments, and when she looked up the Mother of God had gone. After this she awoke, and found it was no empty dream, for although she saw no letter when she put out her hand to take it from the spot she had seen it in, she yet had the feeling of perfect health and strength. She called her nurse, who had fallen asleep on a sofa near her bed, and to her question, if she wanted anything, the patient exclaimed, "Oh, I feel, I feel— —." "Feel what?" rejoined the other, "are you worse?" "Oh, no, I feel so well!" upon which she told her of the dream. Then at once she made trial of her strength, to see if she had really recovered, left the bed without help, and found that all was perfectly true. So exuberant was the delight of both nurse and patient, that it woke another inmate of the house, who slept in the next room, and who wondered what this lively conversation, intermingled with laughter, could mean, when suddenly the late invalid presented herself at the door, and the joy of all was unbounded. But the return of health meant the return of appetite, and though it was the middle of the night they had to warm some soup for her. After this simple refreshment, they united in an act of thanksgiving for the great grace, and said the Litany and Rosary, and during its recital the happy patient was able to kneel without difficulty.

She would have liked to make use of her regained health at once to go to church, and also to begin to labour, but she was kept quiet in her room the first day; but not so the next, which found her standing at the wash-tub as of old, with the other women, and working as energetically as any of them. Four weeks passed, and no sign of her malady was to be seen; not a soul in her little town doubts that the recovery is a perfect one. The words of the Blessed Virgin, "Here is my proof," were more than a product of her imagination, as the result showed, and will prove once more, as it has so often done formerly, that the Mother of God is our surest advocate.

127. The Mother of God at Limbach.

On a pleasant eminence on the left bank of Main, about a mile distant from the parish of Limbach, in a beautiful region, stands the exquisite shrine of our Lady of Limbach. In ancient times there had been a lonely little chapel, with a picture of the Mother of God, whither people resorted in their sorrows and afflictions, in order to implore the intercession of our Lady.

In the fifteenth century, the chapel fell into decay, and the pilgrimages decreased, the real cause being the spread of Protestantism. But in the next century (1630) the people of Limbach returned to the Catholic Church, and at the same time tried to revive the neglected pilgrimages; they even attempted to build a chapel in the village itself, but from various signs that were manifested, they concluded that our Lady wished to be venerated in the old chapel.

Then the miraculous picture, which hitherto had been lying in a corner, was renovated and taken back in solemn procession to its old place over the high altar, and there exposed anew to the veneration of the people. It is carved in wood, and above the head of the Divine Mother, who holds the Child Jesus on her left arm, are angels bearing the crown of twelve stars.

In the year 1727, a wonderful event took place, which was the means of bringing this pilgrimage into renown. A poor shepherdess of Schwalvinger, at Limbach, had just recovered from a severe illness, which was followed by a serious disease of the eye, so that she became very anxious, lest she should lose her sight. In this great distress, she sought mercy and help from our Blessed Lady at Limbach, visited the Chapel of Grace, and prayed most earnestly. During the night, in a dream, it was made known to her that at the foot of the hill, some water had collected in a little hollow, caused by the imprint of an ox's foot. With this water she was to wash her eyes, and sight would be restored to her. The poor suffering woman revealed her strange dream at once to her husband and to others, but she only got laughed at, as no one had ever seen the slightest drop of water on this sandy and arid spot. Nevertheless she did not allow herself to be dissuaded, but asked to be taken to the place, where she actually found the water, washed her eyes with it and was cured.

The spot where the water appeared lies near the high road, about ninety steps from the church of the pilgrimage. Men were ordered to dig the ground in a circle of sixteen to twenty feet, in order to find the spring from which the water might have issued, but no spring was discovered. The poor woman, delighted with her miraculous recovery, spread the facts everywhere, and soon a crowd of blind, lame, infirm and decrepit people came to the spot, where water oozed from the ground. This water has the quality, besides other remarkable ones, that when it is in a clean sealed vessel, it keeps for many years without emitting a bad smell. The many offerings which were now made, enabled the chapel to be repaired, and as the number of pilgrims considerably increased, Limbach was made a parish of its own, in order that it might minister more freely to the many spiritual demands of the pilgrims.

The Prince Bishop Friedrich of Würzburg, had a special devotion towards this favoured place; he visited it frequently, endowed it richly with vestments, and gave twelve thousand florins for the building of the new church, saying: "As I have received from the Immaculate Mother of God, at Limbach remarkable graces in my many infirmities, I have promised as a token of my gratitude, to enlarge this Church of Grace, and put it in good condition."

In the year 1751, the building of the new church began, and, by the help of many benefactors, was finished four years later. Bishop Friedrich consecrated it on the 7th of September, 1755, with the utmost solemnity. It is a large and beautiful building, having, besides the high altar, two side ones; and it is still visited by numerous pilgrims, on account of the wonderful efficacy of its miraculous spring.

128. *The Pilgrimage of "Maria Luggau," in Kärnten.*

Amongst other holy places, where the faithful resort in throngs, in order to partake of our Lady's favours, is Luggau, upon the confines of the Tyrol.

For centuries, thousands of pilgrims have sought and found aid here, in their spiritual and temporal necessities, but as no doubt many of our readers are unacquainted with the origin and history of this pilgrimage, we think a short account will not be misplaced in this little book: —

"Up to the year 1513, Luggau was almost an unknown spot, it owned neither church nor priest; but at last it pleased the Mother of God to dispense her graces on this chosen spot, for, one day in the year 1513, the pious wife of a poor farmer being over-fatigued with her day's work, sat down to rest in a field of wheat; sleep soon overpowered her, during which our Blessed Lady appeared to her, and gave her to understand that she wished a church to be built in her honour in this same field.

"When she awoke, Mme. B— — not wishing to believe too easily in this strange vision, determined to convince herself of the reality of the occurrence by a holy artifice. She placed a lighted candle in the field, with the intention, should it be blown out by the wind, to give no credit to her dream, but should it remain alight, she would know that a heavenly message had been entrusted to her. Three separate times she made the trial, and each time the light burned brightly; so she began at once to collect alms to accomplish her mission, begging from house to house.

"But instead of contributions, she was the recipient of abuse and insult, meeting everywhere with contradiction and opposition. She was even accused of getting money on false pretences, and on this accusation was imprisoned; but after awhile, her real character being too well established amongst the people for this to be long believed, she was set at liberty. Mme. B— — or as she was more familiarly called, Helena, was not easily daunted in her grand enterprise, looking upon opposition, with its long train of intricate difficulties, as a sure sign that the work was blessed by heaven, and more fully convinced than ever of the truth of the apparition. By degrees, and by dint of perseverance and prayer, she succeeded in raising enough money to erect a small wooden chapel, in which she placed with intense joy, a beautiful image of the Virgin Mother.

"As soon as this was accomplished, our Lady deigned to show her satisfaction in the work, by a wonderful favour bestowed on a lunatic, who, as he was passing, suddenly seized the new image and made off with it; fortunately the carpenter, who was at work on the roof, noticed this theft, and calling after the poor imbecile said: 'Fie, for shame! it is our Lady's own image you are taking.' No sooner were the words out of his mouth, than the poor man raised his eyes to heaven, giving thanks to God and the Virgin Mary; for his intelligence had that moment been restored to him.

"Helena was still more encouraged by this wonderful indication of divine favour, and made a resolution to erect a worthier house for the great Queen of Heaven. She went therefore to Pittsberg to see John of Mandorf, the magistrate, to obtain from him the legal forms, as well as assistance for the building of a new church.

"The account of what had taken place with regard to the lunatic, and also the holy fervour of the pious Helena, induced the magistrate to go to Luggau, to see for himself, and make arrangements as to what was to be done. But he met with so much opposition from the greater number of the villagers, that he thought it wiser to give in to them, and let the matter rest. He had not advanced half way on his homeward journey, when his horse, usually a very quiet animal, shied, and he was thrown, but his foot caught in the stirrup, and in this position, he was dragged along some little way. In his danger he invoked the help of Mary, and promised to do all in his power to promote the building of the new church in Luggau, if his life should be spared. Hardly had he made this vow, than his horse stood still, quiet as a lamb, and to his great astonishment, he found he was none the worse.* After he had been rescued by our Lady in such a wonderful manner, he turned his horse's head, and rode straight back to Luggau, in order to settle everything necessary for the building of the church, without paying any attention to the resistance or insults of his opponents. Amongst these were two, who distinguished themselves by making use of abusive and insulting words, but

---

* On the spot where this took place, a chapel was erected, and the walls were decorated with pictures, depicting this wonderful event.

Divine Justice overtook them both, for one fell into a serious and painful illness, which was the means of bringing him to the knowledge of his guilt, and by the mercy of God, he repented; but the other with his whole family, perished by fire.

"The building was at last begun, and on the 22nd of May, 1515, the foundation stone was laid with great solemnity. All the priests of the Lesach valley, John of Mandorf, and numerous pilgrims were present. By means of donations and alms, the church was completed the following year, and the statue of the Mother of Dolours was carried from the wooden chapel to the new church. From this time, the devotion increased day by day, and the wonderful answers to prayer, and abundance of graces received there, brought countless numbers of pilgrims, from far and near, to the Mother of Dolours at 'Maria Luggau.' "

129. A Miraculous Cure.

Elizabeth P— — was the daughter of a respectable carpenter, at Ingolstadt. When she was twenty years of age she became paralyzed, and entirely lost the use of her legs. This misfortune befell her in 1866. Owing to his scanty means her father was unable to have her nursed at home, and she was obliged to go to a hospital. For ten years she remained in a helpless condition, only able to move by sliding along the ground. The doctors unanimously declared her case to be incurable, as they found she had absolutely no feeling in her feet or legs; even when they operated upon her, she could not feel the knife.

Throughout these long weary years her confidence in our Lady never wavered, and she felt convinced that if only she could get to a shrine at Gaemersheim, much frequented by the devout people of Ingoldstadt, her heavenly Mother would cure her. At length a poor widow, whom she knew, offered to wheel her there in a basket chair, which she borrowed from the hospital. Elizabeth gladly availed herself of this offer, and on arriving at the church door, the good widow lifted her charge from the wheel chair, and gently placed her on a bench facing the statue of the Madonna.

Suddenly, an indescribable sensation passed through the poor invalid, and she sank down on the stone pavement, as though helped off the bench by an invisible hand. Her companion hearing her move, quickly turned her head, and seeing her on the ground, went to her assistance, but Elizabeth said she thought she could get up alone, and to prove her words, she raised herself, walked round the chapel, and finally knelt down before the statue of her benefactress, tears of joy and emotion expressing the gratitude her heart was too full to speak.

The basket chair was now discarded, and she returned home on foot, walking the whole distance of six miles without the slightest fatigue; nor was she ever again troubled by a complaint which our Lady had so effectually removed.

130. *The Mother of Grace at Heilig-Wasser.*

Anne M—— —, an orphan, aged twenty years, had been an invalid for many years. In addition to all her other miseries, she entirely lost the power of speech, and the doctor declared her malady incurable, owing to a strange affection in her throat. In her distress, the poor girl had recourse to our Blessed Lady, and determined to make a pilgrimage to the Mother of Grace, at Heilig-Wasser, convinced that there she would find help and deliverance from her pains.

Obtaining an introduction through a friend, she received a hearty welcome, and what she valued more, many joined her in praying for her restoration to health; knowing that where "one or two are gathered together, God is in their midst."

Daily, public prayers were offered on behalf of the poor sufferer, and Anna, herself spent much of the night in prayer, and imploring our Blessed Lady to manifest the wonderful power of her maternal love for her afflicted child. Four days had passed in this way, when the great Feast of Pentecost being at hand, she was incited to still greater fervour. But on the eve of this festival, the invalid was seized with violent spasms, which reduced her to a semi-unconscious state, so that she spent all that night in bed, only able to breathe a few aspirations.

The next morning, Whit-Sunday, Anne persisted in going to the little church to hear Mass and receive Holy Communion. It had always been her custom, when leaving the house each day for Mass, to smile, and make certain signs of friendship to the kind people with whom she was staying, as she was unable to speak to them; but this morning, what was her surprise, to hear herself give utterance to the accustomed greeting of the country: "Blessed be Jesus Christ." A universal cry of astonishment and joy came from the lips of all; Anne, herself, was completely overcome, she joined her hands, raised her eyes towards heaven, and exclaimed, joyfully: "Oh! Mary, my wonderful Mother!" Tears of most fervent gratitude ran down the pale cheeks of the happy girl, and the bystanders could not control their emotion, for help had come at last, and the gracious Queen of Heaven had again manifested her wonderful power. They set out at once for the church, received the Holy Sacraments, and dedicated themselves soul and body, to the holy Mother of Grace, and promised by a votive-tablet, to offer flowers, etc. to perpetuate this miraculous cure. Later, Anna was received, through the influence of a generous and kind lady, into a religious Community, and gave her life entirely to God, and His holy Mother, as a continuous offering of thanksgiving.

131. The Church of our Lady, on the Köhlerberg, near Freudenthal, in Silesia.

Oswald, Baron of Lichtenstein, and governor of Freudenthal, was very fond of hunting. One day, when he was entirely engrossed with his sport, he lost his way, and came to an unknown, wild deserted region. In spite of all his endeavours, he could not find the path which led homewards. The sun set and rose again, and found him still wandering hopelessly, over strange tracts of country. Hunger and exhaustion made him feel depressed, and so discouraged did he become, that he sank down on a stump of rotten wood, which was covered with damp moss, and most ardently implored the "Help of Christians" to come to his assistance. In his gloomy state, he felt that death from starvation was inevitable, and he abandoned all hope of human aid. Suddenly he heard voices—in a moment he had sprung from his seat, and he saw in the distance some charcoal burners, he called out to them, and they turned in astonishment at the sight of a stranger in those parts. They gladly showed him the way to their smoky little hut, and there offered him what scanty food they had. After the much needed refreshment, they once more put him on his homeward path. He ascribed his deliverance to our Blessed Lady, and he built a chapel in her honour on the spot where he had met the charcoal burners, as a lasting expression of his gratitude to her. In addition he caused a beautiful picture of his benefactress to be painted over the high altar.

Many pilgrims began to frequent our Lady's new shrine, and, as abundant alms were bestowed by the recipients of favours and graces, the Bishop of the diocese decided to erect a large church on the site of the former chapel; this was completed in 1758, and a priest was permanently appointed to reside there, and minister to the spiritual wants of the ever increasing numbers who flocked there.

132. The Church of our Lady on the Wanneberg, near Roggenberg.

At the time of the war with the Swedes, in the 16th century, the monks of Roggenberg, in the diocese of Augsburg, were obliged to leave their monastery, as it was very much exposed to the ravages of the enemy; they therefore went to the little town of Weissenhorn, where they had another house of the Order. Only Father Francis Doser remained behind, in order to assist the people with his advice and consolation, administer to them the Sacraments, and take care of the Divine Service, and as it was safer for him to perform his duties in the disguise of a farmer, he was forced to change his habit for the dress of a peasant.

One day, when he was on his way to visit his little flock, six Swedes fell upon him, dragged him up the Wanneberg hill, and bound him to an old oak tree, leaving him to die by inches. Father Francis, who, from his early youth, had been a fervent servant of Mary, experienced in this hour of need, her wonderful benevolence. Our Blessed Lady stood visibly before him, and with her virginal hand prevented the rope from strangling him. One of the soldiers, being seized with remorse for the brutal act, and as it were urged by a supernatural power, ran back, and cutting the rope, released the good monk.

Later, Father Francis was raised to the dignity of Abbot, as our Lady had foretold him, but never, till he was on his death bed, did he disclose to anyone, not even to his Confessor, Father John Sapper, his wonderful rescue from death. He was inspired to do so then, that he might thus add to the glory of his heavenly Mother, and induce others to venerate and invoke her with more confidence.

His successor, the Abbot Adelbert, built a chapel in the vicinity, in remembrance of this wonderful event. This chapel was entirely rebuilt in the year 1794, and, on the feast of the Apostles SS. Simon and Jude, the holy Abbot Thaddeus Aigler, and Father Philip Schafheuth, transferred the picture of "Our Lady of Help" into the newly-built chapel for the veneration of the faithful. The number of pilgrims increased so rapidly, that a great desire was expressed on all sides, to build a yet more suitable chapel, in honour of the Mother of God; and ere long, by means of donations contributed by the pilgrims, the present chapel of "Mary Help" was erected.

In the year 1845, on the same feast, just fifty years after, the image of our Lady was borne in solemn procession from the parish church, where it had been kept during the process of building, to the new chapel, in presence of an immense concourse of people. The Dean of Roggenberg, Reverend Joseph Zanker, performed the ceremony of the Blessing.

As this shrine was raised through veneration and gratitude to Mary, we trust that the same gratitude and love of the

Mother of God will ever preserve it.

133. *The Cave at Carnaxida, Lisbon.*

It was in the year 1822, on the 31st of May, that a number of small boys were engaged in an exciting chase after a rabbit; the poor hunted animal at last made for a hole, where it thought no doubt, to find a safe retreat. Just as it disappeared from their sight, the bells of the village church pealed forth, summoning all to Mass.

One of the youngsters, Nicholas, who was about fourteen, did not wish to miss his week-day Mass, and yet he was very loth to leave the spot at the moment when they had secured their prey. Temptation was strong, but he bravely resisted it, and his good example was followed by his companions, who one and all turned their backs on their prisoner, taking the precaution to block up the entrance, with the faint hope that they would find the rabbit in their possession on their return. How their self-sacrifice and valour was amply rewarded we shall now see.

Immediately after Mass, the boys set out to carry on the hunt, and began to dig an immense hole, in order to follow the track of the little animal, with as much energy as if they had a presentiment they should find something of greater value than a harmless rabbit, as it very soon proved; for Nicholas, who was stronger and more eager than the rest, knocked up against a stone, which, falling down from its place, discovered to the astonished boy a huge cave, large enough to contain over forty people. Without further thought, he pushed his way along, when presently his attention was arrested by a most ghastly spectacle, a mass of human bones and skulls. At first, he recoiled from the offensive sight, and was on the point of leaving the cave, as he felt sick and faint, but looking back for a moment, he suddenly caught sight of a little statue of the Immaculate Virgin, standing in a niche, which was hewn out of the rocky side of the cave, about a foot in height. It was made of burned clay, but quite black and misshapen. This extraordinary discovery soon made him forget his first fright, and being a devout boy, he knelt down to say an Ave to the Mother of God. He now called to his companions to join him, and the whole band of little excavators knelt together in this strange place, where in all probability Mary's image had been hidden for centuries, ever since the first invasion of the Moors into Portugal, and had waited for this act of veneration, rendered to her by these boys, who had prepared themselves by sacrificing a harmless pleasure for the sake of hearing Holy Mass.

Yet this was not all. The rumour that the Blessed Virgin had appeared in the village of Carnaxida spread all over the country, and the people flocked in crowds, bringing their sick and infirm to the Grotto, and all those who entered came out perfectly cured. An altar had now to be erected, then a chapel was built; miracles increased daily, and the offerings of the gratified people overflowed. It seemed indeed, as if the whole of Lisbon moved towards this new sanctuary, so much so, that the Cortes got alarmed, and tried to put a stop to the general enthusiasm, but in vain. At last it was decreed that the black image should be transferred to the cathedral of Lisbon, which was accordingly done in the grandest possible style in 1883. It there found a home, until the completion of a most magnificent church at Carnaxida could receive once again its treasure, for the people had no intention of giving up permanently what they considered their possession.

134. *After Many Years.*

So innumerable are the instances of the power and kindness received from the hands of the Mother of God, even in our own day, both at home and abroad, that it is difficult to select the most interesting.

We do not wish to assert that all these incidents are of a miraculous nature, Holy Church remains silent on the subject, and so do we, but these remarkable occurrences have been, and ever will be, the means of sanctification to thousands, the source of edification, the increase of reverence in our churches and chapels, and the revival of faith and confidence in tepid and lukewarm Christians. Indeed, they cannot fail to benefit souls by bringing home to them the fact that, in spite of the scepticism of the age, in spite of the almost insuperable obstacles we oppose to grace, God's arm is not shortened, the power of Mary's intercession is not lessened.

*   *   *   *   *

The following is one instance, out of many, of a remarkable cure, which happened at a comparatively recent date. It is transcribed from an official account, signed by the parish priest and the mayor of the district:

"Marie Françoise Petitot, the subject of our Blessed Lady's tender assistance, lived at Pont de Roide Besançon, in France. When she was eleven years old, the loss of some near relative, and other troubles consequent upon it, told on the sensitive child to such a degree, that her health was seriously affected. She had never been strong, and now she seemed to lose all vitality, and gradually became a hopeless invalid. For some

251

unexplained reason her feet became so contracted, that she was unable to walk without great pain, and consequently spent all her day on a sofa. After trying every remedy human skill could suggest, she resigned herself to her fate, and remained in that sad and helpless condition for thirty-two years. She had long felt a great desire to make a pilgrimage to the famous shrine of our Lady, at Einsiedeln, but for many reasons, she was not able to carry out her intention. At last, on the 11th of May, 1850, she started, after many wearisome preparations, being drawn in a little donkey carriage; she arrived at her destination on the 18th, and took up her abode at a small inn. The day following her arrival being the Feast of Pentecost, she allowed herself to be carried to the 'Chapel of Favours' to hear Holy Mass, which was said at eleven o'clock. Just at the moment of the Elevation she felt a most extraordinary change coming over her, as if her whole being was transformed, her feet were loosened from their contracted position, and she found she could place them without difficulty on the pavement. She stood up at once, and falling on her knees, gave humble thanks to her Saviour, Who had cured her through the intercession of His Mother. She was now able to return to her lodgings, leaning for support on two friends.

"The news soon spread far and wide, and many were the people who came to see for themselves the truth of this miracle. During the three days she remained at Einsiedeln, she went to church regularly, with only a slight support. On her homeward journey, as she passed through the Catholic cantons of Switzerland, the people came out to greet her, and in fact, her return home was a triumphant procession in honour of Mary. Every now and then she would leave her donkey car, and walk in front of the people to satisfy their devotion. In this way she arrived on the frontiers of France.

"When she had reached her village, which was six miles from the parish church, at Villars-les-Blamont, she was accompanied by an immense crowd, who had previously assembled at the church to hear Holy Mass, in thanksgiving for the wonderful favour that had been vouchsafed to one among them; her own priest had come with the rest, and preached a very suitable and devotional discourse. The news of her arrival had spread throughout all the neighbouring villages, and multitudes hastened to be present at her reception, which was arranged for the afternoon.

"At about two o'clock p.m., a long procession, under the supervision of ten priests, met Marie Françoise, who was being conducted by almost as numerous a concourse of people. When the two processions had met, they united in singing canticles of joy and thanksgiving; Marie descended from her little conveyance, and walked between the two lines of pious worshippers, but after awhile, being somewhat fatigued, she resumed her seat in the donkey car, and then they all proceeded to the church of her native place. But this church was only capable of holding three thousand people, and as the crowd was so immense, many had to stay outside, in the grounds and in the cemetery; the priest being obliged to deliver his address to the people in the open air. He spoke long and fervently on devotion to our Blessed Lady, in such a moving manner that many were quite overcome.

"The ceremony concluded with Benediction of the Blessed Sacrament, which the priest gave at the threshold of the church, and the people did not depart, until Marie Petitot had gone into the presbytery. During this and the following day, she was visited by innumerable people who wished to see and speak with her. Several who had ridiculed the possibility of the cure, were quite won over, and returned full of faith and admiration.

"Next day, a solemn High Mass was celebrated at this church, in the presence of more than twelve hundred people, during which, Marie communicated with great devotion. Every one, now could judge for themselves, that her cure was complete and genuine, as they saw her return from the Communion rails alone. The High Mass, the joyful hymns, the eloquent sermon of the parish priest, again moved all the spectators to tears, and the service ended by a grand 'Te Deum.'

"We, the mayor, and parish priest, of Pont de Roide, declare and testify, that the above narration is true.

"*Pont de Roide, June,* 1850.

"R. P. MENEGAY, *Mayor*.

"P. BOILLON, *P.P.*"

On the last day of August, this favoured one was again in Einsiedeln, and was able to walk without the assistance of her neighbours. Out of gratitude, she made a pilgrimage each year to Einsiedeln, on the Feast of Pentecost, till she died on the 29th of August, 1870.

May this true and simple account, increase devotion and trust in the goodness and power of Mary, who will on her part, never fail to show herself a tender and solicitous Mother to all those who invoke her aid.

"Salus infirmorum, ora pro nobis."

135. At Loretto.

James Margrave, of Ballen, was seriously wounded in an

insurrection that broke out at Cologne, and was in danger of death. He promised that, if he should be restored to health, he would make a pilgrimage, and give a handsome present to our Lady, at Loretto. He was cured, but one of his arms remaining stiff, he desired a more complete answer to his prayers. Feeling confident that our Blessed Lady would not fail him, he set out, full of faith, to perform his promise, and for two days he exercised himself in works of devotion, and grateful visits of love to his benefactress. On the third night after his arrival at the shrine, he had a most consoling dream about our Lady. When he awoke he found he could move his arm without pain, and as freely as the other. He himself related this favour to the then reigning Pope, Gregory XIII, and he has left a document to this effect, testified by many witnesses, in the archives of Loretto.

"Praised be Jesus and Mary!"

136. *The Sanctuary of Pompeii.*

Everyone has read of the ancient city of Pompeii, which was partly destroyed by an earthquake, Anno Domini 63, and later, in 79, was completely submerged by a stream of lava, or shower of ashes from Mount Vesuvius. It was discovered in 1748; but it is not however to this old city of Campania that we wish to draw the attention of our readers, but to the new Pompeii and its sanctuary.

The little village, Valla de Pompéii, lies at the foot of Mount Vesuvius, and for a long period it remained solitary, forsaken, and unknown; many years ago, a lawyer, Bartolo Longo, eminent for his great sanctity, had exposed for public veneration an old painting of our Blessed Lady, with the

Rosary, in the hope of reviving this devotion in the hearts of the people. In the year 1876, he, with some pious and generous friends, bought a site for a church, and the foundation-stone was laid the same year by the Right Reverend Bishop of Nola, Formisano. No one would have believed that such a magnificent temple could have been erected in such a short time, and ever since, the devotion of the Rosary has flourished there, the powerful Queen of Heaven showing, in a wonderful way, how pleasing this devotion is to her, by miraculous cures, and remarkable answers to prayer, in thousands and thousands of cases. The tidings of the heavenly favours she has bestowed on her faithful servants, have spread throughout the whole world. For all parts, gifts for the church, and for the adornment of this most costly of all God's houses have poured in; the piety of the faithful, and the talent of the most renowned Italian artists, animated by faith and love towards the Holy Virgin, have placed here a memorial of religion, which, in future ages, will bear witness to the devotion of the nineteenth century towards the Mother of God. This temple is built of the rarest Carrara marble, adorned with gold and precious stones, and was solemnly consecrated on the 8th of May, 1887. The miraculous picture, before which fifteen lamps burn day and night, in honour of the fifteen mysteries of the Rosary, was adorned with a crown of diamonds, after having been blessed by the Holy Father himself, who also sent a very handsome chasuble, richly embroidered, and bearing the arms of the Pecci family, to be worn for the consecration of the church.

The munificent gifts of the faithful have not only erected this church, but have also founded two institutes for children, one for boys, and the other for girls; an industrial school, a preparatory school for artisans and mechanics, and a printing office, which publishes every month, the magazine, *Il Rosario della Nuova Pompeii*, an account of the almost daily miraculous answers to prayer, and frequent favours of the Queen of the Rosary. An orphanage also is supported by means of the alms received, for destitute girls, who have none to help them. And moreover, a refuge for children of condemned criminals. Here they are trained to be good and useful men, so that they may not follow in the degraded footsteps of their parents. This is indeed a truly noble and excellent work of brotherly love and charity! The faithful come, day by day, as pilgrims to the throne of our heavenly Queen, and all classes of suffering humanity there find refuge at the feet of the Mother of sinners. They stream in from all parts of the world; some seeking consolation and cure in bodily ailments, others giving thanks for favourable answers to their prayers.

Thus, in a few years, New Pompeii has become famous, and can even boast of the modern convenience of a railway-station, as well as postal and telegraph offices. The sanctuary itself is surrounded by workshops and inns, the latter affording shelter for the many pilgrims who visit the church and the adjacent charitable institutions.

A Confraternity has been established under the title of "Our Lady of the Rosary of Pompeii," and devout clients of Mary may get themselves enrolled by applying to the director at Valle di Pompeii, Naples, Italy.

137. Waghäusel.

Among the many miraculous places in Baden, the ancient and widely renowned pilgrimage at Waghäusel, holds the first rank; here for many hundred years, Mary, the refuge of all in distress, has been honoured with special fervor and confidence.

There once stood a little house, inhabited by poor people, in the neighbourhood of which an image of the Blessed Virgin Mary was exposed; but on account of the constant wars, it had been hidden in a hollow oak tree, in order to protect it from any irreverence, or prevent its being taken away. How long this statue remained thus concealed is unknown, but the manner in which it came to light again is too interesting to be passed over in silence. It happened in June, 1435, that a shepherd, who was tending sheep in that district, found a stone image about a foot and a half high, in a hollow oak tree; it was a statue of the Mother of God, with the child Jesus in her arms. Full of joy, the good man carried it home, honoured it by many devout prayers, and considered it a great treasure; the very next day however, it disappeared from his house, and was again found in the old oak tree. No one could tell how it had returned to its old place, and when this was twice repeated, the shepherd fell into such a rage, that he was on the point of destroying the statue, but he heard a mysterious voice calling to him: "Stop, do not break it!" Terrified by these words, he fell on his knees before the image, humbly imploring our Lady's pardon.

In reparation, he determined to erect a little grotto beside the oak; and having completed it, he placed the statue in it, that all those who passed along the road might salute it. Being on the high road, between Spires and Heidelberg, it soon became known and its miraculous discovery was much spoken of, with the result that in course of time, it became a resort of devout pilgrims, miracles were wrought, and wonderful spiritual favours were obtained. At last, the shrine became so famous, and the concourse of pilgrims so great, that it was found necessary to erect a church, and place a resident priest on the spot to minister to their wants.

The church was solemnly consecrated by the Bishop of Spires, in 1473. It was a beautiful little structure, containing four altars, the high altar being built on the site of the old oak tree, and over this the miraculous statue was suitably enthroned. Year by year, as the anniversary of the consecration came round, people would come in throngs to the sanctuary to honour the Blessed Mother, who loves to reveal herself to the humble and simple, and to shower blessings on the little ones of whom her Divine Son speaks. The rich also, came to seek light and assistance at Mary's feet, and left bountiful alms for the adornment of her shrine.

In the year 1616, Bishop Philip Christopher von Sötern sent two Capuchins to Waghäusel, from Spires, who remained for three years, but in 1619, the so-called "Pfalz" war broke out, and Count Frederick making himself king of Bohemia, the Fathers fled with the miraculous image to Philippsburg, where they remained for a year; from thence they went to Mainz, and stayed there until the termination of the war. On the fifteenth of June, 1630, they returned to Waghäusel, bringing with them the wonder working statue; they replaced it in the chapel, and once more began the Divine Service, which had been interrupted for so long. But peace was not of long duration, for two years later, the invading army of Swedes struck terror into every breast, and once more the Fathers fled with the miraculous image to Philippsburg, but returned again to Waghäusel, leaving the image behind at Philippsburg, hoping that the Swedes would not harm them. They were, however, dragged from the altar during the Holy Mass, and clothed in the sacred vestments, put on horses and carried away prisoners. The chapel was plundered, and all the pictures and votive tablets destroyed and burnt.

In the year 1634, a Calvinist peasant of Waltorf, in the Pfalz, happened to pass by this chapel, in company with a locksmith, named Philip Nägler, of Hanau. When the former saw the image of the Mother of God over the door, he became furious, and began to insult it in a most blasphemous manner. Then, taking from his wagon a fork, he struck at it with repeated blows, until at length the statue fell down, and remained neglected and broken on the ground.

But the just punishment of God soon overtook the offender, for he was suddenly seized with such violent pains, that he could not move a step farther. He was lifted into the wagon, and driven home, where he died soon after, amidst the most fearful agony and sufferings. This visible punishment made such an impression on Philip Nägler, that he renounced his heresy, and was received into the Catholic church at Philippsburg. The miraculous image remained at Philippsburg, reinstated in its former position, until that town was also conquered by the Swedes, when it was secretly carried to Spires, where it was exposed in the Capuchin church. Meanwhile Waghäusel was deserted, until in the year 1638, Kaspar Bamberger, the noble commander of the garrison at Philippsburg, invited some Fathers from Cologne to Waghäusel, and promised to build a monastery there. In 1639, the foundation stone was laid, and by this time the pilgrimages were again set on foot; on feast days the people streamed in such numbers to the chapel, that there was not even standing room. Therefore the chapel was enlarged in 1683, by John Hugo, Elector of Treves and Bishop of Spires, who also erected an altar in honour of the Mother of God, and one in honour of

Saint Anthony of Padua. The consecration took place on the Feast of our Lady's Nativity, 1685, the Vicar General of Spires performing the ceremony.

In 1688, Philippsburg was again besieged, and was conquered by the French, on the 28th of September; the Capuchins were therefore obliged to leave Waghäusel, and in 1690, they betook themselves to Kirrlach, not far from Waghäusel. Here they remained for a long time, their beloved church and monastery having been devastated and destroyed. The miraculous statue was once more brought secretly to Philippsburg by two Capuchin Fathers, and soon after, to secure its perfect safety, it was carried to Heidelberg, where it was kept in the Capuchin monastery until the end of the war. Eight years later it was brought back to Waghäusel, to the universal joy of the people, and has remained there ever since. Pious pilgrims have always made it their pious duty to contribute to the preservation and embellishment of this sanctuary.

The Capuchin monastery was abolished at the beginning of this century, for on the 7th of January, 1827, Father Ladislas, the guardian, celebrated Mass there for the last time, and went the next day as parish priest to Neudorf; the monastery was then sold.

The renowned popular writer, Martin von Cochem, died at the monastery of Waghäusel, on the 12th of September, 1712.

138. Our Lady of the Angels, Toulouse.

Pouvoirville is a small parish, not far from Toulouse, it is most pleasantly situated on the hilly side of the river Garonne, and overlooks a beautiful plain.

The chief boast of this little parish is a chapel, dedicated to our Lady of the Angels, which has been favoured by God in a special manner, on account of many wonderful graces He has bestowed on devout pilgrims who have visited it.

It is not known when or how the devotion to our Lady of the Angels was first introduced into this village, but it is generally supposed to have been brought there many centuries ago by some Franciscan friars. It had been more or less kept up among the villagers, and handed down from father to son, so that all were accustomed to invoke our Lady under this sweet title.

The moment however had arrived, when a new impetus was to be given to this ancient devotion, and it was brought about in the following manner:—

At midnight, on the 21st of July, 1856, a young man named Marie Frederic de Bray, lay dying in the castle of Bellevue, near Toulouse. He had long been suffering from a most serious illness. All means for his recovery had been tried; he had consulted physicians from Paris, Montpellier, Turin, and Florence; but human science was of no avail, and even all the prayers said for him seemed fruitless.

But the power of the Blessed Virgin is unlimited! Just as the sick man seemed about to breathe his last, he said with his failing voice to the Queen of Angels: "I make the vow." The condition of his cure was a vow to go on a pilgrimage to the shrine of our Lady of the Angels, at Assisi. He had hardly pronounced it, when to the great surprise of his sorrowing mother and relations, he rose up cured. The family doctor who certified his recovery, said: "This is a real miracle;" and he himself told the Archbishop of Toulouse, that he was "ready, if need be, to attest and sign it with his blood."

Such was the marvel that manifested our Lady's wish to be honoured once more in her sanctuary at Pouvoirville.

This was only two years after the proclamation of the Dogma of the Immaculate Conception, and when the holy Pontiff, Pius IX, heard of this miracle at Toulouse, he at once granted the great favour of the Indulgence of the Portiuncula to the parish of Pouvoirville. The inhabitants were overjoyed at the favour bestowed on them, and celebrated the day with all possible devotion; all field-work was abandoned, and for miles around, the old and young vied with each other in showing their filial love to Mary.

Every 2nd of August called forth the same tokens of faith and love. A congregation has been founded in honour of our Lady of the Angels, which has extended throughout the world, being raised to an arch-confraternity in 1871.

Numerous graces, for both soul and body, have been granted by the Queen of Angels, in answer to the prayers of this arch-confraternity, and new favours showered on rich and poor. It is fitting, in these days of peril, that we should invoke her, under this sweet title, for through it, we enlist all heaven to help us, that we, and all who need assistance in the conflict we have to wage against the powers of darkness, may gather strength and courage, so as one day to be numbered in the "company of many thousands of angels."

XI.

LOURDES.

139. Irma Dubois.

It was on Tuesday, the 30th of September, 1874, towards eight o'clock in the evening, that we first caught sight of the beautiful church at Lourdes, just as the "Magnificat" was being sung by hundreds of voices, resounding through the autumnal air like the echoes of angelic hymns.

It was certainly an impressive moment; but the sight that strikes the beholder most, is the earnest faith, evident on every side, in this most hallowed spot; the absorbed prayer of such a multitude—for each and all seem unconscious of their neighbour, bent only on the one object of their visit—veneration, thanksgiving, and—as is generally the case—petition. If any one has had the privilege to witness either a special grace granted, or a miracle performed, they will have experienced in their soul a sensation of awe and veneration, which thrills through their whole being, bringing with it an increase of faith, which cannot be described.

We will relate a few of these miraculous cures, which we think have not yet been given to English readers, hoping that in spite of their shortness and imperfect style, they will bring home to their minds how near and deeply interested our Blessed Lady is in the welfare of her children:—

Irma Dubois, of M——, being deprived of the use of her feet, hands, and tongue, was brought to Lourdes on the 30th of September, 187—, in such a weak condition that the doctor had to be called in when she arrived, for it was feared she would die immediately. The following morning she was driven as far as the church, and her uncle, Monsieur Dubois, from Bagnères, and Viscount de Fouchecour, from M— —, carried her into our Lady's sanctuary. When Mass was over, the two gentlemen took the invalid to the Communion-rails, afterwards bearing her to the Grotto, there to finish her devotions; from thence they took her to the spring, in order to bathe her feet in the wondrous water. Monsieur Dubois, who had openly expressed his disbelief in the power of the Mother of God, at Lourdes, left his niece for a moment, in order to give the coachman some directions, but scarcely had he reached the carriage when he heard the cry: "A miracle! A miracle!" Then he saw the crowd pressing forward quickly to the miraculous spring, and perceived Irma walking alone, holding her crutches in the air. The miracle had, indeed, taken place, and, coming forward immediately, Monsieur Dubois embraced her, whom he looked upon as his own child; then, falling on his knees, he wept from emotion, exclaiming, "Oh, Mary, I thank thee! Now I believe!"

The Bishop of M— — then dispersed the crowd, in order to inquire into the sudden and perfect cure of one of his flock, and thousands of pilgrims, who were witnesses of this miracle, entoned with the most ardent expression of faith and deepest emotion, the "Magnificat," which arose in a mighty hymn of thanksgiving and gratitude to the ever-blessed Virgin Mary.

Mlle. Dubois was surrounded by crowds of pilgrims, who congratulated her, and presented her with a book in order that she might write her name; everyone wished to have the account of the miracle from her own lips, which until now, had been closed to all. Instead of answering them, she raised her eyes, bathed in tears, to the figure of the Blessed Virgin, which is above the grotto, and exclaimed: "All praise to Mary Immaculate, our Lady of Lourdes!" And this prayer was re-echoed by thousands of voices.

M. Dubois now wished his niece to get into the carriage, for it was eleven o'clock, and as she had eaten nothing since the evening before, he feared she might suffer from a fresh attack of weakness; but she begged so hard to return on foot, that he acceded to her brave request, and all the pilgrims accompanied her, singing the "Magnificat."

140. Abbé de Musy.

The wonderful cure of the Abbé de Musy, which took place at Lourdes, on the fifteenth of August, 1873, is thus related by himself:—

"I had been ill for twenty years, and utterly incapable of fulfilling the duties of my ministry, my sight was so weakened that I could not read my breviary. For ten years I could not even say Mass, and for the same length of time, I had been like a dumb man. I was suffering from disease of the spinal cord, which almost deprived me of the use of my limbs. I had already consulted the most renowned doctors of France, Germany and Switzerland, when our Lady inspired me with the thought of going to Lourdes. I was driven there, helpless as a child, in a little carriage; we arrived early on the 8th of August. I had myself carried to the church, where I daily heard Masses, from five o'clock until ten. I chose a quiet nook at the bottom of the church, in a side aisle, through which the crowd of men constantly streamed, without their being able to see me. By my side was a poor child, who was even in a sadder condition than myself, and who also sat on a wheeled chair, waiting for the 'moving of the water;' here I spent a great part of the day.

"On the Feast of the Assumption, I heard Mass said by a Sulpician priest, who had done much towards promoting our Lady's honour. At the moment of the Consecration, I felt inwardly compelled to throw myself on my knees, human respect made me hesitate for a moment, but at length I yielded to the inspiration; I stood up and cast myself on the ground. At that moment, Mary indeed turned on me a look of pity and of love, for I was cured. A minute before, I had been blind, dumb, and lame; now I saw, I could speak, and I could walk. I at once made trial of my new strength, and descended from the church to the grotto, which is at some little distance. The people who had seen me so terribly afflicted, could scarcely believe their eyes, and with indescribable fervour, the pilgrims entoned the 'Magnificat,' in thanksgiving. Afterwards, every one, wishing to convince himself of the reality of the miracle, insisted on my walking, speaking or writing. For an hour and a half I was employed in signing little pictures for them, and thus doubt was no longer possible.

"In the evening, the ever-blessed Virgin Mary bestowed on me another consoling favour. A man of about sixty years old, was ushered into my room: 'Father,' he said, 'I have seen all that has happened to you, and it has touched my heart. I have not been to Confession for forty years, and I will not go away from here, until I have laid bare my past life to you.'

"Thus, our Immaculate Mother, who had healed my body, wished now to perform another miracle, the cure of a soul dead in sin."

141. Julie de Breuil.

Julie de Breuil, Baroness of Portbriand, was born in the castle of Villeguerin, in the diocese of Saint Brieux (Côte du Nord), on the 7th of March, 1843. On the 15th of March, 1873, she felt violent pains in her eyes, and in April of the same year she underwent an operation for their cure. For a time she did not suffer quite so acutely, but in 1878 her left eye became perfectly blind, and on August the 12th, 1882, she also lost the use of her right eye. Three doctors were consulted, and all declared that this blindness was beyond ordinary medical skill, so they held a consultation on the 14th of August, and advised their patient to consult the celebrated oculist, Galezonski, of Paris. She refused to do this however, preferring to seek light for both soul and body at the Grotto of Lourdes, whither she journeyed on the 29th of August. She washed in the life-giving water of its spring, without however feeling any alleviation. The next morning she received Holy Communion at the Bishop of Baune's Mass, and she at once felt a little amelioration of the pain in the left eye. She then went a second time to the healing spring, and scarcely had she plunged into the water, when she immediately called out, "I see!" A doctor examined her, and pronounced her statement to be correct, saying, "Yes, she sees perfectly." And from that time she has never felt the slightest pain in her eyes. The three doctors whom she had consulted stated these facts in a register kept especially for writing down instantaneous cures, after merely washing in the water of the Grotto.

142. A Girl from Rhodes Cured.

Towards the end of July, 1875, a poor girl, who had been paralysed for five years, was brought to Lourdes. She was in such a state of weakness and exhaustion, that no one would help her into the bath, in spite of her earnest entreaties, for they told her it would be tempting God; so all she was permitted to do, was to drink a few drops of water out of the spring. At first, she could only take very little, which she swallowed with difficulty; then, having recovered her breath, she drank a whole glassful. She had barely finished this, when in the presence of all, she jumped out of the carriage, exclaiming: "I am cured! I am cured!" and threw herself into her sister's arms. Everyone was moved to tears, for it really seemed as if she had risen from the dead, so like a corpse had she looked on her arrival. For the two following days, this young girl carried the banner at the head of the procession of pilgrims from Rhodes, from the parish church to the Basilica, without feeling the slightest fatigue.

143. Only a Taste of Lourdes Water.

A Jesuit Father writes the following account to a religious paper:—

"The horse which was to have brought me to the railway station, fell on the slippery streets, and so I missed my train. This was indeed very vexing as I had taken every precaution to be in time. We arrived at the station just as the train was moving off; regrets were useless, so I patiently submitted to my lot, and thought I would say my office during the time which would elapse before the next train, which was due in about an hour. This was no easy task in a busy station, but if I went away, I did not know what to do with a large bottle of Lourdes water, which I had with me. To put it in the luggage room did not seem quite reverent, but I noticed in the corner of the waiting-room, a man, closely wrapped up, who, to all appearances, meant to sit there for several hours. So I walked up to him, and asked if he were going to remain there for some time? 'Yes,' was the reply.

"This 'yes' was uttered shortly, and signified, rather, 'what does it matter to you?'

" 'Are you going to stay till eleven o'clock?'

" 'Yes,' was the curt rejoinder. His voice sounded still gruffer.

" 'If I leave this article here, will you look after it?'

" 'What is it?' he asked.

" 'Oh, nothing very particular; but will you have the kindness to take care of it?'

"In a sulky voice, I at length got the reply 'Very well, leave it there.' I then went off to a quiet spot under some trees, near the station. Having finished my office, I bought a newspaper, in order to pass away the remaining twenty minutes. Scarcely had I begun to read, when I seemed to hear a voice saying to me: 'Go and see what has become of the bottle!' 'Stupid bottle!' I could have said, but the remembrance of its contents restrained me. I wanted to read, but the voice seemed to repeat: 'Go and see what has become of your bottle!' I could stand this no longer, so I went; the man was still there, the man of the slow, rough and morose answers, but he sat with his face buried in his hands, and the tears welling through his fingers.

" 'Oh, Father,' he said, 'I will tell you all, yes all.' (How I wondered at this unexpected manner of address.) 'You see that

I am already an old man. I was born and baptized in the Catholic church, and until the age of eleven, I practiced my religion; then I lost my mother, and my father being already dead, I was left alone in the world. Fortunately, I was in the hands of a good master, but he was a staunch Protestant, and he eventually constrained me to embrace his religion; and to please him, I became a Protestant. Later on I married, and God gave me a good Catholic wife, who continually entreated me to return to the religion of my childhood; but I put it off from year to year. When you went away, leaving this bottle standing here, I was curious to know what it contained, and to try what a papist priest's brandy tasted like, but I soon perceived that it was only water after all. As soon as I had taken a mouthful, a change came over me, I felt determined to become a Catholic once more; and I will do so immediately. So I beg of you, Father, to hear my confession.'

"This announcement was so strange that at first I believed the good man had been drinking something more than my water, and so I wanted to get rid of him.

" 'We have not any time now,' I replied, 'for the train will be here in a few minutes; besides, this is not the place for such things. Come to me at X— —.'

" 'Now, Father, now,' was the rejoinder. 'I cannot come to X— —; do hear my Confession, and I promise you that I will go to church next Sunday with my wife.'

" 'Do you know,' I asked, 'where this water comes from?'

" 'No,' he replied.

" 'It is from the miraculous spring of the Immaculate Mother of God, at Lourdes.'

" 'Well then, it is the Blessed Virgin Mary who has obtained this grace for me,' he said. Thereupon I lost no more time, and

271

before the train left, I had reconciled this aged sinner to his God."

144. *Another Conquest of Grace.*

Father Antonius, a Capuchin, relates the following incident:—

"A grey-haired sinner had come from a distance to the sanctuary of Lourdes, merely out of curiosity. We met in the crypt, and, offering me money, he said: 'Father, I have been commissioned to have a Mass said at this sanctuary, and here is the money for it.'

" 'I do not want money, my friend,' I answered, 'but the salvation of your soul. Have you been to confession lately?'

" 'Father,' he replied, 'I am certainly astonished at your question! No, I have not been to confession, and I made it a condition when I was persuaded to join the pilgrimage: that they would leave me in peace about confession. Besides, you do not even know me; and for you to speak of confession to me is rather too much for a fellow.'

" 'Not so, my friend,' I rejoined; 'but it is too much to come to the Grotto with all your sins, and to carry them always about with you. You do not yet know the power of our dear Lady of Lourdes. Have you even prayed at the Grotto yet?'

" 'No, Father, for I have only just arrived.'

" 'Well, then, come down with me, and I will show you the way.'

"He followed me, and we went down together. As usual, the place between the little stream and the Grotto was filled with pilgrims. I showed him the Grotto, and we then went in.

" 'What must we do here, Father?' he asked.

272

" 'We must first of all pray, my son,' I answered.

" 'But it is at least fifty years since I did such a thing, and I have forgotten all my prayers.'

" 'So much the more reason to begin them to-day,' I said to him.

I then threw myself on my knees, and he submissively followed my example. This man, who had not prayed for half-a-century, remained a long time in this devout position, his eyes fixed on Mary's image. For my part, I most earnestly entreated grace for this soul, through our Lady's intercession, and by the influence of the rays of maternal love, which here almost visibly eradiate from her heart, I felt that the fruit was ripe for gathering.

" 'My friend,' I then said, 'if anyone prays to the Blessed Virgin in the way you are doing, could they have the heart to refuse what she asks and desires?'

" 'Yes Father, I know well what she has desired of me for a long time; but can an old sinner like me really find forgiveness still? Why, I need at least a whole year to prepare myself for confession!'

" 'A year, indeed, if you had to do it alone,' I replied; 'but if the Immaculate Virgin is with you, and you have the happiness of being in her favoured Grotto, you will find one minute quite enough; try, at any rate.'

"I then took him by the hand, and led him to the confessional behind the altar; he there knelt down, and began his confession. What passed in the soul of this poor sinner, God, our Lady, and the holy Angels witnessed. Afterwards he wept, from sheer joy and happiness, for in that one brief moment, Mary, our Immaculate Queen, had converted him, and raised him to a new life."

145. Conversion of a Jew at Lourdes.

Eleanor von Grey, when still quite young, had married a Jew. Although a Catholic, she had not hesitated to unite herself with one over whom the waters of baptism had never flowed. But as years went on, and he showed no signs of relinquishing the religion of his ancestors, his wife became more and more anxious, and the very thought of his dying an alien to the true Church, and deprived of all the Sacraments, was a source of much trouble and anxiety to her. She therefore prayed much, and earnestly, to Mary, the Queen of Heaven, on her husband's behalf, trying, at the same time, to win him over by persuasions, and explaining to him the truths of our holy religion, but it was all to no purpose.

God blessed their marriage with a little girl, but soon after her birth M. von Grey became seriously ill, and the doctors could not come to any decisive opinion with regard to his complaint. One day M. von Grey, quite unexpectedly, proposed travelling in the neighbourhood of Lourdes, "in order," as he said, "to inhale there the pure, fresh mountain air, and thus perhaps restore his shattered health." His wife was delighted at this proposal, for she inwardly hoped for more than restoration of health; she yearned for the enlightenment of her husband's soul, and did not delay the journey a single day. It was the beautiful month of May which they were to spend at Lourdes, and this alone was a propitious sign in the eyes of the anxious wife.

They arrived on the last day of April, and found the town in festal garb, in preparation for the opening of the May devotions. The crypt above the Grotto was especially attractive and pretty; long wreaths of flowers and green foliage were hung round the windows, and festooned from point to point; every vein and cornice seemed garlanded with leaves and flowers. Lights, plants, and bouquets of the rarest and most beautiful flowers adorned the Sanctuary itself, whilst our Lady's image literally stood in a bower of magnificent roses.

Every day the invalid, accompanied by his wife, was present at the religious celebrations, and an undefined hope of her husband's ultimate recovery began to spring up in Madame von Grey's heart, for although he was not actually better, still he was none the worse for his unusual exertions. She even ventured one day to say something of the kind to him; but he gazed on her with such a look, that the words died away on her lips. He knew better, and was not to be deceived; he felt his days were numbered, and it was not for his recovery he was now spending these long hours in prayer in the crypt.

They generally made their first visit about the time of the first Mass, and the second at two o'clock in the afternoon, which was the usual hour for the May devotions. One day they could not enter the crypt at once, owing to an immense gathering of nine hundred pilgrims, which had arrived from Bayonne; but happily our two travelers had not to wait long, for, after a time of most earnest prayer, the pilgrims again formed in procession, and marched in perfect order through the cloister of the crypt, going from thence down to the Grotto by the zigzag route. There they knelt down for a moment, after which this vast crowd arose, and in one voice entoned a glorious "Magnificat," which re-echoed among the rocks of Massabielle, across the river Gave, and softly died away over the meadows below Lourdes. After Benediction, the pilgrims returned in time to catch the evening train.

During the whole of this particular afternoon, M. von Grey

remained silent and motionless in his chair near the Grotto, at times noticing the pilgrims as they came and went, but mostly absorbed in deep reverie. When this crowd of devout people had at last dispersed, his wife tried to persuade him to leave also, but he seemed disinclined to do so, and as his wife feared to interfere with the workings of Divine Grace, she left him undisturbed for a time.

The shadows of evening gathered around, and one star after another appeared in the purple sky, but M. von Grey, apparently, had no eyes or thought for outward things. He never raised his eyes, except to gaze on Mary's image, which glittered like silver in the light which was reflected from the dark damp wall of rock behind. At length his wife noticed that he was becoming restless, and following the direction of his eyes, she saw that the wind had blown one of the candles on the pyramid all on one side, and that it was on the point of burning itself down; M. von Grey pointed to the candle, at the same time touching his wife's arm. "Shall I fetch another," she whispered, with a mingled feeling of hope and fear. He answered by a smile, in the affirmative. Mrs. von Grey made a sign to a servant to fetch another, and before the former had time to take it, it was already in her husband's hands. "Will you put it up yourself?" asked his wife, in joyful surprise, scarcely believing that such a thing was possible. He smiled again, and, leaning upon his wife's arm, M. von Grey staggered through the Grotto. The servant hastened to open the grated door, and then, giving the sick man an arm, drew him gently forward, and helped him to arrange the candle; then the Jew knelt down to pray, and after some little time, he stood up. Leaving the Grotto with the aid of the sacristan, he returned to his wife, but could not utter a syllable. She looked anxiously at him, and saw a bright light shining from his eyes, while a smile hovered on his lips; the soft, gentle look in his eyes, seemed more of heaven than of earth.

"Yes," he gently whispered, in answer to the enquiring look of his wife, "Your prayer is heard, Eleanor! From henceforth I am a child of Mary." And so indeed it was. In a short time M. von Grey was received into the Church, but only lived for six months after, continually thanking God for the great grace bestowed upon him. He was a daily communicant, and his piety, faith, and love, from the moment of his baptism, were touching to all who saw him, and his wife, being resigned to the Will of God at his death, considered that a more consoling miracle had been wrought than if his health had restored him to her for many years to come.

XII.

RETRIBUTIVE JUSTICE.

146. A Blasphemer's End.

SOME years ago, an old gentleman named X——, died on the 8th of December. For more than thirty years he had not been to his duties, and took special delight in uttering blasphemies against the Mother of God. Some weeks before his death, being already troubled with a cough, he happened to be taking a walk in the neighbourhood of the pilgrimage, at N——. Meeting a peasant, he scoffingly remarked, "I must go and pay the Mother of God a visit soon." On the 8th of December, as he was sitting in the evening in his arm-chair, he heard the bells ringing out joyously; he asked his nurse the meaning of it; on receiving the answer that, "to-day was the Feast of the Immaculate Conception," he uttered such a shocking blasphemy, that the attendant dared not repeat it. Scarcely had he spoken the words, when his face became so distorted, that his little grandson called out, "O, look at grandpapa, how ugly he is." And he died the same instant. As he could not be interred in consecrated ground, his Protestant son took care that he should be buried with music and every mark of distinction. At the grave, a friend of the deceased, who also prided himself on his scepticism, pronounced a panegyric, and in conclusion, suggested satirically, that as the Church refused to pray for the soul of the departed, they had better pray in silence. Upon which, another anti-Catholic stepped forward and said, "No, rather let us pray all the more loudly." So saying, he began the "Hail Mary," but he became so puzzled that he could not remember what followed, and was obliged to give it up. As the dead man had dishonoured Mary in life, it was not fitting that God should allow the beautiful words of her prayer to be pronounced over his corpse.

147. Retribution and Mercy.

In the year 1793 there was living in the south of France a well-known doctor, named Tabas, who was fond of relating the following story:—"One day he came across a soldier, who seemed to be suffering much from his leg. The kind doctor asked to look at it, and see if he could not relieve him. When he had undone the bandages he found a bullet-wound, which was alive with worms. The doctor was horrified at such a sight, and wanted to apply remedies, but the soldier assured him that every possible remedy had been tried in vain, and that he felt convinced that he would carry the horrible sore to the grave. On being asked how he came to have such a wound, he replied: 'In Spain; but you have not yet heard *why* it will never heal, so I will explain it to you once for all.

" 'I was twenty years old,' he proceeded, in a hesitating voice, 'and it was in '93 that I joined a regiment bound for Spain. There were two others from our village, Thomas and Franz, and we had grown up in the reckless spirit of the age, and were three unbelieving, or rather, godless fools, who prided ourselves on caring neither for God or man.

" 'We were in great spirits, and the journey was made cheerfully enough. Not far from our destination we passed through a village, where we noticed a statue of the Mother of God, which was held in such veneration, that in spite of the Revolution, it stood quite uninjured on its pedestal over the porch of the church. The unholy thought crossed the mind of one of my companions to insult the statue, in order to scoff at the peasants' 'superstitions;' he acquainted us with this profane resolution, and Thomas proposed to shoot at the statue; Franz answered with an approving laugh, and trembling and full of anxiety lest I should appear less courageous, I tried to dissuade them, for my conscience was opposed to this action, remembering my dear mother's teaching; however, I was only laughed at. Thomas aimed, and shooting, the bullet hit the statue on the forehead, Franz also shot, and hit the breast; 'Now then,' they said to me, 'it is your turn.' I dared not protest, and shutting my eyes, I tremblingly aimed, fired, and hit—

" 'The leg?' asked the doctor.

" 'Yes, just above the knee, that is where I hit it, so you see that I shall never be cured—

" 'After this *heroic* deed, we continued our march. An old woman who had seen all, cried after us: 'You are going to the war, are you? but what you have done will not bring you luck!' Thomas threatened her, I felt very low spirited, and Franz was rather uneasy.

" 'That same evening we halted with our regiment, and a few days later we were suddenly engaged in a skirmish. I must own I felt somewhat disconcerted on going into battle, and more than once thought of that statue of the Mother of God. However it went well with us, for we were on the winning side, and Thomas distinguished himself. Then the engagement being at an end, and the enemy in full flight, the colonel was just going to give the command to halt, when a shot was fired from a rock, Thomas reeled, and then fell on his face to the ground. We rushed forward to help him, but he was already dead, the ball had struck him in the middle of the forehead, between the eyes, in the very place, where, a few days previously, he had hit the statue. Franz and I looked at each other, without saying a word, pale as death.

" 'In the bivouac, Franz was with me, but he could not sleep. I waited for him to speak, and would have advised him to pray; he remained silent however, and I dared not speak of the thought which kept us both awake.

" 'The next day, the enemy returned 'en masse.' As soon as they appeared, Franz pressed my hand, and said: 'It is my turn to-day; you are happy to have aimed badly.'

" 'The wretched man was right, for on our return, Franz and I, who were without wounds, were walking together, suddenly a shot was fired from a ditch, where a wounded Spaniard lay hid, and Franz was hit in the breast. Ah! doctor, what a death! he rolled on the ground, calling out for a priest. Those who were near raised him up, but he soon expired, and we left him lying in the road.

" 'From that moment, I was convinced that I also should not remain unpunished, and I resolved to confess my sacrilege to the first priest I met, unhappily I did not find one. Meanwhile, after many battles had been fought without any evil having happened to me, my anxiety gradually vanished, and with it my good resolution also. On my return to France, I had quite forgotten all about the incident; but it was recalled to my memory, when during the march over the frontier, we arrived in the very village where the mutilated statue was. By some unaccountable accident, the gun of one of my comrades went off, and I was hit here where you see the wound. So the prediction of the woman was in truth fulfilled, which she had uttered after the perpetration of the sacrilege (I seem to hear it still): 'You are going to war. What you have done, will bring you no luck.' Both of my companions were now dead, and I was wounded. At first the wound did not appear to be very bad, and the army-surgeon thought a few days rest in the hospital would put one to rights. I believed it too; his surprise was as great as my horror, when he saw worms issuing from the wound. For twenty years, doctor, I have borne this punishment, I have tried every remedy, but find it all of no use. Indeed, I do implore my cure of God, and ever hope for it through His mercy, but I must not complain, and I do not complain. This wound has brought salvation to many souls, to mine in particular; should it remain with me to the last, and my end be a Christian and a penitent one, I shall owe all my happiness to this dreadful wound. I shall still congratulate myself, even if I shall have to limp the rest of my days, for I doubt of my cure, but not of my forgiveness, and I confidently hope to die in the grace of God, through the intercession of her whom I have injured.' "

148. God Protects the Honour of Mary.

Many remarkable instances prove that God nearly always punishes quickly and severely blasphemies uttered against His Saints, and especially those against the ever-blessed Virgin, the Queen of Saints. An instance of this kind is inscribed on a very ancient votive tablet, which hangs near our Lady's Altar, in the parish church of Gesecke, in Westphalia. It is related in very old style, and runs as follows:—

"In the year 1633, on the 29th of October, a Hessian musketeer, named Louis Ladeler, after having uttered blasphemies against a statue of the Mother of God, which was placed in a niche, shot at it from a house in Helwig street.

"He hit the statue on the left shoulder, but was at once seized with a frenzy which lasted for three days, during which time he cried out, unceasingly: 'Heal the woman! Heal the woman!' and after three days, he gave up his soul in most dreadful torments."

The statue was afterwards carried to the parish church, which was near, and placed over our Lady's Altar. In remembrance of this event, an annual religious feast is kept at Gesecke, which the people call "Maria Schutz" (Mary shot). The votive-tablet concludes with these words: "And the shot can still be seen, whereby you must acknowledge the Almighty Power of God, fear and love Him, and reverence His loving Mother. Amen."

149. *Our Lady's Refusal.*

The well-known Padre Segneri relates how three youths set out one night, with a sinful object in view. On the way, the light which they carried with them went out. They then came upon a picture of the Mother of God, in a little corner of the street, before which a lamp was burning. One of them went up to it, with the intention of re-lighting their lamp, but he had scarcely drawn near, when the light went out. He returned and at once the little lamp before Mary's picture, rekindled as brightly as before. And as often as he made the attempt to light his lamp, the same thing always happened. Then he recognized how true it is, that our Lady will always be a light for us as often as we turn away from sin, but never, when we deliberately stray from the right path.

150. *Salutary Punishment.*

For some time we had been climbing the steep path which leads to the crater of Mount Etna, when our guide told us that we had now left the cultivated portion of the mountain, and that the rest of our way lay through a thick growth of fir trees. We heard this announcement with some relief, as we had been walking under a scorching sun, and were beginning to long for a little shade. Everything around us now seemed silent and solitary, no living creature appeared to dwell in the woodland solitude, almost deathlike in its peaceful stillness. Involuntarily the thought of brigands came into our minds, we knew that the whole of Sicily was infested with them, to the terror of travelers, and this forsaken region would offer a good shelter to those who prefer to lie hid.

"Are there any robbers about here?" we enquired of Beppo, our guide.

"No sir, the banditti do not frequent these heights; you are safer here than in the streets of Palermo, but there is a hermit right at the top."

"A hermit! Beppo?"

"Yes, but no one knows anything about this extraordinary man, signor. He lives on the other side of the forest, and is never seen in the villages around, for he shuns the dwellings of men. In storm and rain he wanders about, and even in thunderstorms and tempests he is ever fearless and tranquil. There is also a chapel at the top, said to have been built by him, where he spends long hours in prayer. The shepherds take this hermit for a spectre, perhaps even for the devil in bodily form."

"Oho! Beppo! have you ever seen this wonderful person?"

"I met him once, signor."

"And what did he say to you?"

"He asked for an alms, and then vanished."

"But, Beppo, just think for a moment, the devil would not live near a chapel, and a spirit has no need of alms. You Sicilians are a superstitious people, and no mistake."

"You may laugh at me, if you like, but the extraordinary apparition has not yet been accounted for."

"Well, then, you shall have a lire as a reward if you will take us to this stranger."

We had now left behind us the forest region of Etna, and after long and laborious mountain climbing we arrived at the end of our journey—the grand and awful crater was within a few yards of us.

"Signor, I have won my lire," hastily exclaimed our guide, "for there is the hermit."

Yes, there he was. He was sitting quietly on the edge of the fiery gulf, and was peering into the depths below. He was still young and of noble bearing, but there was an air of sadness about his features. The wind played with the folds of his garments, and drove the sulphurous vapours unnoticed into his face; nor did they seem to trouble or disturb him in the least. When he heard our guide's voice, he slowly raised his weary head, but our presence did not disconcert him; on the contrary, he came up to us and humbly asked a small alms. This awakened and increased my interest in this strange man, for there certainly must be some mystery attached to him. I gave him an alms, at the same time entering into conversation, to which he seemed in no way averse. Finally, I asked why he led such an extraordinary life.

"My good sir, in order to make that clear to you, I must relate my whole history, and I will willingly tell you all, both as

285

a warning to others, and to make reparation for my crime.

"I need not tell you my name; you are ignorant of it, and it is not necessary; but what you should know; is that in the world, I was thought much of, and held a post of honour. But withal, I was, like many of my equals, unbelieving, godless and proud. I led a life after the manner of those who forsake their God and forget their religious duties. About fifteen years ago, I travelled through Italy and Sicily, and made the ascent of Mount Etna, in order to contemplate this beautiful but awful scene. Two of my companions, as godless and immoral as myself, were my fellow travelers. On the way, we came across a wooden crucifix, and near to it, a pretty little way-side grot, containing a picture of the Mother of God. This was too much for me and my scoffing companions, so we wickedly resolved to insult, profane, and destroy the picture. No sooner said than done. We overthrew the wooden cross, broke open the grot, and then, with mocking laughter and coarse jests, threw the cross, grot, and picture, into the very midst of the subterranean fires.

"After this so called heroic deed, we began to descend the mountain. I had perhaps gone a hundred paces, when I slipped on a dangerous place, and was hurled into a huge saucer-like cavity, at one moment poised in mid-air between heaven and earth, at another precipitated from rock to rock, from one point to another, and a hundred times I should certainly have been dashed to pieces, had not God's divine Hand, and the arm of His Blessed Mother, saved me. Then my eyes were opened, and in that same moment, the danger of my infamous life passed before me in all its atrocity, and in the midst of all this horror rose up before my mind the wooden cross, the grot and picture of our Lady, which in our

286

wickedness we had destroyed. It seemed to me that if I could only cling to this cross, I should be saved. Then I silently prayed thus: 'O holy Virgin Mary, Mother of God, come to my assistance and save me; I will promise to build a chapel where your picture once stood, which our blasphemous wickedness has destroyed and profaned.'

"All this was the thought of a moment. I then lost consciousness, and when I came to myself, I felt like one wounded and bruised all over, lying in the immeasurable depth of this mountain pass. It was several hours before I could recover from my fright and fall, but during that time my perverted heart became entirely changed, and my resolution remained firm and unshaken to say farewell for ever to the corrupt world which had ruined me, and to expiate my sins and crimes in the very place where the Mother of Mercy had awakened in me the desire of a new life.

"Then I gathered up all my strength, and scrambling out of this strange hollow, I hid myself for some time, for I felt certain that my companions would soon come to look for me. And so it was; for several days they searched the rocks and ravines with guides and peasants, but they did not find me. Their investigations and inquiries were fruitless, so they gave me up for dead. So indeed I was, now that I wished to remain forgotten by the world, and had awakened to a new and spiritual life.

"Later on, I descended into the valley, and sought a neighbouring monastery, where I cleansed my conscience by a general confession, and returned to the mountains, converted, consoled, and at peace. Roots, wild herbs and the beggar's bread were now my food and sustenance; but I could not longer delay the fulfillment of my vow, so I built the chapel which you see up there, with blocks of solid lava, on the very place where the crucifix once stood. A statue of our Lady, which the Superior of the monastery willingly gave me, adorns the little sanctuary, and before this picture of the Mother of God, the Refuge of Sinners, I bewail and lament the wanderings and sins of my early life, and thank the Mother of Mercy for my wonderful conversion."

The hermit having now come to the end of his history, took leave of us, and soon disappeared from our sight.

I remembered afterwards that about fifteen years before, the newspapers had announced the death of the young Count Von G— —, who had perished in the ascent of Mount Etna.

THE END.

MARIA SANCTISSIMA,
ORA PRO NOBIS.

Made in the USA
San Bernardino, CA
26 January 2019